THE SELFIE GENERATION

EXPLORING OUR NOTIONS OF PRIVACY, SEX, CONSENT, AND CULTURE

ALICIA ELER

Skyhorse Publishing

First Paperback Edition 2019

Skyhorse Publishing books may be purchased in bulk at special discounts for sales promotion, corporate gifts, fund-raising, or educational purposes. Special editions can also be created to specifications. For details, contact the Special Sales Department, Skyhorse Publishing, 307 West 36th Street, 11th Floor, New York, NY 10018 or info@skyhorsepublishing.com.

Skyhorse® and Skyhorse Publishing® are registered trademarks of Skyhorse Publishing, Inc.®, a Delaware corporation.

Visit our website at www.skyhorsepublishing.com.

10 9 8 7 6 5 4 3 2 1

Library of Congress Cataloging-in-Publication Data is available on file.

Cover design by Erin Seaward-Hiatt
Front cover selfies courtesy of: Emma (@emmanent.dogmain), Betty Aloysius Bamford Cassidy, Ray Anthony Barrett, Janna Avner, Marilyn Bamford, Maria Bamford and Scott Marvel Cassidy, JB Brager, Gaby Cepeda, Ihsan Eler, Alicia Eler and Jerry Saltz, Lauren Elizabeth Neal, Priscilla Frank, Nikita Gale, Andrea Gyorody, Peregrine Honig, Alex Huntsberger, Rebecca Kling, Che Landon, Bronwyn Lundberg, Hannah Miet, Maggie Miller, Shera Morgan, Anne Orchier, Eve Peyser, Munib Raad, Brannon Rockwell-Charland, Elaine Romero and Brad Eggers, Dorothy Santos, Sarah Seidelman Bamford, Tiffany Sum, Mark Tilsen, Ben Valentine, Hrag Vartanian, David Wellman and friends campaigning with Hillary for America, Lauren White, An Xiao Mina, Jenny Yurshansky, Sarah Zucker

Print ISBN: 978-1-5107-4285-7
Ebook ISBN: 978-1-5107-2266-8

Printed in the United States of America

Praise for *The Selfie Generation*

"Eler's book alights on the source of the selfie's power: It is the easiest way to assert one's humanity in our hyper-networked world. Perhaps our much-fussed-over narcissism is not a flaw but a survival tactic."

— *The New York Times*

"Through a mix of reportage and personal reflection, Eler gives a snapshot of the snapshot, situating the selfie in a variety of cultural milieux: intimacy and relationships, journalism and activism, memes and savvy advertising."

— *Los Angeles Review of Books*

"I am taking a picture of myself as I write this blurb about Alicia's neat new book addressing the joys and hazards of phone-operated self-reflection. And in taking this selfie, I find my selfie."

— Maria Bamford, comedian

"Eler is a selfie semiotician. Her book is in defense of millennials and all those who dare to take a selfie."

— *Wired* magazine

"In this kaleidoscopic exploration of the selfie, Alicia Eler challenges the popular view of the selfie as a narcissistic act. Part Millennial apologist, part cultural sage, Eler transforms this work of personal memoir into a meditation on the deep need of human beings for social connection. *The Selfie Generation* exposes the level of privacy we're willing to sacrifice in order not only to meet our basic need of food and shelter, but one another."

—Elaine Romero, playwright, associate professor, School of Theatre, Film and Television, University of Arizona

"Fascinating, provocative, entertaining and enlightening, and likely to be the foundation of all future books on this subject."

—*Chicago Tribune*

"Alicia Eler breaks with clichés to imagine the selfie as a double-edged sword, at once an empowering and vulnerable phenomenon, characteristic of the digital age."

—BBC

"A timely addition to growing research on selfie culture. Weaving first-person narrative and conversations with tech and social media experts, the Minnesota Star Tribune journalist offers a wide-ranging exploration of the effects of the selfie on our cultural relationship to technology, privacy, and gender."

—*Chicago Reader*

"From activists recording themselves through what Eler calls 'sousveillance' to artists exploring how social media users craft their own self-image, *Selfie Generation* uses these images to explore the boundaries of the Internet and the physical world, along with questions of consent and copyright. Through interviews with both professionals and friends, Eler toes the line between a personal essay and a scholarly resource."

—*Minneapolis Journal*

THE SELFIE
GENERATION

For my cousin Sinan Eler,
whose selfies will always be remembered.

Sinan pictured with his mother, my aunt Hülya Eler.

Contents

An Introduction to the Selfieverse

"Selfie." The singular mention of that word elicits an opinion from everyone. The selfie is contentious and controversial because its boundaries aren't known yet. In the age of social media, the very existence of the selfie has raised questions about how much of peoples' lives should be shared on the Internet and social media. While the desire to connect with others is natural, how much is too much (#overshare) and what does that say about this cultural moment?

This is not an idealistic book about social media and technology. But it's also not meant to alarm you. It's a story of necessity and social rewards, of complacency and complexity. It's a story about what happens when you join a social network because you want to connect (#connect).

I've combined memoir and analysis in this book. It feels necessary to talk about my own selfie-ing experiences in the context of the selfie as an image-object that is also a noun, verb, form, action, aesthetic, and an embodiment of surveillance culture, adolescence, and celebrity.

Originally when I started writing this book, I had three main questions in mind: How has the rise of social media changed notions of online privacy? Why do people selfie? How has social media created hyperpersonalized advertising based on the information we feed the network? I was also interested in how social media was portrayed in TV and pop culture, since so many around the world are influenced by these media images.

Plus, I wanted to explore how representations of the selfie and social media on TV shape popular notions about the "right" way to selfie. The jury is out on that, though it's clear that someone who sits around constantly posting selfies will inevitably be labeled narcissistic. To bring all of these questions together under the umbrella of selfie as a teen/celebrity phenomenon and understand how the selfie came to be what it is today is, ultimately, the goal of this book.

Oh hey, what exactly constitutes a selfie tho?

The word "selfie" can mean both an action (to selfie) and a form (the selfie). To selfie is a verb: it means to take a selfie. Selfie is a noun: it is an image of your face shot with a front-facing smartphone camera. In the selfieverse, there are two types of selfies we see most frequently.

The *recognizable-as-selfie* marks itself aesthetically, either through the long arm, duckface, off-kilter gaze, bathroom mirror, #aftersexselfie, survival selfie, disaster selfie, before death selfie, #wokeuplikethis in bed from above angle, gym selfie, etc. It is often hashtagged #selfie when shared on social media.

The *unrecognizable-as-selfie* image attempts to hide or evade its selfie-ness through lack of visual markers. It usually ends up being a close-up of the face.

The selfie is primarily visual, but it can also be textual. A self-referential tweet or status update is a verbal selfie. As Ruth Peyser, my writer colleague/collaborator/friend Eve Peyser's mom, once tweeted: "A tweet is a verbal selfie."[1]

> **eve peyser** ✓
> @evepeyser
>
> *Following* ⌄
>
> mom just tweeted at me, "tweets are verbal selfies." she is an accidental web theorist and she's smarter than us all.
>
> 9:47 PM - 13 Oct 2015
>
> 21 Retweets 90 Likes
>
> 💬 3   🔁 21   ♡ 90   ✉

The very nature of the selfie is that it's shot with an awareness of *potential publicness* even if it is saved to a phone and never shared or leaked. The selfie distorts ideas of "public" and "private," merging the two to create a virtual existence. This messes with ideas that the private is a privileged space, and that the self offline is the only "real" self.

Another issue that the selfie—in this case, one that's shared to the Internet rather than stored on a phone—brings up is its obviously performative nature (#performativity). Once the selfie is shared, it's easily seen by practically anyone online, making it vulnerable to, among other things, facial recognition technologies, which are increasingly troubling for activists working online. Facial recognition technologies on social media and on our phones use those images to identify us, making us easily and simply trackable. In the project *Facial Weaponization Suite* by artist Zach Blas, he creates collective masks made with aggregated facial data to fight back against biometric facial recognition.[2] This is seemingly opposite of the selfie, which is complicit with and integral to facial recognition technology and surveillance culture.

The other type of "privacy" that people bring up when discussing the selfie and social media is Internet privacy and surveillance, which will be the main focus of chapter 2. The selfie is often thrown into the Internet privacy conversation because it is integral to social media culture and the Internet and fuzzies the line between private and public. Someone's online personality often won't match their offline self. A person who is extremely friendly and engaging on social media could be completely anti-social in real life. The selfie creates space for presenting a new version of one's self, protected behind screens. What you see is not always what you get in-person. (If you ever meet in-person, that is.)

Selfie feelings

I say I never liked taking selfies, but that's simply not true. I love taking and posting selfies when I'm feeling good and open to onlookers. But I didn't love the technology that made selfies super ubiquitous. I first started self-imaging as a teenager using film camera.

Self-imaging has sped up through technology. The year was 2009, and I was holding out against what everyone around me seemed to imply were requisite technological updates to life. I proudly owned a silver flip phone—a.k.a., "dumb phone"—its cover chipped and worn because I dropped it so often. I was on the family plan, and our data was limited. Two friends of mine had recently purchased iPhones. They both made more money than me, and were admittedly kinda "nerdy." The iPhone seemed like something for them, not me. I was just a poor post-college grad.

At cafes, I'd sit close to them, watching as they tapped out texts. I didn't want to read the texts—I just wanted to watch their faces as the messages appeared on those tiny screens. These little thought bubbles turned into back-and-forth conversations that could happen at any time. It reminded me of AOL Instant Messenger chats I had with friends as a teenager, except for those I had to be sitting at my computer, which I didn't like to do for very long because I got restless, and I didn't like the screen. The bubble of the text messages reminded me of the ways that cartoon characters have thoughts that appear on-screen, and only the viewer is privy to them. They are interior thoughts. The characters don't say them out loud to one another. As the scene shifts, the thought bubbles leave the screen. The characters say something else aloud—not the thoughts that they were thinking.

Texting annoyed me. It seemed like a waste of time communicating something that could've been shared much more quickly through a phone call. Plus it was more time looking at a screen. I would've rather been reading a book or magazine, or taking pictures. This was before phones had cameras in them, anyway. But as it goes with all things social, admittedly I began to feel left out.

Yet the idea of spending $600 to have a mini-computer in my pocket was clear evidence of a techno-capitalist imperative that I did not want to literally buy into. I didn't even want to own a phone, it turned out. Yet, despite my disdain for the iPhone on several levels, eventually I acquiesced. Why? Because I kept receiving texts on my flip phone from someone I was crushin' on. I'd call her, and she'd text me back.

I wouldn't reply to her texts that often because my phone sucked. But there was something intriguing about the pace of texting, and the ways it interrupted otherwise quiet time, time spent in transit, in thought. Still, I didn't reply. Then we'd see each other in-person and she'd ask if I received her texts, and I'd say yes. Why didn't I reply? She seemed sad about my lack of response. I felt bummed about that. I'd say that I didn't know what to say, and my phone sucked so . . . why did she keep texting me? #justcallmeplz

Still, I wanted to #connect too, before it was a hashtagged thing on social media, and so eventually I took the leap. I bought a cheap used BlackBerry from eBay, which was not *nearly* as cool as the iPhone, but it could send and receive texts, I could check email, the Internet worked, and it had an okay camera. Now I had a big dumb phone in my pocket so I could . . . text her? Something still didn't make sense to me, but before I could think that through I got swept into some text conversation, forgetting about what felt pressing. Instead, a sense of complacency sunk in. I was the cartoon character thinking bubble thoughts but, before they could disappear from my mind, I'd share them with her. It created a sense of intimacy and vulnerability that I hadn't previously experienced through writing. It felt more exciting than talking on the phone. Before long, I was hooked!

A year or so later, I upgraded to an Android and then, eventually, saved some money and bought an iPhone of my own. This 4G version had a front-facing camera, and also connected to the Internet without so many delays. It seemed far more worth it. Facebook also had an app. I became more active, and then I started reconnecting with a lot of friends from college and high school. It was fascinating to see what they were up to. Soon, I began posting pictures to Facebook.

Since I'm totally a closet theater person—I did performance art in college, and do some stand-up comedy here and there when I'm not being a hardcore reporter—I liked the sense of posting selfies or pictures of myself to the Internet because it mimicked the experience of being onstage and performing. I felt seen and liked, and I didn't need to learn lines or write out jokes or show up anywhere outside of my computer screen or smartphone. Plus, I could control the narrative. It seemed like an exciting and weird social experiment. I was game.

Previously, Facebook was just some Internet thing that my friends and I made fun of. At Oberlin College, many of us joined Facebook in 2004, when it became available to liberal arts college students. I posted maybe three times between 2004 and 2008. By 2010, Facebook had become relevant. People left Friendster and MySpace and hopped on Facebook. I thought it was gonna come and go like those other networks. Boy, was I wrong.

The once antitechnology Alicia was now on Facebook. Then she joined Twitter, posted likable pics to Instagram, reluctantly joined Snapchat and Periscope and Tinder, owned a smartphone, and felt ready to #connect.[3] But what did that even mean? And did I want that? I wasn't sure, but there I was—and my friends and crushes were around too, all seemingly just a click away.

Take a break from selfie-ing and read this book about selfies

The selfie is an extremely polarizing topic. Everyone has an opinion on the selfie, with some claiming it is the downfall of the "kids today," who live their lives online and have lost in-person social skills, while others laud it as a way to connect, to share a moment and a feeling, and to literally give face time. Because the selfie is still fairly new and technology is increasingly personalized to the ways individuals use it, the selfie triggers questions about what is socially acceptable to share, when, with whom, and why. The purpose of this book is to shed some light on how the selfie came to be, what it means on a scientific psychological level, and then answer questions about why it's become such a polarizing topic. Lastly, I consider what the selfie means for the future of communication, privacy, and surveillance.

In Chapter 1, Screen Kween!!!, I focus on the neuroscience and psychology of selfies, in order to answer the question of "why do people selfie?" in a hardline, science-focused way from the get-go before getting into more of the cultural implications. The selfie is largely both an adolescent and celebrity social phenomena, because both categories of people are intensely focused on how they are perceived by others. Celebs and teenagers both want to be adored; being liked is the ultimate reward. After all, the selfie goal is to capture the attention of onlookers in the way that the person wants to be seen. The selfie generation includes anyone who can achieve this aspiration. Keeping this in mind, the selfie is both a form and an action, a noun and a verb. The selfie generation includes anyone who selfies, but it is typically more associated with people under the age of thirty-five. Of course, privacy implications differ based on age. And that's the focus of the next chapter.

Chapter 2, Privacy Settings, argues that we have traded our notions of Internet privacy for products, deals, free services and, most of all, convenience, making us complacent with surveillance culture. I recall a time before social media when it wasn't ever expected that photos I took would end up anywhere else; those developed moments were private. But with the rise of social media, I became preoccupied with the privacy settings and options that social networks offered all their users. How could a photo that I once kept so private that it was almost a sacred object become something that could easily be shared with peers through digital means? How could so many people become willingly complacent in the surveillance state, in the collection of our very personal data by corporations and the government, without wondering where it will end up, or who will see it? Selfie performance is predicated on relinquishing privacy. For that reason, this chapter also discusses security culture, which is antiselfie and recognizes how deeply surveillance is embedded into our everyday lives—especially for those who engage in dissent.

So where would consent come into this equation? Chapter 3, Consenting to the Image, approaches the selfie and Internet image/meme culture from a feminist perspective with a focus on questions of digital consent. That is, what do we really consent to when we post and share images? Copyright law means almost nothing on the Internet, where remix culture rules, fair use sometimes works, and social media sites take little to no responsibility for the content that is posted and instead require users give the network a limited license of their own content. When the digital content is of a sexual nature—such as nudes or sexts—questions of consent become intertwined with trust, much as they do offline, but with far higher risks because of how easy it is to post anything to the Internet.

The rise of the selfie as a cultural phenomenon has also became a literal "beat" for media outlets. Any headline with "selfie" in it will inevitably become newsworthy. In Chapter 4, The 24/7 Selfie News Cycle, I delve into how selfie news generated its own buzz, making for clickable headlines even if the content itself is actually antiselfie. A headline with "selfie," especially "selfie death," is guaranteed clickbait for an Internet news economy. Any selfie can easily become recontextualized within the context of the selfie-as-trend. In this chapter I pay particular attention to types of selfies that were especially sensationalized in the media, from sexist readings of the selfie, to survival selfies, faked survival selfies, daredevil selfies, teen risk-taking selfies, #funeralselfies, selfies at death memorials, #aftersex selfies, and more. "Selfies are not meant to be passport photos," said Rob Horning, an editor at *Real Life* magazine and *New Inquiry* who has written extensively about selfies. "They are meant to broaden the possibilities for what sort of self you are to yourself and your friends."

Such ways of curating oneself for their social network, to catch peoples' attention and to be seen, echo the purpose of advertising. And naturally, as the selfie trend snowballed and became totally mainstream, questions of how it became used as an advertisement and in advertising began to change. Chapter 5, Meta-Selfie Advertising, lol, continues the focus on the crossover of selfie into media consumption and production. The selfie taker is both complicit in the use of their selfie within the network's circulatory nature, and also happily hashtagging away—either literally or ironically—offering additional free, word-of-mouth advertising for the product, place, or thing. This circular nature creates a self-fulfilling advertisement prophecy of person as both consumer and advertiser, making market research data even more accessible.

As if that weren't enough repurposing of the selfie (#selfie), Chapter 6, Video Killed the Radio Star, Selfie Killed TV, looks at the ways that the selfie and social media are portrayed on TV, which adds to how people then perceive and understand the selfie. Showrunners approach social media and technology in two ways. In the "exterior approach," technology is viewed as separate from the individual, a force to be reckoned with. The Internet is a place where people create an alter-ego or persona where they are anything but their "real" self. The "interior approach" views technology as part of everyday life. Often what is transmitted through technology is just a reflection of the character's interior processes. There is no one right way to portray technology on TV, much as there is no one right way to take a selfie.

The last section of the book shifts the focus back to the selfie-taker, and looks toward the future. In Chapter 7, Selfie Gazing, I dissect the ways that the gaze used in the selfie narrates how onlookers are supposed to look at the subject in the frame. Whether the selfie is a #bathroomselfie, #mirrorselfie, or #gymselfie, the selfie-shooter controls the viewer's gaze. Ultimately, the selfie-shooter controls how they are perceived. Aesthetically, the selfie is a form of photography, but it is also complicated because as soon as it's posted, it is also both "live" and archived. The selfie may appear raw and vulnerable, but it's also curated as such. By posting the selfie to a network, the person who shares makes their image surveillable and vulnerable, yet the selfie also creates a space for personas, and plays with fantasy, desire, and projection. The selfie becomes an image on to which others project. And as it goes in selfie culture, the social validation and connection is worth the reward.

Chapter 8, Fake News and Selfie Journalism! Read All About It!, veers back into the media, but this time with a focus on fake news and the possibility of selfie journalism, which breaks with the tradition of the selfie as image of oneself shot with a smartphone camera. Instead, selfie journalism is a type of social media commentary through recontextualized images, posted through an individual's social media account.

Chapter 9, The Authentic Selfie, reiterates and finishes the argument about what the selfie actually is. The selfie is an aspirational image, but it also an integral aspect to socializing, interacting, and being seen by others online. In an attention economy of likes that demands performance and absolute connectivity, the selfie is a way to visually grab someone's attention, mimicking a face-to-face interaction. In order to exist, the selfie most be continually produced by the individual, and seen by the network. The selfie is a continual piece of content, yet once posted it is also immediately archived within the network, to which the user licenses their image for repurposing—an infinite mirror loop.

THE SELFIE GENERATION

Chapter 1

Screen Kween!!!

THE SELFIE IS YOUTHFUL. It's a teen thing, it's soooo millennial, and yet it's also wrapped up in ideas of celebrity culture. Kim Kardashian became famous by crafting her persona on social media after her sex tape was leaked.

The selfie is both an adolescent and celebrity social phenomena. Both teens and celebs have an intense focus on self-appearance, and how they are perceived by others. As a teenager, being liked and popular is the ultimate reward; likewise, celebrities are often adored, but at the very least they must garner attention. The trap for both teenagers and celebrities is getting too caught up in other peoples' opinions. And now, of course, much of that feedback loop and commentary happens on social media, a space that is monitored. For teenagers, social media is where their friends hang out; for celebrities it's where others talk about who they are and what they should do, projecting opinions onto these people.

"I think that many things about being a celebrity are a lot like being a teenager," said Carrie Bearden, PhD, professor in the departments of psychiatry and biobehavioral sciences and psychology at UCLA. "It's a lot focused on your own presentation, and sort of you're in that space of constant self-presentation and just being seen by the public, or however the public sees you is very critical. For people who are not in the public eye, that kind of dies down. As a teenager, everyone feels like they're in the spotlight all the time whether or not that is true."

The selfie is a photo taken of oneself and, often, though not necessarily always, posted to a social media site. People snap selfies with their smartphones that they don't ever share. I can recall countless experiences of waiting for a friend to find a photo on their phone that they want to show me and, while watching them scroll, I notice a large number of selfies in their photo album. I also have other peoples' selfies on my phone—either selfies they shot with my phone, or selfies I've received from others.

The selfie as an aesthetic is often, but not always, recognizable as such. Sometimes the person's arm, holding the phone, makes it into the photo. Other times the selfie is shot in front of the mirror so that the smartphone is visible. The selfie is a mirror; the shared selfie is then a shared mirror, reflecting the moment it is taken. Selfies are an important though completely optional part of a person's social media presence and of their digital communication.

The selfie is also a way to #connect—adding the hashtag means it will also be searchable with other images that have the same hashtag. Selfie-ing means putting one's image out onto the Internet, or it can be wasting time, a random act of vanity, pausing to acknowledge boredom or some other momentary self-reflection, or reaching out for a sense of digital community, to be seen by others within a social milieu. Regardless, the selfie is a way to be seen. But bear in mind that the selfie is not the self. The selfie is an image of oneself. Selfies are indicative of a cultural shift in how people socialize through technology. Gen Z and Millienials certainly use technology more than other generations, but the cultural shift of socializing through technology is experienced by people of all ages. It's all very different from the days of analogue photography past. Previously, a printed photograph sent might receive a verbal affirmation or a written response. In contrast, an image posted or shared online will receive some type of "like"—some immediate, general reward from an onlooker, someone who is watching albeit not necessarily paying attention. The affirmation one receives from a well-liked selfie triggers the rewards area of the brain—unlike a "bad" selfie that doesn't receive many likes. But sometimes you just have to upload that pic. YOLO!

People take selfies for many reasons: to see how they look (to themselves if kept private, or to others if shared), to receive validation from others, and to be *seen* in a superficial sense. (Hello, don't judge a book by its cover but *obviously we all do*.) Selfies that are shot but never posted are simply part of an individual's momentary self-reflection and navel-gazing. That friend with lots of selfies in their phone photo album thinks about their self-image and how they appear to others. It's fun to selfie alone, snapping away while lying in bed, inside a public bathroom, in places where people find themselves with an impulse to share, as if these images were secrets or something previously referred to as "private." The bathroom mirror selfie is basic yet always has a risqué feel to it.

I can recall my first art school renditions of what are now known as bathroom selfies—they were self-portraits taken in a bathroom mirror. I took off my shirt, gazed at myself in the mirror, and snapped pictures. Not that I shared them with anyone outside of people in my photography class, though. Those were never meant for the Internet, and they were not taken with the perceived publicness that we see with selfies today.

Selfie hatin' on Kim Kardashian

The selfie as narcissistic self-promotion is attributed to Kim Kardashian, who has used and continues to use highly curated images of her life to capitalize on her own self-image. She is the embodiment of selfie. Even though Internet celebrity has become a normalized aspiration for people around the world—to become famous is a desired accomplishment—the process to get there, which includes successfully capitalizing on your own image, is considered a narcissistic impulse. To be a culture that celebrates individualism yet also casually labels that individual narcissistic is awkward. Kim K embodies all of those contradictions, and that is why she is the selfie kween!!!

In the article "Toward a Unified Theory of Kim Kardashian" for *Brooklyn* magazine, Ruth Curry explains the ways Kardashian crafts celebrity through her social media:

> Kim Kardashian—and maybe Kim Kardashian alone—has figured out how to make a fortune on the countless hours of emotional labor most women are expected to perform for free: smiling, looking pretty, being accommodating, being charming, being a good hostess. These are the skills a celebrity appearance entails.[1]

Kim K's selfies offer fans a voyeuristic look into her life, curated by her. Some teenagers idolize and imitate her, social media solidified her fame, and her book *Selfish* is a rich compilation of all that, as Nancy Jo Sales explains in her book *American Girls: Social Media and the Secret Lives of Teenagers*:

> In 2006, [Kim] had just 856 friends on Myspace—where she announced her profile, "I'm a PRINCESS and you're not so

there!"—and now she had 31 million followers on Instagram, second only to Beyoncé, whom she would eclipse in a few months, climbing to number one. She had 34 million followers on Twitter, where she posted more selfies daily, most of which got thousands of favorites and retweets.[2]

Selfish is literally a collection of Kim's selfies over a period of eight years, documenting her public ascension to celebrity that coincided with the rise of Instagram. Not only did Kardashian solidify the importance of the selfie, she also defined it, using it as a way to both create and commodify her own image.

There's a sense of unspoken social jealousy from onlookers toward anyone who takes a moment to selfie while out in public, in the world with other people, rather than asking someone else to take a photo of them. Why, just the other day I found myself feeling salty about some wedding selfie-takers. They were standing on a bridge all dressed up as bride and groom, and then they paused to take a selfie together even though they had a photographer with them. It's not that I was jealous of their wedding. Rather, it's that they took a moment in public, while everyone else was around, to selfie and thus block out the rest of the world when someone else could have documented them. They stepped out of the moment and into a selfie—or rather, into their own selfieverse.

The same type of jealousy I felt about their moment is what I've heard described in misogynistic terms toward teenage girls—that they have the audacity to *ignore the world around them and take pics together!!!* That they don't need someone else to do it for them. And thus the individual who would've been included in that experience by photographing them is now rendered obsolete. The out-in-public selfie-taker doesn't care about other people around them in that instant. They are doing what they want to do. Rather than understanding what this person is doing when they selfie, a jealous onlooker will label them a narcissist in a sort of knee-jerk kind of way.

In reality, I get that the couple wanted to take an "usie." I actually prefer taking selfies to having my picture taken simply because I have a lot more control over the image, angles, and my expression. It's easier than asking someone else, who probably doesn't know how to take a good picture. True, the selfie may also create a sense of antisocial behavior, but who said that photography was social? A selfie makes clear how someone sees themselves in that moment, then gives them the option of whether or not to share. A picture by someone else demands a relinquishing of that pleasurable control of the image. And in the age of protected, curated social media accounts, where social media privacy settings are apt to change without warning, we do seek the illusion of control over our online lives. Or at the very least, our images.

So, it's important to distinguish between having control over how an image looks—that is, using the selfie as a way to create a self image as one sees fit—and an utter lack of control over how or where that selfie will end up. All too often questions about social media privacy, spurred by Facebook, are conflated with actual Internet privacy laws. While these do overlap, they are not one and the same. Social media is always an optional space for sharing, whereas Internet privacy has broader definitions and implications.

I KNOW you like my face ;)

Images of peoples' faces are the most liked of any type of visual content because they mimic looking into someone's eyes, face-to-face and in person. In looking at a selfie that's making eye contact, you do feel like you are looking at the person. Though it's just an image, the emotions you get from looking at that image are real. In a 2014 study out of the Georgia Institute of Technology and Yahoo Labs, researchers combed through 1.1 million photos on Instagram and discovered that pictures with human faces in them were 38 percent more likely to receive likes than those without. Additionally, they're also 23 percent more likely to garner comments. And the next detail is even more surprising: the age and gender of the people in the photos didn't matter. Pictures of kids or teens aren't more popular than images of adults. Furthermore, when it comes to receiving likes, men and women are on par. It would seem that the selfie is the great equalizer; a face is just a face, and we are just people wanting to connect. Chill out on the *kumbaya*s though—"connecting" online is not the same as doing so in-person, and researchers identified a few other factors that drive engagement rates for online connectivity.

Constant posting is not the way to achieve more likes. In fact, according to Saeideh Bakshi, a PhD candidate at Georgia Tech College of Computing, who ran the study with Yahoo Labs, posting too frequently doesn't necessarily mean more likes at all.[3] In fact, posting constantly to Instagram could actually lessen the amount of likes per photo. "The more you post, the less feedback you're going to get," said Bakhshi in a Georgia Tech News article. "Posting too much decreases likes two times faster than comments."

But why would faces consistently get more likes than other types of images posted to Instagram? For one, face is the place. Before we walk, talk, or write, we know how to see. We come into this world, open our eyes, and look around. "Faces are powerful channels of nonverbal communication," said Bakshi. "We constantly monitor them for a variety of contexts, including attractiveness, emotions, and identity."

Interestingly, though, any images that are liked often, whether or not they are selfies, will attract more likes regardless of the content. In a study out of UCLA's Department of Psychology, "The Power of the *Like* in Adolescence: Effects of Peer Influence on Neural and Behavioral Responses to Social Media," scientists set up an experiment to see what types of images would get the most likes based on previous likes. The participants volunteered pictures from their own Instagram accounts. Then as they scrolled through, they either had the option to like or not. The images ranged from mundane pics of food and puppies to people participating in "risky" behavior like smoking, drinking, or dressing in provocative ways.

"We saw the typical behavioral effect that one might have expected, meaning that the participants were much more likely to like a picture that received many likes by a prior participant than the one that received few, irrespective of the quality of the pictures," said Mirella Dapretto, one of the researchers. But this was not so with images of risky behavior that received many likes.

According to the study, even if the risky behavior photo received many likes—which would suggest that the brain receives more rewards activation by liking it—the region that controls good judgment and restraint appeared less active. In other words, seeing risk-taking is not inherently rewarding for that area of cognitive control. Still, if such content has already been liked by others, it will continue to get liked: A fast and easy recipe for going viral.

#tbt the good ol' selfie days

I don't post a lot of selfies these days—not like I used to, anyway. Nowadays, my selfies tend to be commentary on the selfie, probably because I've thought about selfies so much as the result of writing this book that I've just gone totally meta. But that's me. Still, regardless of how many arguments for the selfie we have, posting constant selfies inevitably sends a visual message that a person is self-involved. This is definitely a limiting takedown of the selfie. To take time to admire and share an image of oneself to a network of people shouldn't imply immediate narcissism. It's bizarre to make sweeping, unscientific, nonpsychological conclusions about someone's personality based on how often or how rarely they post selfies.

In any case, I love a good selfie, and I love posting one when I am feeling inspired and in the mood for some likes. I stagger my Instagram so that it's not all selfies all the time, because that's actually not very visually or thematically engaging for me or, I think, for viewers. But mostly, I use stories way more than posts.

I don't want to photograph myself that much. A great selfie takes work. You rarely get a good one on the first try. Selfie sessions can last anywhere from one minute to one hour. Your phone memory may fill up. You have to delete more to keep taking more. And at times, it seems like the perfect selfie is just a click away—but is it? Or is it impossible? There are times when I've self-imaged more than others, like during emotionally difficult transitions. Regardless, posting and receiving validation is not a bad thing. It's human nature to #connect, to want to be seen.

That said, I notice that if I get likes on selfies, I do feel a sense of validation. And I feel good—science has proven it so. Selfies provide me a quick affirmation, like receiving a smile from a stranger. The well-liked selfie also provides conveniently quantifiable results, giving me a moment of connection with the outside world even if I'm truly in my head. After the deed is done, I can just put the phone away and it's gone, making the whole process as convenient, quick, and easy as I want it to be. Like deciding when to respond to a text message, I enjoy that sense of control over my technology rather than allowing it to control me.

But, when I use the quick hit of selfie validation too often, something else starts to happen. Too much looking in the selfie mirror can warp my perception of self, sending me into a downward spiral rather that the reward of pleasant reflection. For me, the key to selfie-ing is enjoying it in moderation, like I would with chocolate. Otherwise, I start to self-objectify in a way that can start to feel dysmorphic or dissociative. When that happens I feel trapped on the screen, caught up in some sort of social media vortex. I find myself there, waiting for the rewards, and that's inevitably when they don't arrive. This is not narcissism. This is a selfie mirror trap.

Let's take a moment to think about the common "selfies are narcissistic" blanket statement.

Selfies can be self-indulgent when taken frequently, but there are also plenty of actual narcissists who don't take any selfies at all, that hate the Internet, and that are paranoid about privacy. So, take your "all selfie-takers are narcissistic" statement and *eat it.*

"If people who take a lot of selfies are narcissistic, therefore I have just said that everyone under thirty is a narcissist, which is ridiculous," said Pamela B. Rutledge, PhD, MBA, and director of the Media Psychology Research Center and faculty in the media psychology program at Fielding Graduate University, who also writes the column "Positively Media" for *Psychology Today.*[4]

"It makes perfect sense that young people would take more pictures of themselves because they're never gonna look that good again," she said. "I would be taking a lot more selfies if I were twenty. At fifty, it's way less interesting and purposeful. At twenty, it was about social connection. It has much less social use now. You would still do it to share within a family, 'here's the three of us missing the other seven of you'—so certainly do it then—but it's not the same. There is a long list of reasons that people under thirty would take more selfies than people over fifty. They look better, and they're also more social than people who are in their fifties."

Send me a selfie, I want to #connect

There are other reasons for taking and sharing selfies that have less to do with public, social validation on Instagram, Facebook, Snapchat, WhatsApp, or whatever other social media platform.[5] Sending a selfie to someone who you know wants to see your face is another form of a virtual hello. Surely, the crowd on social media may *like* your selfie, but receiving an unexpectedly cute selfie is more intimate. The recipient may imagine making eye contact with you, as if the two of you were actually face-to-face, gazing into each other's eyes.

Regardless of the distance, whether the exchange takes place across the same city or across the country, selfies make the connection feel more immediate. Receiving a picture delivered to the phone in your hand—the same hand that could be holding theirs in this moment—suggests your beloved is right there with you even though they are not physically there. This can be achieved through texting or some other form of communication, but because the selfie is of the face, there's something else more human happening in the exchange.

In relationships of any kind, selfies become part of a way to communicate, to stay in touch. Even though your person is far away, you still want to see their face, to get a glimpse of them. Selfies could become an integral part of staying in touch. Marissa Douglas of *Odyssey Online* endorses sending selfies on the daily for people who are in long-distance relationships:

"Sending selfies to your partner will always be a must but with long distance relationships, it can help that void of not being with each other. Send one on your way to work, class or before you go to bed to make your partner feel like they are there and they get to see you in every aspect of your life even though they can't be there to witness it for themselves."[6]

Karen Krausen is a teacher who currently lives in Chicago but grew up in Los Angeles. She and her partner, Avi, were in a long-distance relationship for almost two years, and they sent a lot of selfies. But it didn't start out that way. The two first met when they were both living in New York City. They were neighbors, traveled in similar social circles, and eventually became friends. "There was an attraction there but the circumstances weren't right," Karen said. Fast-forward six years. Karen was traveling through Chicago from Los Angeles, en route to Urbana, and remembered

that Avi was living in Chicago. She recalls that they m͏
she was on her way to Urbana from O'Hare Airport,
nected during that time. "We were both in relationships," she said.
"Then, a few months later, we weren't in relationships."

Avi had planned a trip to LA to visit some friends, so they decided to chill. Then he emailed her to say that he couldn't come. That put the two of them in touch via email, and then they started emailing regularly. Eventually, he booked a trip to Los Angeles, and she booked one to Chicago. Karen and Avi stayed in touch for about a year and a half, from the end of October 2014 until August 2016, when she moved to Chicago, where he was living. As Karen tells me, selfies became an important part of their long-distance intimacy.

"I would definitely send selfies when I thought I looked pretty, like 'hi, I look cute, this is me in my office. Good morning.' Just to say hello and have that," she said. "It was a really easy way to connect because we weren't able to FaceTime at work, and it was a way for me to see his face and peer into his world without being on the phone or FaceTiming or texting. It was a way for me to share pieces of my life."

Karen admitted that at the beginning, she used selfies as a method of luring him in since in-person techniques weren't available. She recalls a photo that she took at the beginning of their relationship.

"I have a memory of two specific photos where it was a holiday party at the house and I was cooking brownies with my friend's kid," she said. "I took a selfie with me and his toddler and another of me and his baby. It was my way of saying 'Hey, I look cute with these kids, do you want kids? I do!'" she said. "When I took these pictures I know that was clearly my intention."

The couple is no longer long-distance, but the selfie sending continues. Even after moving in together, they still enjoy sending selfies because it's become a part of their intimacy. "I was out and about at the beach the other day, running errands, kayaking, and then I sent him a selfie of me kayaking, like, 'Hey I'm doing things, I am doing something for me,'" she said. "And he'll send back a picture of him at work being like, 'This is me, wishing I was with you.'"

Karen and Avi selfie, courtesy of Karen Krausen.

Beyond the affectionate use of the selfie here, as a sort of quick love letter postcard, there's also a sense that this sort of communication has become natural for them. "I think there's a piece of it that, once it becomes a part of the communication, it's not like it's ending," said Karen. "It just became another dimension in the texts that are going back and forth. We'll text and send photos, articles on Facebook, and an Instagram photo. It becomes a multidimensional way of communicating."

Similarly, Andrea and her now-husband, Todd, dated long-distance for a year and change. Like Avi and Karen, their relationship began in-person, but quickly shifted into long-distance before they came back together in a new location, Los Angeles. They moved to Cleveland in March 2017 when Andrea got a job elsewhere.

"We met when I was living in Berlin and he was living there also," said Andrea. "We dated for four months, from April until I left Berlin at the beginning of August. That's when I told him I was moving to LA in August for a job."

Rather than part ways indefinitely, they decided that they wanted to stay in touch and make it work. Since they both traveled often for work, they figured that there was a way to manage the relationship. And indeed they did. He went to LA for six weeks at one point, and eventually moved there; his job let him work remotely. During the long-distance period of their relationship, they sent selfies.

"He would occasionally send really funny ones. I would send more frequent, serious ones, generally taken in my apartment," said Andrea. "Not like sexy selfies—nothing inappropriate. I'd send him selfies maybe once or twice a week."

Whenever something becomes a consistent element of a relationship, one begins not just to expect it, but also enjoy it. "If I would go for a while without sending them, he would be like, 'Are you going to send me more?'" Now that they live in the same place and wake up together, there's "no need to record my face for anyone," said Andrea. "Occasionally we'll be out and take one together."

Since the selfie habit became so ingrained for Andrea, now it feels strange for her to go without them. Why quit something that's fun and gratifying like selfie-ing just because the physical circumstances that previously necessitated the practice have now changed? Because she enjoyed it, Andrea decided to keep selfie-ing even after she and Todd began living in the same city.

"I tried to take one the other morning—he was in Canada last week. I was like, 'I feel like I've gotten out of the habit of taking them and I don't look as good in the morning because I'm not trying to take photos of myself,'" she mused about her selfie-ing, reminiscing on how things have changed.

If you thought those selfies were just for Todd, though, you were wrong, dear reader. They were not, and will not remain, *exclusive content!*

"I would reuse selfies maybe 30 percent of the time," Andrea said, casually. "I would try to make sure I sent them to him first so he didn't think I was recycling my Instagram content for his pleasure. Occasionally, he'd be like, 'Oh and you wanted to share that one [to Instagram] too?' and I'd be like, 'Yep!' He was slightly put off when it wasn't exclusive content, but he got over it."

Over that sixteen-month period, Andrea mastered her selfie game. At their wedding, everything changed.

"We got married a month and a half ago, and it was really hard—I didn't have my phone most of the day. We took one selfie after we got married. The rest was professional photographers chasing after us," she said. "I know how to pose for a selfie—I can take a really good one—but I don't usually let people take photos of me. I was like, 'I know we're paying you thousands of dollars, but I need direction—I know what to do when I am looking at the phone, but not when I'm looking at a camera five feet away.'"

Kyle Benson, a relationship coach based in Seattle, had a similar experience with selfies and getting to know someone long-distance. He and his girlfriend met in Mexico, and when he went back to the US they began exchanging selfies.

"I think they can bring a new level of intimacy," said Benson. "She'll have a terrible day and something happened with her business or in her life, and she'll be really upset, and I'm like 'Is there anything I can do?' and she's like, 'Just shoot me a picture of you smiling.' It's the same thing for me. For some reason people see selfies as just sexual; I think for me I find it as a way that's sweet and comforting, too."

Sending selfies gives a sense of increased connection, in part because you directly get to see the other person's face. "When I receive a selfie, it's like, you get pictures and text messages and then you get that selfie, and I notice for me I feel more of a connection with it," said Benson.

"The selfie is more expressive than many of the kinds of communications that we are used to because it shows the face and the eyes. And because our bodies respond to that as if it were real," said Dr. Pamela Rutledge. "People don't routinely send each other selfies when they can talk. My perspective of technology is people use whatever is available to them to create the most closeness."

Perhaps that's why we react so strongly to selfies that we receive one-to-one on our phones, or that we catch on social media. It feels real because it's a way to be present together, no matter the location.

Selfie game STRONG!!!!!!!

There's the person who posts a lot of selfies to their social media, and then there's the private Instagram account @WrongEye4, created by LA-based Sara Apple Maliki, where people can find a bunch of weird selfies captioned randomly. Well, mostly selfies—the account also includes other obscured body parts, just not straight-up nudes. One pic is a close-up of a girl's ass clad in a black thong, with the words STAY RAD written on one cheek. The caption reads "bully you into buying." In another selfie, a guy wears a smug look on his face, posing in front of ocean-themed wallpaper. He looks tired—bags linger under his eyes. The caption on his pic randomly reads "my little pony theme song." In another image, there's a bathroom mirror self-ie, of a woman obscuring her face with a smartphone and her pants down, ass hanging out. This one is captioned "Wayne Gretzky pushed me down the stairs." This account has evolved to include a collection of submitted selfies, but that's not how it all started.

"[The account] began because a handful of girlfriends and I would send nudes we didn't want to send to guys to each other," Maliki said. "I realized the aesthetic value of the photos and asked if I could post them on an Instagram account. They all agreed as long as the photos remained anonymous. That way there was instant gratification without the negative feelings or association."

Maliki started the first version of this account in 2013, but because of the nude content it got deleted several times. It came back in various iterations over the next two years, with names such as @Wrongeye, @wrongeye_ and @privateeyecount. But even when she edited out the nudity, the photos got reported. Eventually, she gave up on this version of the account. After none of these versions worked, she started @WrongEye4 in October 2015. On this account, she sometimes posts nudity in the IG Sto-ries section, where photos and videos disappear after twenty-four hours. The captions for the photos come to her "completely at random from my imagination," she said.

Selfie courtesy of @WrongEye4 / Sara Maliki.

People interested in checking out @WrongEye4, which is a private Instagram account, have to ask permission for access. If they're allowed in, they'll encounter these selfies, and can also choose to submit their own. The @wrongeye4 bio reads "if ur feelin urself . . . I wanna see . . . ANONYMOUS SELFIES! LOVE YOU ALL! Please DM submissions & any questions you may have x."

In this regard, the account functions as a destination for selfies that would otherwise have no place to go, or that could end up on the wrong phone, much like the nudes that inspired this account in the first place. To some, the selfies come across as digital detritus, but to others they're a fascinating peek into ways that people self-image, documenting a version of themselves, and deciding to post that, somewhere, for someone to see.

"To me, the online world is an extension of our social world," said Dr. Pamela Rutledge. "The interesting thing is that it happens when people don't see it as the same—they see it as 'some other place.'"

Online and offline worlds are intrinsically linked, with a fluid interchange occurring between the two. Behavior that happens online reflects offline, and vice versa. For accounts like @wrongeye4, the collective act of feelin' yourself is made performative and visible to others who are allowed access to the private IG account. It was set up so that this group of women could receive validation from each other for hot nude pics, rather than risk sending those images to guys who could just as easily post them publicly to the Internet, or share them with an unintended recipient. Today, the account is more of an experiment into what the selfie is or could be. It's an opportunity to play with self images, to have fun, and to not be judged for taking them.

Despite delightful accounts like @wrongeye4, there's still a prevailing notion that people were inherently different before smartphones. Surely, communication wasn't as instantaneous, but that doesn't mean it was necessarily "better" before. In this "gold standard" argument, what was happening back in the day was right, and the way things are now is somehow wrong or unacceptable. Basically, this is an argument for the "good old days," and it's about as tired as nostalgia for nineties television or favorite childhood films. "We are measuring that distance looking for what's wrong," said Rutledge. "So I think that's what we see all the time in selfies, measuring that distance as if how we were behaving before was the right kind of way."

Lez stay in touch :)

For myself, another important motivation for posting selfies or even sharing anything to Facebook is staying in touch with people who I can't see on a regular basis. It's always nice to receive a gentle like from a faraway friend or a family member thousands of miles away who I don't chat with regularly, but still care about.

Staying in touch and socializing online are largely what teenagers do, because the Internet is another place where their friends hang out. Why give an entire generation these types of digital tools and then attempt to shame them for using them exactly the way that they were designed? Yet again, adults forget that they were once teens, and the media sensationalizes the ways that teens behave during this intense period in their life when they are figuring out who they are as social beings. No matter what time period, teens will always be teens.

"We overinvest too much meaning in selfies when we think of them as social malaise and narcissism," said Rutledge. "The receiver views that as a trigger of social validation. It doesn't mean we are hanging around looking for likes, but it does imply a positive social connection. It triggers the rewards sector of the brain as much the same way as when you run into a friend and they look happy to see you and you feel rewarded."

Naturally, much of the blame for the "downfall of society as we know it" lands on teenagers, as it always does because *oh jeez, the kids today!* No matter the generation, there's always something to worry about. I always think back to Larry Clark's 1983 photography series *Teenage Lust* and 1971's *Tulsa*, which portray a life of adolescent drug use and sex encounters. Teens were doing a lot of the same "bad behaviors" back then, but without the help of social media to document all of it. Usually, participating in these "bad behaviors" are about finding one's self within the community of their peers. Such acts of yesteryear—whether they be doing drugs or just going to an ice cream social—are much like today's acts of participating in a specific behavior, and taking selfies as a way to socialize and also show off. Larry Clark documented this long before it was possible to find these same types of images on Instagram or Snapchat. Thanks to technology, they're now readily available, hashtagged, and searchable, perfect for great Internet listicles like #funeralselfie, which were heavily criticized in the press but, to me, seemed like pretty normal teen behavior.

In a post I wrote for *Hyperallergic*, "Stop Freaking Out About Funeral Selfies," I explained the backlash to funeral selfies, wherein teenagers were hashtagging pictures #funeralselfie of themselves either at or on their way to funerals.[7] I thought about the ways that an inherent part of adolescence is how a teenager shares their feelings and what they're up to with friends. The fact that these images of teens' lives are publically available and viewable by adults and randoms alike is what makes them appear more shocking. Normally, adults and randoms online are not privy to the social lives of teenagers.

Julie Weitz is an LA-based artist whose work explores what it's like to exist digitally or, as she puts, it "the experience of embodiment in the digital realm."[8] She also happens to teach at community colleges in the LA area, a high school in South Central, and a nonprofit high school program at Otis College of Art and Design, so she has another view into the world of teenagers and social media. For Weitz, the difference she notices in how the "kids today" use technology has much to do with economics and what their parents use. That is, if the parents aren't using the technology, it's less likely that the kids will.[9]

"The more privileged students have access to up-to-date technology and their parents are more likely to use it, hence making them more digitally savvy," she said. "For my students who have less access to the Internet and advanced technology, their use seems more innocent. One student is an active blogger about video games, another student photographs and posts her artwork from the class online. Among this demographic, I see less of a change. The awkwardness of adolescence seems the same."

Weitz was first introduced to Finstagram when she was teaching at a private high school in Brentwood, a wealthy area of Los Angeles. "A student introduced me to the concept of 'Finsta' or fake Instagram, which she explained to me was the normal Instagram you share with everyone which shows you in your best light, whereas your real Instagram is the one you share with your 'soul sisters' as she put it, and exposes you in all states of being—ugly, emotionally distressed, etc. This idea impressed me—the students recognized the inauthenticity of sharing yourself on social media, and repurposed it for a select few—keeping in mind the importance of friendship and trust."

Clearly, teens are social media savvy. Certainly, #funeralselfies became a thing before Finstagram was invented. But how do teens learn how to use social media?

"If the format of Instagram is about projecting an image for quick consumption, the question is: how do you feed the feed?" asked Weitz. "For teens tapped into that kind of self-awareness, social media can be an open space for sassy attitude and authentic creativity. The critical distinction is to recognize the difference between the persona they project in bits of information versus their complex, constantly growing selves. In this sense, socializing IRL [in real life] will always be more productive and full."

Socializing is no longer relegated to on or offline; instead, it is part of a continual fluid interchange. Or maybe you become close to someone in another country who you won't immediately meet IRL. Or maybe you swipe on Tinder in cities thousands of miles away that you're considering moving to, just to see who's out there and to get the place's vibe. When I was a teenager, AOL Instant Messenger was just becoming a thing, and I recall having a lot of chat sessions with friends. I'd leave the chat on and walk away from the computer, only to return and find messages waiting for me. It was exciting, immediate, and social. I try to replicate that excitement sometimes with text messages, leaving them hanging for hours or days because the anticipation itself makes the message arrival that much more fun. But that was a time when such technology was still super new, much slower, and not on smartphones.

"Teens today are at a period of their life where finding their place in a peer group is their primary developmental task," said Rutledge. "They aren't addicted to likes, but they are focused on finding their social milieu, and at least half of this is happening online."

Professor Catherine Liu, who recently taught a class at the University of California at Irvine on the history of selfies, likens young people and selfie-taking to the communalism movement of the 1960s.[10]

"The moral panic about youth culture replicates the youth culture panics that took place around rock 'n' roll—these knee jerk reactions about 'out of control' young people who don't care about privacy and are addicted to this thing," said Liu when we spoke via phone. "This is reinforced from the cinematic network, from *The Social Network* to *The Bling Ring* and *Unfriended*, in addition to unsubstantiated memes about cyberbullying and cyberstalking."

In addition, explained Liu, selfies also represent the fall of an industry that was built in the twentieth century: the family-oriented photography industry that centered around Kodak and Polaroid. "Early advertising of Kodachrome is very similar to Facebook and Instagram, with the goal of wanting to capture your memories." Except the early Kodachrome ads were all of white, middle-class women doing domestic, family things all with the ease of their cameras, notes Liu.

"The problem is that we do give our data away," said Liu. "Facebook is building our world, but the exchange still comes out on the side of the positive in terms of connectedness rather than being lost in the world of surveillance and narcissism."

Enter my queer selfie ZONE, y'all

Many of the selfie studies out in the world approach gender as binary, which is very limiting and, frankly, annoying! Gender exists on a spectrum and it, along with race, class, sexuality, socioeconomic status, etc., all affect how and why people selfie. In the article "Of Selfies and Queer Folk" for *Photoworks* (UK), a development agency focused on photography, Sharif Mowlabowcus carves out an explanation for queer peoples' deep-seated relationship with selfies—as a way to be seen by others in the networked community, and to exist authentically in spaces where otherwise one is either overlooked or shamed:

> LGBT folk gravitated towards digital forms of communication and identity performance with a deep sense of investment

much earlier than their heterosexual compatriots. The queer self became 'networked' far earlier (and far more easily) than the straight self. In part this was due to necessity. Being seen as queer is never easy when the world one lives in is coded as a priori heterosexual. But there was something more in this migration to the digital, this leap into cyberspace. There was a gravitational pull that promised unprecedented visibility to the queer individual and the illusion of self-determination in how one might be seen by others.[11]

Similarly, on the brilliant blog livingnotexisting.org, created by geoff, a mixed-race genderqueer filipinx living in Toronto,[12] they wrote:

> Selfies are acts of resistance that disrupt normalized beauty, gendered and sexualized representations in mass media. They empower individuals to be active agents in defining their own beauty, gender and sexuality. Selfies provide visibility to non-normative bodies underrepresented and misrepresented in the media.[13]

There's a lot more to a selfie than meets the eye. In fact, sometimes you wouldn't know any of this from the surface, particularly from individuals who experience queer invisibility on a daily basis. That is, they are not read as queer out in the world. There is a privilege to being read as heterosexual, of course, but at the same time there is a sense of erasure. I was wondering about the ways that selfie culture could be used to help queer people connect. I've made a few queer friends off Tinder, but mostly I've used it for its main purpose: dating. I wondered if queer connections could happen via Instagram, specifically by using hashtags as a way to be visible.

In fact, the answer to that question arrived. I received a follow from the account @babetownnyc, a pop-up supper club for queer women, trans and nonbinary people. They'd liked a selfie I had taken with my friend Kait Schuster at LA Dyke Day, which I'd hashtagged with #dykeday, making it easily searchable for queer companies like this one. I was being marketed to, and it worked. The account was a dinner party in Brooklyn for queer women, femme women, and gender nonconforming etc. . . . and they found me through a hashtag from the photo with Kait. (I did not go to the event.)

I thought more about the question of queer connection in relation to Kait's Instagram (@kaitshoes), with whom I selfie-d that day. Her IG is mostly pictures of her, selfies or otherwise. She's a queer femme and cisgendered (lady) who is also a writer, performer, and visual storyteller based in Los Angeles. We talked selfies one day by phone.

"I think social media is a really helpful tool in breaking the isolation of queer fear. If people are willing to be visible, using a hashtag can connect them to other people where even ten years ago we had only MySpace searches," she told me. "It's getting easier and easier to find people who are in similar boats as you. I think selfie culture is really helpful for that."

Kait is one of the most empathetic people I know, and I wanted to understand her intention, aside from queer visibility, for wanting to hold this selfie space for herself on Instagram. Practically every photo on her account is of her. Was she anxious about possibly being called self-involved or narcissistic?

"It's this weird low-brow / high-brow thing that happens, where I think about self-obsession in what is to me a pretty sophisticated way," she said. "I am self-interested, and I do have that anxiety that people think that I'm self-interested. I kind of stopped the obsession around that by being like, 'That's true, but what if that's not bad?' I think there's a lot of stigma around self-interest and what that means. At the same time, I don't know anyone who is interesting to me who isn't self-interested."

The selfie can also be a way of attempting to externalize the internal, allowing for a specific type of self-expression. It's another element of selfie-ing that Schuster told me she thinks about often.

"I'm so interested in myself and what motivates me, and I feel like my Instagram and my selfies are another expression of that," she said. "I do so much internal work on myself—therapy, talking with friends, self-help books—and so taking selfies, using self-timers, and people taking pictures of me is almost like, 'What is my internal movement doing for my external life?'"

There's a specific gendering to referring to selfie-takers as "narcissistic" that I also want to point out as well. Generally, it's men telling women that they are narcissists for selfie-ing, something that critic John Berger recognized decades ago in his iconic book *Ways of Seeing*. He points out that in Western art, women have historically been subjects for the male gaze, with little control over their bodies or subjectivities.

Considering the gendered active/passive relationship, women are the objects of desire and inspiration for the male gaze, and to act of their own accord is, as Berger described, somehow suddenly labeled as narcissistic within the patriarchal viewing culture by the very men who want to retain control. The same holds true, decades later, for the majority of selfie critiques issued by men about women taking selfies. Writes Berger of the contradictions inherent in a man painting a woman versus allowing her to view herself: "You painted a naked woman because you enjoyed looking at her; put a mirror in her hand and you called the painting 'Vanity,' thus morally condemning the woman whose nakedness you had depicted for your own pleasure."

In another condemnation of Western art history's paintings of nude-women-by-men paradox, Berger famously notes: "Men act and women appear. Men look at women. Women watch themselves being looked at."[14] A woman taking a moment to actually look at herself is not only brave, but a threat to the patriarchal order. To quell that feminine threat, men immediately labeled her as vain, as someone who is crying out for attention (from men, because obviously who else could save a woman from herself?!). At the same time, the selfie taker captures the gaze and loves it. The selfie serves and it is pleasure, attention, and validation all in one. The super-liked selfie WINS. Period.

A real BFF narrative . . . on social media?????

When I told my BFF Che Landon that I was writing a book about selfies, she asked me if the book would be about constructing a narrative around the selfies I've seen in my years of research. I told her that sort of, sure, that's what the book would be about. How can it not be, really, since we're living our lives but also posting about them, too? This made me feel like the selfie whisperer. It was after or around that point that we started taking usies together. An usie is just a selfie of "us." We wanted to document our friendship, too, and it would've just felt unnatural to ask a stranger to take photos of the two of us together. We knew how we felt about our friendship, and it was for us to capture—not some outsider. I don't like being that sentimental on social media, but Che really does and so she posted pics of our friendship to IG and Facebook.

One evening when Che was out of town, I found myself missing her a lot and actually feeling sentimental. Lying in bed with my phone in hand, I started scrolling through my photo collection. I'd been delaying transferring the photos to my computer, not wanting to send my memories to a new portal, and I was unwilling to try and figure out how to work my iCloud despite the neverending stream of notifications that said: "Your iCloud storage is full!" My phone told me that I was holding on to too many photos, but I didn't care. There was a point in time when I was diligent about always transferring my images to the computer, never letting my phone get full. But then I realized that I could have entire photo albums of my life on the phone, easily accessible whenever I wanted to show them.

So, it happened that evening I was lying in bed and came across a cute usie of Che and me at her place in LA, cuddling on her bed and generally having the best time! I selected the image, and then glided over to Instagram. I posted it along with an emo note full of hashtags, which is how Che always posts her social media pics both for fun and so they'll be more visible on the platform.[15] My overuse of hashtags was a direct reference to her style—a social media shoutout. After posting it, I felt better for a moment.

aliciaeler   ...

Liked by **chelandon**, **kaitschuster** and **19 others**

aliciaeler Awwww #tbt #missu #chillin #homies #bae #selfie Che Che @chelandon 😊 💯 😂

chelandon 🖤 🖤 🖤 🖤

But why did I need to make these images of longing public to my entire Instagram feed, or anyone on the Internet who Googles my Instagram? Somehow, it felt more meaningful to me to post our friendship on the Internet and have others see it, bear witness to it. That validated the friendship in a more performative way than if I'd just texted her individually. It brought up the question of: Are we taking photos to take them, or are we taking photos in order to share them and get that extra validation from other people? It felt like a very teen phenomena, but also Che is an actress and I enjoy playing with the performative space of social media. So this felt like an extension of that creative performative work. It made me think about how much Che enjoys sharing photos of her and me. But it also made me think about our friendship differently at times, because we began creating a public narrative about our friendship on social media. It was performed and crafted for social media, but it's also real life.

Chapter 2

Privacy Settings

My mom likes to tell me about what a private person I was in high school. "I barely knew who you were," she said to me while we're sitting at the dining room table of my childhood home in Skokie, a Chicago suburb. We sipped bitter black Starbucks coffee. My parents' elderly German Shepard, JoJo, slept lovingly at her feet. Only the mention of a walk would rouse him. My mom gazed serenely down at JoJo, and then looked back up at me. "You were just so . . . in your own world," she said.

I came of age before the rise of social media. The idea of privacy was different in the nineties, before easy Internet access. My dad had a dial-up Prodigy account, which I used to go on AOL Instant Messenger and chat with friends, but my life was mostly offline, and not so easily surveillable online, like the lives of teenagers today. As an adolescent, I also knew how to keep things from my parents, the original Big Brother. I simply went into my bedroom and closed the door, which was covered in ominous-sounding, adolescent-outcast-type phrases like "Welcome to the Freak Show!" and "Enter . . . if you dare!!" that I wrote with permanent marker. It pissed my parents off—it was typical teenage behavior. But every time I went into my room, I felt like I was in a universe entirely of my own—that I had a private life. To match the permanent marker scrawlings on the door of my bedroom, I drew lyrics from my then-favorite singer, Ani DiFranco, on my dresser, along with other random words like "AC/DC," which was how, at one point, my dad decided to define my sexuality. (I didn't object, but I did laugh at that terminology.) My room offered me a sense of privacy.

The words "Welcome to the Freakshow" are still
on my door, despite being painted over.
Here's a photo of it by my dad, Ihsan Eler.

When I was alone in my room, I also took self-portraits using a film camera. I tried on different outfits, stood in front of the large mirror that hung to the right of my closet, and snapped pictures.[1] Later, I walked a few blocks to the local Walgreens and dropped them off to get developed. There was a time lag between shooting the pictures and seeing what they looked like. Nowadays, that is not the case. If I were a teenager and these were selfies today, I would have seen the results immediately, and it's likely that I would've posted at least a few of them to Instagram and Snapchat, where my friends hung out. I would've saved some of the images for myself, too. There would be many outtakes. But back then, I showed my photos to no one at all, chatted on AIM with friends, and hung out with friends at school. The self-portraits I took were my own reflections. They were for me; they were a way for me to see how I appeared to myself and, ultimately, an attempt to understand how others saw me.

I participated in the rise of social media and shift toward sharing what I remember as private moments. I became preoccupied with the privacy settings and options that social networks offered users. How could a photo that I once kept so private that it was almost a sacred object become something that could so easily be shared with peers through digital means? How could so many people become willingly complacent in the notion that the audience for shared selfies wasn't easily determined, and that these images would become data on the networks where they were posted? In our hypersocial networked era, we've traded the notion of "privacy" for products, deals, free services, and, most of all, convenience. Selfie performance is predicated on relinquishing privacy.

Yet we rely on these technologies to communicate with the people in our lives, and abandoning them completely would inevitably make our communications increasingly difficult. Backing out of this would pose a major inconvenience.

Many of the conversations around social media come back to privacy. We buy something online with a credit card, post some thoughts to Twitter, drop an image on Instagram, and search through various news sites. These digital activities make up sensitive, trackable information that can now be sold off to third parties, such as advertisers, without notifying the consumer. Yet here we all are, posting selfies to social networks, texting with friends, emailing away thoughts. Simply put, it is how we live today.

But what are the proper definitions of privacy? At a basic level it can be defined in the way that we are using it here, as *one's right to privacy*, as "freedom from unauthorized intrusion."[2] In the definition of privacy in terms of secrecy, privacy is also defined as "a private matter: secret." In Black's Law Dictionary, the notion of "privacy" is broken down specifically as it relates to the law:

> The right that determines the nonintervention of secret surveillance and the protection of an individual's information. It is split into 4 categories (1) Physical: An imposition whereby another individual is restricted from experiencing an individual or a situation. (2) Decisional: The imposition of a restriction that is exclusive to an entity. (3) Informational: The prevention of searching for unknown information and (4) Dispositional: The prevention of attempts made to get to know the state of mind of an individual.[3]

Despite what we know today about privacy, there's still an acceptance of giving up privacy for convenience, whether it's in communications or consumerism.

"Many of us have become complacent today—that is, when we are not actively craving publicity, or learning to love what we can't do without. We have gotten accustomed to the commodification of privacy, of autonomy, of anonymity—to the commodification of what DA Miller refers to as that 'integral, autonomous, secret self,'" writes Bernard Harcourt in his book *Exposed.*[4]

The notion of privacy can be broken down into three tiers: online privacy as it is defined by corporate social networks, how telecommunications companies buy and sell the data we share online, and privacy as it relates to information that the government is able to obtain about its citizens under the surveillance state in a post-9/11 world.

After Snowden's revelations about the NSA, it became clear that we were already living in a postprivacy world in which it's even more important for people to understand their constitutional rights, and purposefully and stealthily navigate the highly surveilled Internet and social networks. Yet many people do not care, and don't question giving up their data because they feel they have done nothing wrong and thus they have nothing to hide. It would appear that the idea of privacy has become a moot point.

"With the increased commodification of things today, though, privacy has itself been transformed into a type of good that can be traded, bought and sold," writes Harcourt. "Rather than a *human* property, privacy protections have become *private* property. Privacy has been *privatized.*"[5]

Still, the question of *why* privacy is important seems to evade many well-meaning people. Beyond the point about privacy being privatized and, thus, commodified, Harlo Holmes, director of newsroom digital security at Freedom of the Press Foundation, breaks down why the "I have nothing to hide" argument is defeatist and, ultimately, useless.

"Despite the fact that *everyone* has something to hide, and to say otherwise is futile, when your privacy is breached, and all your information laid bare in front of others, you never get to choose how that information will be used to tell a story about you that might be very far from how you, and others in your life, know you," said Holmes. "You never get to choose; someone else does. That's the point."

Privacy before Facebook:
Expanding the surveillance state, Post 9/11

I was seventeen years old, a junior in high school, when 9/11 happened. This was pre-Facebook, social media, and smartphones. I had what we would now consider a really rudimentary cell phone that, at the time, felt very high-tech. I walked into Spanish class; it was a class with a teacher I didn't like, and who also didn't like me. My accent sucked, and she picked on me about it, even though I loved the class. (Don't worry, my accent has really improved!). French was my first foreign language, which I abandoned because Spanish seemed more practical to learn in the U.S. I was always trying to make the more "practical" decision. I spaced out a lot in that class.

I remember, however, that I was not spacing out on 9/11 as the class listened intently to voices of panic on the radio—turned on reluctantly by that Spanish teacher who told us to stay calm, that it was a false alarm, and we should just keep learning today. But we did not, and it was not. What happened that day would have massive repercussions for how we interpret and sense our own privacy, and the idea of privacy altogether.

It's impossible to talk about privacy without discussing 9/11, the destruction of the Twin Towers in New York, and the loss of 2,996 lives and injuring of another 6,000. The events following 9/11 changed ideas of privacy by justifying expansion of the government's domestic surveillance abilities, and the ability to label and prosecute everyday people as "terrorists." As we know, 9/11 was declared a terrorist attack, and the White House quickly took legislative action by passing the PATRIOT Act on October 26, 2001.[6] It was done hastily, a little more than a month after 9/11, and it vastly expanded the government's ability to surveil the average American.

"Employing an absurdly broad definition of 'domestic terrorism,' the PATRIOT Act turns almost all forms of vigorous protest and minor criminal conduct into prosecutable acts of terrorism," explain Michael Ratner and Margaret Rather Kunstler in their book *Hell No: Your Right to Dissent in Twenty-First Century America*.[7] "For example, the act labels what would normally have been standard Gandhi/King-like civil disobedience as domestic terrorism. Had the PATRIOT Act existed in 1999, protestors opposed to the World Trade Organization who technically engaged in trespass in demonstrating at the WTO conference in Seattle conceivably could have been charged with 'domestic terrorism.'"

The intention of the PATRIOT Act was to give the NSA more access to citizens without issuing search warrants for the purposes of stopping another terrorist attack from happening. Searching inside Americans' private lives made them potential suspects to the US government. Then President George W. Bush explained that privacy could be violated—no warrants necessary—for the "purposes of preventing a terrorist attack," which is vague language. But with the expansion of the PATRIOT Act, much human rights and domestic advocacy work could fall under "domestic terrorism" and thus become equated with terrorism.

"The PATRIOT Act granted the government remarkably intrusive powers: to invade the privacy of Americans and others living in this country, and to find out what individuals are saying, thinking, and doing. Broad new wiretapping provisions [. . .] means that our conversations on the telephone and our emails are not protected."[8]

In a 2005 article for the *New York Times*, "Bush Lets U.S. Spy on Callers Without Courts," James Risen and Eric Lichtblau reported: "Bush authorized the National Security Agency to eavesdrop on Americans and others inside the United States to search for evidence of terrorist activity without the court-approved warrants ordinarily required for domestic spying, according to government officials."[9] These steps were supposedly part of an effort to track any possible links to al-Qaeda, and included the monitoring of international phone calls and emails, as well as domestic communications.

Previously, the NSA's mission was to spy on communications abroad, not domestically. The PATRIOT Act changed all of that, significantly stretching the Fourth Amendment, which protects against unreasonable searches and seizure of a citizen's private home, to electronic surveillance and wiretapping. "Unless an exception applies, law enforcement agents are required to obtain a search warrant to conduct a search," write Ratner and Kunstler.[10] "Search warrants must be supported by probable cause, with facts sworn to by the officer applying for a warrant."

The application of the Fourth Amendment became a topic of fierce debate after former NSA contractor Edward Snowden leaked classified NSA documents to the *Guardian* and the *Washington Post*. The first document that Snowden leaked to the *Guardian* detailed a secret court order from the NSA to major telecom provider Verizon, ordering collection of telephone records of millions of US customers.[11] Chair of the Senate intelligence committee, Senator Diane Feinstein, who initially defended the NSA, stated that the surveillance program only recorded the metadata—the phone numbers of calls placed and received, and the time of calls and duration—rather than the data itself, as in what was said. However, that metadata also includes personal information, which can offer a more detailed profile of the individual than the actual content.

"[T]he government has surveilled virtually all Americans. We know it did because of the Snowden leaks, and because it has argued in court that no volume of surveillance violates a reasonable expectation of privacy when it comes to metadata," writes Sean Vitka for *Slate*. "While one program—the telephone metadata dragnet—was technically ended (and in some ways codified) by the USA Freedom Act in 2015, another law is still on the books with virtually no limits."[12]

Snowden brought to light evidence that the NSA had collected telephone records of tens of millions of Americans. But that was not all. Through the creation of PRISM, the "downstream" surveillance program of the NSA, Internet firms, Facebook, Google, Microsoft, PalTalk, YouTube, Skype, AOL, Apple, and Yahoo provided all types of electronic information, including emails, chats (voice, video), videos, photos, stored data, VoIP, file transfers, video conferencing, notifications of target activity (logins, etc.), and, of course, online social networking details.[13]

Not every company complied with NSA requests to access data. Ladar Levison, founder of Lavabit, a privacy-focused email provider, shut down the service rather than comply with federal agents' demand to give them the master encryption keys.[14] Rumor had it that Snowden had an email account through Lavabit, and later an accidental government leak in 2016 confirmed that indeed, they were after Snowden's email.[15]

The following year, the *Guardian* and UK's Channel 4 News reported that the NSA had also collected nearly two hundred million text messages a day from around the world, extracting data such as location, contacts, and credit card information.[16]

After Snowden's whistleblowing, the US Senate passed the USA Freedom Act of 2015 forcing the NSA to stop bulk collection of mass phone data collections.[17] This would be the United States' first significant surveillance reform since 1978.[18] Under this law, the NSA could only obtain data about specific individuals with permission from a federal court.[19] But as the *Intercept* reports, that's a pretty low bar—a very small step toward dismantling surveillance programs.[20]

"It's a testament to the significance of the Snowden disclosures and also to the hard work of many principled legislators on both sides of the aisle. Still, no one should mistake this bill for comprehensive reform. The bill leaves many of the government's most intrusive and overbroad surveillance powers untouched, and it makes only very modest adjustments to disclosure and transparency requirements," writes Jameel Jaffer, the American Civil Liberties Union deputy legal director.[21]

In the midst of all these NSA leaks, social media had already become a means for sharing pretty much anything, and the common understanding of privacy seemed to be about what people willingly or unwillingly shared online, rather than about how easy it was for the government to request information about any individuals using the PATRIOT Act.

All of these shifts in privacy occurred before the rise of social media. So where does the selfie fit in to all of this? The selfie arrived at a time when mass surveillance and data collection had already become the norm. In their essay "Selfie Control" for the *New Inquiry*, JB Brager covers these questions about the rise of the selfie that happened to be raised at the same time that the public began learning the extent of mass surveillance: "The rise of the selfie coincides with revelations of mass surveillance: We have all started taking more photos of ourselves as we've become subjects to the government's massive recording apparatuses. . . . The technology that makes the selfie possible is also the technology that makes mass surveillance simple."[22]

The selfie and the expanding field of biometrics, which uses technology to identify individuals based on biological traits such as retinal or iris scanning, facial recognition or fingerprints, were signs that people were becoming even more easily trackable based not only on what they posted to social media, but also just by being out in a public space.

In this way, the selfie acts almost as a moment of defiance mixed with an awareness of just how surveilled our lives are today. The selfie is a declaration of an already data-exploited self online, and one that is also imaged even through simple situations such as security cameras in stores, at airports, or in other public spaces. In posting a selfie, a user attempts to claim space in an already oversaturated social media environment. Yet the selfie is always under surveillance; it signifies what Bernard Harcourt refers to as an aspect of the expository society, in which we now have a platform for "unprecedented levels of exhibition, watching, and influence that is reconfiguring our political relationship and reshaping our notions of what it means to be an individual."

The public knows about surveillance culture thanks to the Snowden leaks and the countless articles that have followed, but the point is that even though we know, apparently many do not care.

The compulsion to share and communicate is exciting and addictive. People feel that they have "nothing to hide," so why should it matter what is shared? We're all so used to communicating on our phones—what would we do otherwise? Sharing to social networks also allows for a specific version of a curated self that is fascinating to watch, particularly for those who are natural voyeurs. It also makes connections fast and easy. But it can become a lonely space if you get sucked in and can't stop scrolling. Despite the uses for social media, it seems as if no one is protecting digital privacy. Not the telecommunications companies who were handed a major win on March 28, 2017, when House Republicans dismantled the FCC's Internet privacy protections.

Verizon, AT&T, and Comcast would "no longer be limited on what they could do with a lot of customer data, including browsing habits, app usage history, location data and Social Security numbers."[23]

The Electronic Frontier Foundation (EFF) is concerned with digital privacy. The organization has remained at the forefront of these questions since the first reports of the NSA's domestic surveillance activities appeared. The domestic spying program works in a variety of ways: major telecommunications companies such as AT&T, MCI, and Sprint handed over "call-detail records" of their customers, which included customers' names, street addresses, and other personal info. The government received access to all of the calls made. They did not have to have a warrant in order to access this information.

The NSA also installed surveillance equipment at telecomm companies, giving them access to communications in real time, such as emails, through 'fiber-optic splitters' that made copies of the data that was then passed along both to the government and the person for whom it was originally intended. Mark Klein, a former AT&T technician, turned over documents to the EFF that explained the fiber-optic splitter that had been installed by AT&T at 611 Folsom Street, which is AT&T's switching center in San Francisco.[24] "They are collecting everything on everybody," Klein said in a *Wired* magazine article.[25]

The splitter enabled the company to "makes copies of all emails, web browsing, and other Internet traffic, to and from AT&T customers, and provide those copies to the NSA." These documents fueled a lawsuit that ultimately led Congress to pass legislation immunizing AT&T and other telecoms companies from being sued for working with NSA's dragnet surveillance program. So, EFF went ahead and sued the government in the dragnet surveillance case.

In May 2014, the Utah Data Center, a fully operational data center built for the NSA, was completed. "[There] will be all forms of communication, including the complete contents of private emails, cell phone calls, and Google searches, as well as all sorts of personal data trails—parking receipts, travel itineraries, bookstore purchases, and other digital 'pocket litter,'" said longtime national security author James Bamford.[26] An NSA spokesperson refuted claims that the NSA would be "unlawfully listening in on, or reading emails of, U.S. citizens."[27] But as *Wired* reported closer to the original intended September 2013 opening of the center, it was "in some measure, the realization of the 'total information awareness' program created during the first term of the Bush administration—an effort that was killed by Congress in 2003 after it caused an outcry over its potential for invading Americans' privacy."[28] The Utah Data Center stands as a symbol of big data and surveillance culture, stationed out in the desert, hard to enter, but an existence that is impossible to forget. But aside from listening into phone calls, and collecting emails and texts, how does the government obtain data? Through companies that collect data.

Since 2011, the EFF has conducted annual "Who Has Your Back?" privacy reports detailing how private companies, ranging from social networks to telecommunications and sharing economy apps like Uber, protect or release data to the government. The majority of Americans remain complicit with the surveillance state. In a culture of big data and expository culture on social media, the selfie becomes another symbol, much like the NSA Data Center.

On this level, with the sheer glut of selfies proliferating on the Internet, the selfie also functions as a sort of digital detritus, or trash. That is, we are living in a culture that's so overexposed and surveilled that of course there's already surveillance footage of us out there in the world, captured by cameras we're either seeing or not noticing at all. So what does one more image of our face even matter?

The publicness of broadcasting a reality-TV-esque version of ourselves brings us back culturally to Kim Kardashian and other viral social media celebs. Internet visibility and a lack of personal boundaries get conflated and, ultimately, rationalized because the government is already surveilling you even if you never post to social media. To this extent, it feels impossible to beat the system, and so submission and complacency appear to be the only way to survive.

Facebook defines privacy, not you

Facebook has a consistent history of changing its privacy settings without notifying consumers, prompting headlines like FACE-BOOK CHANGES PRIVACY SETTINGS, AGAIN; YOU SHOULD GO CHECK FACEBOOK'S PRIVACY SETTINGS; or other, more alarmist articles. In a sensationalist-sounding 2011 article on the tabloid-y site *Daily Mail,* a brash headline declared HALF OF FACEBOOK USERS 'CAN'T KEEP UP' WITH SITE'S SNOOPING POLICIES AS PRIVACY RULES CHANGE EIGHT TIMES IN TWO YEARS.[29]

It was not that long ago, however, when Zuckerberg declared in 2010 that privacy was "no longer a social norm" at the Crunchie awards in San Francisco. "People have really gotten comfortable not only sharing more information and different kinds, but more openly and with more people," he said. "That social norm is just something that has evolved over time."[30] Except it's not at all. Instead, Facebook decided to change the ways people think about privacy because it is a service that makes money off of people releasing their information.[31] Users did not ask Facebook to shift ideas of privacy. Rather, Facebook shifted its ideas of privacy, and users went along with it or quit the network altogether. It was, in a sense, forced complacency.

Because of Zuckerberg's blanket statements about the changing nature of privacy on social networks, many users became wary of the network. The first level of "privacy," according to how Facebook defines it, occurs in Settings: Privacy, and involves three categories: Who can see my stuff, who can contact me, and who can look me up?[32] Thus, privacy is considered in relation to the content users post to the network, and other people with whom the users connect. It's about other people's access to your stuff, or rather how much access to you and your stuff you give other people. Making friend lists and curating content so that only specific groups of people can see it is one way to go about creating a sense of social digital privacy. That is, shielding some social content from certain people, and showing it to others.

The next level of "privacy" as defined by Facebook has to do with the advertisers, search engines, and authorized applications that have access to your data. Facebook is a free service, and one way it pays its bills is by selling the data of users. The price of free is never free, but somehow people are still outraged when they learn that their data is being monetized. Any time you log into an app or web service through Facebook, you give that third-party access to your Facebook information, including bio info, links you click, and stuff that you like on the site. This makes it easier for the site to feed you targeted ads and relevant news articles.

Disconnecting your Facebook account from these third-party services is possible, but the nature of the social network makes it that much more inconvenient and labor-intensive to do so. And who has time or interest to do it? Simply put, it's less involved to just take the easy way out and give Facebook what it wants: More access to your data. Ultimately, when you use Facebook, or any social network for that matter, you relinquish your definition of privacy—it becomes what the network defines it as, something that's easy to forget.

Facebook's rise marks this disintegration of privacy standards, indicative of what Holmes calls a "flip" in technology that occurred about ten years ago, when the value of privacy became clear.

"'It just works!' is the primary drive of capitalist enterprise in tech, and so it benefits no one but them when we push, and internalize, that narrative," says Holmes. "Something flipped when tech aged about ten years, and realized that privacy violations were the quickest way to monetize, especially because everything on the Internet was free (as in beer!) to consume. But this wasn't the first flip, and it isn't like our generation first discovered the tension between free services and capitalism; baby boomers had their own awakenings to this as well, with questions about how the Internet could remain a free (as in speech!) place if you didn't pay to click on hyperlinks."

One more visible aspect of Facebook's investment in recycling users' data is the Facebook Memories function. It's evidence that we consent to have Facebook treat our potentially personal information in whatever way they want. We agree to this simply by signing up.

Facebook presents Facebook Memories as a cheerful, uplifting way that the network is helping you remember something that, perhaps, you forgot happened in the past at annual intervals. But it doesn't take into account the fact that users may not want to remember these things, for personal reasons. Or maybe it's just not something to think about. Unlike a memory raised by some outside trigger—a scent, visual cue, or perhaps that déjà vu moment when someone you meet reminds you of someone you already know—the Facebook Memory is served up by the network, without warning and seemingly out-of-context from its original location. It's a calculated and algorithmic memory, served up Facebook-style!

Facebook also assumes that by posting content to the network, the user consents to re-experiencing it at a later date without any prior notification or suggestion. Here's a suggestion: Facebook, why not ask users if they want to receive Facebook Memories?! Often, the content that's reshared back to us is of a sensitive, personal nature. For example, how about a selfie that you shot with a romantic partner who is now an ex? Or what about that selfie with a relative who passed away? A sentimental picture of a cat that ran away surfaces just a year after kitty disappeared. Seeing this may not be something you want to relive.

Some Facebook Memories are pleasant reminders of a sweet memory. Facebook recently reshared an image of me and my friend the playwright Elaine Romero, who I haven't seen in person in a while but am in touch with regularly. It was nice to see that image of us together, beaming and excited, before the premiere of her play "A Work of Art" at the Chicago Dramatists.

The present social media sharer isn't taking into account how they may feel in the future. Why would they? Life is life and the future is unknown.

Certainly, the Facebook Memory could bring up a whole new slew of emotions. If the content is emotional and unexpectedly reexperienced during a moment of vulnerability, it can send one into social media fatigue. In today's hypersocial networked world, it is just one more digital space to manage. Ultimately, Facebook Memories serves the network. It causes reengagement with older content that would otherwise get sucked down the Timeline. And so the network serves it up, and we look and stay longer, staring at the screen and remembering the good old days.

Responding to surveillance
through planned sousveillance

All of this information paints a very bleak picture of the future. To live without a sense of hope, however, is to live in constant fear or doom. Artists have taken it upon themselves to ask these questions about the nature of surveillance in order to start a conversation about it. Additionally, sousveillance can bring to light events and actions otherwise hidden.

In the age of surveillance, sousveillance is associated with selfie-ing—it is the act of recording oneself through small or wearable portable personal technologies. Sousveillance is considered the inverse of surveillance. In French, the word *sur* means "over" or "above," and thus "surveillance" is roughly translated as "watching from above." *Sous* roughly translates to "under" in English; sousveillance is being watched from under, the act of one taking a camera onto themselves, and pressing record.

Sousveillance can also bring justice. For example, a home video camera in 1991 exposed the Los Angeles Police Department in the Rodney King beatings, and a cell phone video camera caught a UC Davis police officer pepper spraying students. Nowadays, anyone can sousveil themselves and quickly post it to the Internet. Women who get cat-called on the street can pull out their phones, record the act, and then post that to HollaBackNYC .com. It is a way to expose predators and people committing wrongful acts to the greater Internet public. But sousveillance sometimes does nothing at all. On July 6, 2016, officer Jeronimo Yanez pulled Philando Castile over in the St. Paul suburb of Falcon Heights, a suburb of St. Paul, Minnesota, because of a nonworking brake light. Yanez suspected that Castile was one of two men from an armed robbery that occurred four days earlier. As the *Star Tribune* reported, "six seconds after Castile told Yanez he had a firearm, Yanez shot him."[33] Yanez fired seven times, killing Castile. Castile had a permit to carry. The aftermath of the shooting was livestreamed to Facebook by Castile's girlfriend, Diamond Reynolds, which included her narration of the event. The police dashcam video was released after a jury arrived at a not-guilty verdict on June 16, 2017. Neither video changed the verdict.

In another instance of sousveillance, Los Angeles artist Jennifer Moon voluntarily sousveilled herself throughout her day, both inside her home and in her car. As an individual who spent time in prison, she already understood what it meant to have all aspects of one's life surveilled and controlled by the Department of Justice. Moon was sentenced to eighteen months after a two-month crime spree that she went on with her then-boyfriend. Together they ran around high on heroin and crack, attempting to rob people at ATM machines using pepper spray. She served half of her time, nine months, in the maximum-security Valley State Prison for Women.[34] In prison she fell for another inmate and discovered a sense of community, which sounds very *Orange is the New Black*, but was actually the artist's real life.

In her project, *Will You Still Love Me: Learning to Love Yourself, It Is The Greatest Love of All* (2015), she plays with the idea of self-love and surveillance.[35] Viewers got used to watching her go along with her day, and if they kept watching they became familiar with Moon on a level that felt intimate yet distant. Viewers ate with Moon, drove to work with Moon, and even went to the bathroom with Moon. What were once private moments that she had, alone, doing regular things, became a reperformance of her time in prison, and potentially data that the NSA would have been interested in given her criminal background. Ultimately, it doesn't matter how the watching occurs—it matters who has access to the data, and what they plan to do with it.

Selfie "privacy"

Not every selfie taken is shared publicly. A selfie doesn't have to be seen or shared to be a selfie. For this reason, the selfie has roots in the self-portrait; but it is not the same because selfies, as a rule, always have a potential of publicness, of being shared, whereas a self-portrait does not carry that implication.

In the days before the PATRIOT Act, before Instagram and front-facing cameras in every smartphone made the selfie a ubiquitous cultural phenomena, the self-portrait suggested a sense of slowness, of careful meditation on one's own image. Plus, the time lapse between taking a photograph and dropping it off somewhere differs from the immediacy of the selfie. Fuji introduced the disposable camera in 1986, and it became popular in the early 2000s, around 2002–2005.[36] Critics of the disposable camera feared that people would be hastier with their shots—that speed would usurp quality. Proponents of the disposable camera were excited about its reasonable price and wide accessibility. No longer would people need to buy a camera before even thinking about purchasing the film.

With high-quality digital cameras in smartphones, it's become that much easier to selfie. The financial bar to entry is now just the expense of the phone itself. And no need to print out any photos, an additional cost that was necessary for every photographic development. Now the only thing needed is additional storage, enough data to save your precious moments—or rather, every moment deemed worthy of documentation. Thus came the birth of the selfie.

Nowadays, to *not* tell one's own life story through pictures on social media seems not only old-fashioned, but almost questionable—as if to say "yes, I do have something to hide," or that one is paranoid about being seen or discoverable online. But to not have a right to privacy is the problem here. Or, if you aren't sharing those life gems online, are you really even living it? (#picsoritdidnthappen) Of course you are, and the argument of "I have nothing to hide" is not the point. Privacy is not an inalienable right.

The US Constitution does not contain an express right to privacy, and while the Fourth Amendment does protect the privacy of a person and possessions against unreasonable searches, this does not guarantee an overarching right to privacy. With our data being harvested at an unprecedented rate, and as we continue to share information via social media, we are in fact offering ourselves up as data sets to the NSA and the corporations, Facebook included, that market products back to us. It seems like there is no way out of this matrix.

Of course, it is not as easily explained as that—many have experienced a real disconnect between the connectivity of social media and the realities of giving up privacy and data in exchange for a free service. Again, however, it comes back to convenience in an increasingly networked world, one where technologies that "connect" seem to be the only way to stay in touch. Writes Bernard Harcourt in his book *Exposed*:

> There are many of us who are confused and torn between, on the one hand, the desire to share our lives with loved ones and friends, to video chat on Skype from anyplace on earth, to freely share photos on Flickr, and, on the other hand, the discomfort of seemingly undressing ourselves in public or entering our private data on commercial websites. And yet, even when we hesitate or are ambivalent, it seems there is simply no other way to get things done in our new digital age.[37]

So what is the solution? To continue using the networks to stay in touch in a more "authentic" way, or to create a persona online? Selfie performance is predicated on relinquishing privacy.

Certainly though, as Harcourt explains in his book, we are not only exposing ourselves to others in our network, but also to the NSA and surveillance programs. It seems like there is no way out of this—unless you want to ditch your iPhone for a burner phone or just basically live without access to the Internet. But even those "dumbphones" are trackable. Freedom, as the old saying goes, ain't free.

Social media is an opportunity to exercise First Amendment rights, which include freedom of speech and freedom of the press. But at what price? In the surveillance state, social media is very easily trackable, and people are, knowingly or unknowingly, branding themselves online.

In 2014, after two grand jury decisions not to indict police officers for the murders of Michael Brown in Ferguson and Eric Garner on Staten Island, organizers of the Millions March set up a Facebook page for a protest that took place on Saturday, December 13, 2014, in New York City. By clicking "yes" or "accept" on the event, participants were also publicly identifying themselves as participants, making their participation publicly available to whoever searched for them. While this Facebook organizing was a show of solidarity, it also further exposed people who dissented. After being identified, an intelligence officer could quickly discover any of their digital information, as Harcourt explains in his book, and then monitor relentlessly.

It takes little imagination to think of the ways that such a list could be exploited: as a background check during a police-civilian encounter or stop-and-frisk. As a red flag for a customs search at the airport, or a secondary search at a random checkpoint. As part of a larger profile for constructing a no-fly list, or for attributing a lower priority to a 911 emergency call . . . as part of a strategy to dampen voter turnout in certain precincts.[38]

Nate Cardozo, a senior staff attorney at the Electronic Frontier Foundation's digital civil liberties team who focuses on free speech and privacy litigation, echoed these sentiments at a talk in 2015 in Santa Monica, California. "Without privacy we cannot have social change or even democracy," he said.[39] Yet privacy is exactly what we are trading for products, deals, free services, and, most of all, convenience.

One example of active surveillance through social media platforms is police use of the tool Geofeedia to track protestors, particularly at protests in Ferguson and Baltimore. It's a reminder of the amount of immediate location data that is available through phones and social media, as reported by the *Washington Post*:

> The companies provided the data—often including the locations, photos and other information posted publicly by users—to Geofeedia, a Chicago-based company that says it analyzes social media posts to deliver real-time surveillance information to help 500 law enforcement agencies track and respond to crime. The social media companies cut off Geofeedia's access to the streams of user data in recent weeks after the ACLU discovered them and alerted the companies about looming public exposure.[40]

It was no surprise that only a day or two after Trump's victory, more articles started coming out about ways to protect against a snooping Trump Administration, which is intent on further enhancing the surveillance state. Trump has publicly spoken out about revenge against his enemies, his accusations that the "media is rigged," and even tweeted his disdain for protestors—or really anyone who doesn't agree with him—before someone on his campaign team probably told him that protesters were just exercising their First Amendment rights. He quickly wrote a more congratulatory tweet about protestors. A few days later, Trump promised that he would be more restrained on Twitter, only to later write a rant blasting the *New York Times* with more false accusations about the media when in fact he had no facts to back up his claims.[41] With this type of unpredictability from a president, those who oppose his administration and are publicly protesting or planning operations must be even more careful.

On November 12, 2016, the *Intercept*'s Micah Lee published an article called "Surveillance Self-Defense Against the Trump Administration."[42] In it, he lays out practical ways to protect against surveillance. He explains that encrypting phones is very important, including using a long, random passcode of at least six digits, and never using Apple's fingerprint technology to unlock the phone. This is because of a 2014 ruling, in which Circuit Court judge Steven C. Frucci in Virginia stated that "a criminal defendant can be compelled to give up his fingerprint, but not his pass code, to allow police to open his cellphone," according to a report from the *Virginian-Pilot*. The rationale behind this was that a fingerprint is "akin to providing a DNA or handwriting sample or an actual key," which is permitted by law. "A pass code, though, requires the defendant to divulge knowledge, which the law protects against, according to Frucci's written opinion."[43]

One of the other most important things to do, Lee writes, is not to bring your phone everywhere—especially not to sensitive activist planning meetings. Our phones track our every move, and they know our exact location when we decide to take them with us. In the surveillance state, they are like little navigation tools that follow us everywhere, that know what we're up to and report it back. "If one phone has been hacked, it could be recording the entire conversation without anyone knowing," Lee writes.

But at the same time, is it too late for this because we have already exposed ourselves through social networks and our selfies? In Henry A. Giroux's essay "Selfie Culture in the Age of Corporate and State Surveillance," he argues that the selfie is not just a fad enmeshed in popular culture.[44] It is a statement about a lack of interest in privacy, but also a site of struggle—it can be used as a means of empowerment and a vehicle for social change. But is that what it will become?

On the contrary, selfies are less about entertainment and vanity then they are symptomatic of a retreat from privacy rights, an intense site for the commodification of the self, and a veritable resource for the surveillance state and its national intelligence agencies such as the National Security Agency.

To get off the network, to stop seeing one's selfie in the networked mirror, is a challenge unto itself. It may be the only way to go in the era of increased surveillance during the Trump Administration. The Obama and Bush Administrations have unfortunately set up the best possible situation for an increase in mass surveillance—and for a power-obsessed, autocratic president like Trump, that does not fare well for citizens.[45]

At the onset of full-on selfiedom in early 2014, shortly after OxfordDictionaries.com declared "selfie" the 2013 word of the year, the selfie still occupied a space of spontaneity, freedom in taking and sharing the image.[46] By May 2015, when Kim Kardashian released *Selfish*, the sense of the selfie shifted. It was clear that the selfie was like any other curated image of the self online—there was a staged quality, a sense that we should "take a selfie and capture this moment" before it's gone, and that the goal was to take the perfect selfie. I recall taking selfies before 2014 that felt more innocuous, less staged, perhaps even innocent. But come 2016, that had all but vanished. The selfie had become ubiquitous, and gone totally mainstream. Selfies marked events, friend hangouts, weddings, nights out, nights in; any moment, anytime, anywhere, had become potentially 'grammable either in the moment or as a #latergram. Only the best selfie should be posted. Today, the selfie is anything but instant and spontaneous; it is the epitome of a selfie-focused mono-app culture.[47]

Anyone with access to a social network can post selfies. In doing so, that person is essentially creating themselves as a product or brand, but also as a highly visible set of data. The interchange between social and performative is solidified in the selfie. With the advent of the selfie, consumer and social identities now comingle within the context of surveillance culture.

Data brokerage: The companies that own us all

The term "big data" is often thrown about, but the most troubling privacy invasion can be attributed to data brokerage. Data brokers are businesses that collect personal information about consumers and sell that data off, without consumers' permission, to other brokers or businesses. It's permissible because privacy laws don't guard against this. This information includes things like public records, Internet searches, and even who you talk to on social networks. Individual companies, such as Acxiom, make public what types of data they collect about consumers, but others do not.[48] Using ad blockers like AdBlock help, but they don't matter much in the grander scheme of data brokerage.

"Data brokerage is one of the most privacy-piercing technologies because of the way that advertisers treat users' information despite massive protests from people within and who do scholarly research on privacy," said Harlo Holmes, director of newsroom digital security at Freedom of the Press Foundation. Holmes works with journalists and media organizations to secure their communications within the newsroom, with sources, and with the public. "It's the most worrisome because it is so intertwined with the financial and capitalist imperative—the techno-capitalist imperative—and it's hard because that's money on the line. A lot of money."

Yet without online privacy laws to stop this, data brokerage continues. In that way, one type of privacy has already been eroded, becoming tradable for new products or services or apps, even if the consumer doesn't know said app's purpose, where their data is going, or how it will be used. An article in the *Economist*, "Big data, financial services and privacy," notes that people are unaware of where their data ends up: "According to the European Commission's statistics agency, Eurostat, 81% of Europeans feel they don't wholly control their online data; 69% worry that firms may use their data for purposes other than those advertised."[49] And that extends into social media, too. "Firms such as Facebook, which have people's names and other personal information, insist that they respect users' privacy when selling advertising space."[50]

Social media users make themselves trackable, visible, and searchable. Privacy is indeed a "fluid concept," but not because users want it that way; rather, because that's what works for the corporations. Users of Facebook and Twitter dump information, from ages to friends and interests, all of it usable and accessible to advertisers.

This reminds me of an amicus brief filed by Snapchat in the state of New Hampshire, where ballot selfies had been banned. Snapchat argued that ballot selfies were "the latest in a long historical tradition of voters sharing their civic enthusiasm—and their votes with their social network," and should thus be legal in the state.[51] The argument against ballot selfies claimed that they could be used as a means of voter intimidation, or a way to buy votes. Eventually the ruling was overturned, making ballot selfies legal in the state of New Hampshire. Obvious praise came from Chris Handman, general counsel for Snapchat, who claimed that the court recognizing ballot selfies was a "victory for free speech in the digital age." What he left out, of course, was the corporate data ownership piece of it. With this win for Snapchat, the company can now do as they please with the information about users, which includes who they voted for and their political beliefs.

"The thing I keep thinking about as you talk about this is the corporate data ownership piece," said Emi Kane, an activist/researcher whose work focuses on privacy and surveillance in communities of color. "We have this sense of agency and how we are presented [on social media], but at the end of the day the corporations own all of that data so we actually have zero control—even less than what we think."

Notes from the history of surveillance

Long before 9/11, civil rights leaders such as Martin Luther King Jr. were labeled as "suspects" by the FBI's domestic intelligence, who referred to him as "the most dangerous . . . from the standpoint of. . . national security." The NSA had wiretapped King in the late 1960s, a fact that they have disclosed.[52] But of course, not everyone is surveilled equally. If selfie culture has taught us anything, it's that some people don't need to worry at all, simply based on their white privilege. In his essay "The Color of Surveillance" for *SLATE*, Alvaro M. Bedoya, executive director of the Center on Privacy and Law Technology at Georgetown Law School, adjunct professor of law, writes:

> There is a myth in this country that in a world where everyone is watched, everyone is watched equally. It's as if an old and racist J. Edgar Hoover has been replaced by the race-blind

magic of computers, mathematicians, and Big Data. The truth is more uncomfortable. Across our history and to this day, people of color have been the disproportionate victims of unjust surveillance; Hoover was no aberration. And while racism has played its ugly part, the justification for this monitoring was the same we hear today: national security.[53]

And certainly, that surveilling post-9/11 has focused more heavily on Muslims, who have been surveilled by the NYPD with help from the CIA. And when news broke in June 2013 that the NSA was logging everyone's calls, it was not surprising to learn who were the targets first. "We now know that the NSA's call records program—the single largest domestic spying program in our nation's history—was effectively beta-tested for almost a decade on American immigrants," writes Bedoya.

Media reports over the past couple of years have described surveillance on members of the decentralized movement Black Lives Matter, which began in 2013 on Twitter through the hashtag #BlackLivesMatter after the acquittal of George Zimmerman in the killing of seventeen-year-old Trayvon Martin.

The police use the same "terrorism" language to justify the spying that they are doing, effectively labeling activists as terrorists. This is alarming, and it is happening.

From a 2015 report by the *Intercept*:

In an MTA document from January 12, D'Angelis, the NYPD counterterrorism division liaison, shared pictures that an unnamed "activist posted" of police milling around Grand Central. The photos in the email appear to be from the Twitter account of Black Lives Matter activist Keegan Stephan. Just beneath the photos, D'Angelis's email claims the document is for "deterring, detecting, and preventing terrorism."[54]

Similarly, the Department of Homeland Security and private security firms monitored the social media accounts of Black Lives Matter's DeRay Mckesson. At one point Mckesson started talking with Snowden on Twitter about guarding against surveillance.[55]

In more reports that came out in 2017, undercover cops in NYC had begun infiltrating BLM members' groups and obtaining access to their text message threads.

"That text loop was definitely just for organizers, I don't know how that got out," said Elsa Waithe, a Black Lives Matter organizer, to the *Guardian*. "Someone had to have told someone how to get on it, probably trusting someone they had seen a few times in good faith. We clearly compromised ourselves."[56]

But it was unclear how the NYPD gained access to those text threads. More likely, it seemed as if someone had hacked a phone, or perhaps walked nearby using a body camera. Uncle Sam was watching.

"Security culture is anti-selfie"

That's what Mark Tilsen, a poet and educator who is Lakota Oglala, from Pine Ridge, South Dakota, said to me about three hours into our conversation. It was a brisk summer afternoon in Minneapolis, and I'd gone to meet Mark at the Lowry, a local diner where you'd find those typical diner aesthetics of booths, loud music, and a sense that no one is in a hurry to get you out the door.

Mark and I originally met in Los Angeles after a panel conversation about the future of Standing Rock at the Depart Foundation on a busy strip if Sunset Boulevard in West Hollywood. Mark had been at Standing Rock for about four and a half months. On that panel about the impact of the Dakota Access

Pipeline sat Standing Rock Sioux tribal chairman Dave Archambault II, Robert F. Kennedy Jr., Bruce Kapson, Jane Fonda, and moderator Jon Christensen.

Questions followed the panel conversation. One of the very last came from Mark, who passionately asked: "What if we lose the political and legal fights, and have to stop the pipeline physically, with our bodies?"

I approached Mark after, telling him I was writing about the panel for *LA Weekly* and I would quote him in the story.[57] As it goes with many sources and people I quote in journalistic stories, I didn't expect to see him again. But sometimes, the first quote is the beginning of a relationship.

On the stroke of luck alone—or perhaps, synchronicity—I happened to be editing this chapter at the same time he was staying in the Twin Cities. Upon emailing him to see if he'd like to talk about surveillance at Standing Rock, he wrote back and said that he was in the Twin Cities this weekend, and would I like to meet for coffee?

Six months later there we were, sitting across from each other at the Lowry. It was PRIDE weekend, and rainbow flags were out everywhere. But I didn't have time to celebrate this year. Mark wore suspenders and spoke with an air of confidence and a sense of fearlessness, having been through near-death experiences at Standing Rock. He lead actions with others, fighting to stop the pipeline from being built under Lake Oahe, the water source for the Standing Rock Sioux Tribe. The pipeline threatened their water supply. When it leaked, it would ruin the lake, and from there oil would flow into the Missouri River, contaminating the drinking water for millions downstream. The pipeline would also destroy sacred sites, violate land treaties, and threaten the environment. Energy Transfer, the pipeline company, denied that the pipeline would break, but a history of pipelines breaking and contaminating water sources showed the severity of this matter.

For a five-week stretch, Mark slept only three hours a night.

His experiences at Standing Rock were deeply intertwined with the web of intense surveillance led by Tigerswan, a privately owned counterterrorism contractor hired by Energy Transfer Partners.

Tigerswan conducted surveillance of all the protestors. Helicopters flew over the camps. Phones were jammed and tapped. Cell service was spotty, with texts not going through and phone calls getting dropped. Sometimes there was heavy breathing on the line during phone calls. The nearby Prairie Knights Casino was tapped, with a federal agency command center from the Bureau of Indian Affairs stationed in the parking lot. Surveillance changed depending on the timing, size of the camp, and actions that were happening.

"Their primary focus was to monitor the size of the camp and also have a psychological warfare component of continuous observation," said Tilsen. "They would observe, from our understanding, through a Stingray, which is a device that can be fitted on a helicopter that scrapes all the metadata of any phones in the area. Not only that, but for night vision they would be using FLIR, which is a type of infrared."

"Dropped calls were a certain thing—that happened when people started switching over to Signal, which has end-to-end encryption that to the best of our knowledge is still solid," said Tilsen. But despite having more secure messaging, the resistance at Standing Rock noticed something else: Denial of service altogether.

The aggressively dropped calls and active surveillance increased, Tilsen explained, in early September, the day after unlicensed Dakota Access security guards attacked protestors with dogs, shortly after a delegation of Palestinian youth started working with them.[58]

"Now we understand that it fit into this narrative that Tigerswan was constructing about the camps—that we are somehow violent or terroristic and they specifically used the word 'jihadi,'" says Tilsen. "And the way that the Palestinian Movement for Liberation is maligned in mainstream media, it's an easy sell when we are starting to work together."

"Whenever we are on phones, we just learned to assume that anywhere within earshot of a telephone, we are being tapped," said Tilsen. "So we learned how to not have important, strategic, or tactful conversations around telephones regardless of if the battery was dead, or if it was in your pocket."

Some people took additional measures to ensure that no information was getting out through their phones. Putting phones far away and walking away, or lining tackle boxes with tin foil to block the signal or other types of boxes or cages that blocked signals. Even with Signal end-to-end encrypted calls, the metadata makes it possible to "basically figure out what is being talked about," said Tilsen, unless people are using really elaborate IPs. At camp, they didn't have that capability.

The Palestinian youth who came to camp to be in solidarity with the water protectors encountered even more bizarre and, as Tilsen describes it, surreal interceptions and surveillance.

"A few of them had their calls intercepted and were answered by impersonators speaking as if they were people from camp," said Tilsen. "Which is a surreal move. As a tactic it is not gonna work but essentially what it does is show people 'not only can I interfere with your conversation to your family and your people, I actually already know who you are talking to in camp.' And so it is a type of threatening surveillance, or interference at that point."

Through all of the surveillance techniques, Tigerswan attempted to track down some type of leader. But in a decentralized movement, there is no leader. For example, other decentralized movements like Black Lives Matter publicly came out in solidarity with water protectors at Standing Rock.[59]

At certain points, I recall following along from Los Angeles with what was happening at Standing Rock through friends who had gone out there and were posting about it. There were several Facebook check-ins going around, one that was north of the Cannonball community and south of Fort Rice. But there were also check-ins at Sacred Stone Camp and Standing Rock Indian Reservation. The latter two were fake, set up by Tigerswan. A viral message circulating around Facebook read:

> The Morton County Sheriff's Department has been using Facebook Check-ins to find out who is at Standing Rock in order to target them in attempts to disrupt the prayer camps. SO Water Protectors are calling on EVERYONE to Check-in at Standing Rock, ND, to overwhelm and confuse them. This is concrete action that can protect people putting their bodies and well-beings on the line that we can do without leaving our homes.[60]

The Morton County Sheriff denied that they were doing this. But of course, police regularly scan social media accounts.[61]

"That was the entire idea around the check-ins, to create the illusion that there is this massive amount of people in camp," said Tilsen. "And then Tigerswan is just over the ridge so they can see no, there are not one hundred thousand people in camp. But it did help raise awareness."

And so I began to wonder how social media was actually being used at the camp. Everyone I knew from LA who went out there was posting frequently, but I suspected they were not in the thick of things. If they were, how could they be posting? Mark told me that there was a relative divide at the camp between people who were using social media, and people who were not at all. Those who used it frequently became public faces of this (decentralized) movement.

"While I was at camp I added maybe one hundred people, and they were all people who I was working with. There are people who started adding thousands of people to create a following, and that was one strategy, to create as much social media imprint as possible."

But that wasn't everyone there. Plenty of other people had little time to check social media, let alone even participate in it for a variety of reasons.

"The other side of the coin is we have people who, they are too busy doing the work to check in on social media—like that is its own thing—that we had very serious people who accomplished many days of heroic actions and were part of doing beautiful resistance who, you're not going to know who they are. And these are the people who are probably going to be able to do the work for decades and decades, and not be caught in these goddamned surveillance sweeps."

And those who didn't have social media profiles and did mask up couldn't be seen as faces of the movement, but also were more likely able to evade the continued surveillance.

At the end of the day, security culture is antiselfie, Mark told me. Security culture is "a set of customs shared by a community whose members may be targeted by the government, designed to minimize risk."[62] Creating this type of a culture makes it possible to not constantly worry about how much potential danger you are in, and worry as much about people being potential informers, saving time that would otherwise be spent feeling paranoid or panicked.

Rather than refer to this as "protocol," which outlines procedures or systems of rules for governing, a culture becomes both "unconscious, instinctive, and thus effortless," so that "once the safest possible behavior has become habitual for everyone in the circles in which you travel, you can spend less time and energy emphasizing the need for it, or suffering the consequences of not having it, or worrying about how much danger you're in, as you'll know you're already doing everything you can to be careful."[63]

"One of the guiding rules of security culture is, if you don't need to know, you shouldn't have that information," Tilsen explained.

Yet how might security culture make sense within social media? First, it's important to understand that security culture arose not only in response to surveillance culture, but also to the "criminalization and violence that comes with it," said Tilsen. But by that same token, there were plenty of Facebook Live feeds coming out of the camps that informed people who were watching from far away and wanted to know what was happening.

"FB Live was one of the biggest ways for us to get our story told, and it was [also] the largest way for Tigerswan to scoop up intel on our actions and everything," said Tilsen. Some people were even retroactively arrested because of imagery captured on Facebook Live feeds. With all of that in mind, why would anyone who is protesting or doing activism post anything that would make them appear more visible?

Toward the end of our convo, Mark quoted something from the Zapatista Movement: "Only after we become faceless are we no longer voiceless," he said before taking a swig from his glass of sazerac. But clearly, Mark said he had a social media profile, and he had appeared in several documentaries about Standing

Rock, and I'd quoted him in an article too. How could the idea of facelessness hold true, then?

"For myself, I have always felt more powerful without a mask than with it. But to stand in solidarity with the people who operate masked, I mask up at times."

So I asked him why he felt more powerful without a mask.

"Because I am Oglala Lakota," he said, beaming. "My name matters to me. My family matters to me. My history matters to me. And I am very proud of it. I come from a line of resistors from both sides of my family. "

So when would the fight against DAPL end? I wondered, since at the time of this writing, oil was pumping through the pipeline, and protestors had been pretty much entirely kicked off the land. What would a real victory look like?

"Shutting down the pipeline permanently," Mark said, not even batting an eye. Then he turned up a *Godfather* sounding voice, cocked his head, and recited his favorite quote from all this: "'It's not over till I'm smoking cigars on the drill path.'"

"Going back to old school"

Is it worth it to master all of these new ways of communicating when few of them are secure? We were on one of those not-secure communication platforms, the phone, when organizer Amin Husain told me: "The easier way to do it is to go back to old school." The "it" referred to best ways to communicate when it came to organizing actions. "I think that's the easiest and safest, and in fact it embodies the type of politics that is necessary, which is for bodies to be in a space or for maintaining—in a way it actually changes your relationship to time, it allows you to slow down in relation to these things. Rather than say no to technology or operate in fear, you just operate more informed."

Amin Husain and collaborator Nitasha Dhillon work on Decolonize This Place, a space in New York located at 55 Walker Street that's action-oriented around Indigenous struggle, Black liberation, Free Palestine, global wage workers, and degentrification.[64]

Decolonize This Place operates from a space of security culture. In addition to creating training, they also had a core group of trusted people, who would in turn bring their trusted people. Whoever came in and out of the space was accounted for. That way, they would know when the police came.

"There were situations in which two or three were clearly cops," said Husain. "Their story didn't fit at all, and we had pushed them out at different nights. That happened maybe twice."

Amin assumes he is tracked, and operates within that.

"The assumption is that we don't know how much they know, and we know that we are active, and so that is not a battle we can win," he said. "So then the battle I can engage in is to assume that the police are there, and then to think about if they were there, how do we communicate."

Trusting people over time, and moving away from technology altogether are two of the aspects that he highlighted. Social media may be used in organizing actions, but in ways that are intended to throw the police off.

"We can do publicity that is really heavy around something, but really that's actually a decoy to another thing that is happening in parallel."

For an action at the American Museum of Natural History in New York City, they used social media to get the word out about an alternative tour, which would bring in more people to the museum. It was actually going to be something else, but gathering people for the alternative tour would bring them into the museum. But the action they were doing was outside, separate from the "alternative tour."

"It was advertised as a tour so nobody knew what was going to happen," said Dhillon. "The moment we got there, the entire museum staff knew and the police were everywhere, paddy wagons, all of that was there—so that was something we had to deal with while doing the action. So that's why what we announced in advance was we were doing an alternative tour, and that we are gonna just walk slowly."

The "alternative tour" was pushed as a public event, one that was very low-risk and got people engaged, but didn't give away the action, which is higher risk.

"The higher-risk engagement is parallel to that, and uses the kind of push on the public sphere that would allow for something else to happen. And in that other context, we don't use Internet, we don't use credit cards if we need to purchase something, we don't use phones, we meet in person with phones away. For things that are even more involved, we actually just write out a note in physical form with a pencil and then erase them, burn them, do those kind of things."

Like Tilsen, Husain and Dhillon recognize that both Signal and WhatsApp do still allow for a lot of information transmissions, so the move is away from technology altogether. Security culture is antiselfie.

But social media is still of use to them—not for actually organizing any actions, but for spreading the word, for visibility of social justice campaigns.

"We did a campaign called Dignity Strike in support of the Palestinian Hunger Strike, that was completely a social media campaign," said Dhillon. "We used Facebook, Instagram, like everything possible to actually get the word out, and it was part of asking people to collaborate on a daily basis. In terms of actions, when it comes to creating narratives and content about what we are doing, then we use social media."

There are other strategic ways to use social media, and before we hopped off the phone Amin pointed to the use of social media in the 2011 Egyptian Revolution that took place in Tahrir Square.

"There was a Facebook page called April 16. That Facebook page did not specify anything other than Tahrir—it did not specify where the march was going to go. It was actually meant to overstretch the military and the police, and then the splinter marches actually began in neighborhoods. So that is an example where, rather than try to abandon social media or these areas, or these tiers of surveillance, in a way you kind of use them to your advantage that makes sense."

"The police are always [surveilling]—we know this because we put a Facebook page together in a park for some kind of event—and there are police. So we know that is it coming from my phone or someone else's phone or my computer—who knows? That's not a good question to be asking at this point. But it's like 'oh, that can happen, so how can we use that?'"

The selfie as indicative of state/corporate surveillance and control

The selfie is, of course, yet another instance not only of surveillance, but of self-surveillance (sousveillance). Constant surveillance normalizes self-surveillance (sousveillance), and the types of behaviors that arise because of it. Regular selfie-ing becomes the norm when others in your social milieu are doing it, too.[65] Selfies serve as ways to self-surveill, surveill others, and in turn keep a constant watch on everyone else socially, causing further insulation.

In his 2015 essay "Selfie Culture at the Intersection of Corporate and Surveillance States," Henry A. Giroux writes:

> While selfies may not lend themselves directly to giving up important private information online, they do speak to the necessity to make the self into an object of public concern, if not a manifestation of how an infatuation with selfie culture now replaces any notion of the social as the only form of agency available to many people.

In the age of state/corporate surveillance, the selfie also functions simultaneously as a way for people to also surveill others, mirroring the idea of "if you see something, say something" that police ask citizens to do about so-called "suspicious activity" in public. Except the selfie in this way is disguised under the banner of "social," masking its overtly political undertones. Let us never forget that the personal is political.

"'Selfie' by itself is an orientation, it is constantly self-checking and self-policing," said Hamid Khan, Campaign Coordinator for Stop LAPD Spying Coalition. "How am I looking? Who am I with? What does it allow me to do? What kind of space can I navigate? How am I moving through these spaces? So I think there is definitely a very deep connection to the constant policing, the commodification of our lives, how they play out so deeply in these as well of just the objectification of life as well. And in that vein, how does the corporate profit?"

Chapter 3

Consent to the Image

Sexts can happen at any time. One time I was deep into some heavy texting and it quickly turned sexting. Then she asked for a pic of my pussy. It seemed like a normal, par-for-the-course sexting request. But it was something I had never done. My heart beat faster and my hands shook a bit, the phone gingerly resting in the sweaty palm of my left hand. I wanted to give her what she wanted. I took off my pants, angled the camera down, pressed the shutter a bunch of times, and fired away! My breath caught in my throat, and my heart beat even harder in my chest. I'd sent it—an erotic pic. The mix of fear and lust caught me off guard, and also turned me on. Sexting!

Even though I trusted her, the clit pic felt like some next level sexual textual vulnerability. Who's to say it would only ever be for her eyes? It only takes a second to forward an image to someone else, or post it to the Internet. Had my lust gotten the best of me?! Probably, but in that instant I simply didn't care. I paused for a moment, deciding that I would not follow that thought to a devastating, catastrophic endpoint of the entire Internet seeing my wet, pink, hairy pussy. I thought of all the other vaginas that were publicly visible, how actually common it was to depict the pussy in art. Detaching from the image in this way soothed my anxiety. I trusted her.

It's common knowledge that you should be aware of what you post to social media and what you sext to others. It's a source of techno-cultural social networked anxiety, understanding what even makes sense to share—if anything at all. At the same time, anything posted can easily be used and reused by another entity.

This lack of control led me to resist social media and smart-phones for many years, even though my work as a writer online required me to become fluent and popular on it (#millennial-problems). I would've much preferred to be left alone to read a book and write in my journal. It was what I'd been doing since middle school, after I got kicked out of the popular girls' group, like many "nerdy" or smart girls my age, and so I retreated into books as an adolescent.

With that memory of being shunned from the popular clique, I wondered: Wouldn't participating in social media just replicate my teenage experience? After all, social media easily lends itself to adolescent behavior, like gossiping, oversharing, and shaming. But I kept seeing writer friends getting jobs and projects through finding their voices and becoming personalities online, and so I begrudg-ingly strode into what felt like the end of my career as a writer because there I was, giving away my thoughts and ideas to randoms on Twitter and my "friends" on Facebook, all the while building my "online brand." (FML—or Fuck My Life, in case you did not know.) With every post, I anxiously hoped for the best, which I fig-ured meant some likes, comments, and maybe even a share.

Thankfully, the people who followed my work on social media sites were not the popular girls, and so I didn't have to cater my interest to them and staying in their lame club. Over time, however, I began to learn which types of posts did well with my audience, which was made up of anything but the "popular girl" types. Despite the anxiety of social media, which I eventually got over, I found my public speaking voice through writing for Facebook and Twitter, posting to Instagram , and writing personal narrative essays. But I was also aware of being watched by others, and that sometimes the nuances of my writing would be lost on social media. Ultimately however, like everyone else, I began deriving satisfaction from a well-liked post, a large number of retweets, and witty comments dropped on a reactionary whim.

Then I predictably became pretty obsessed with social media.

It became a skill, a game, something to master. Like any skill, I began to home in on the specific type of short writing that worked well for social media, and I started to enjoy it. People who liked my writing and sensibility began following me, liking my stuff, and engaging with the content I produced. Soon, I found my niche online, and I was "popular." The sad seventh grader who got shunned for being queer/weird/other/different was now way cooler than *all those bitches*. Rather than sitting in a corner in an empty science classroom and reading a book, I could sit in a corner, read a book, and then tweet or Facebook my thoughts not only about the book but about other social, political, and cultural issues—thoughts that were on my mind all of the time anyway. It all felt great! I was a poster child for successful social media. I attracted followers, fans, and even some friends and dates.

But ultimately I felt like a slave to social media. It had become a necessity—now I needed it for both my social and professional lives, especially as a freelancer. I didn't post as many selfies as some of my friends, but I posted enough to know what would engage people.

The selfie to me also became not just an image of myself—that was far too simple—but also akin to a status update or a tweet, which is a textual version of me, carefully curated and posted for the purpose of entertaining, which usually results in getting likes (#rewards). To nail that selfie moment, one where I'm not only interested in being seen but also feeling *good enough* to be seen, is a powerful thing. Likable content is monetizeable, marketable content, and also triggers the rewards center of the brain.

"The same brain areas [that are activated for food and water] are activated for social stimuli," said Mauricio Delgado, associate professor of psychology at Rutgers University, in an interview for the American Marketing Association.[1] "This can be a smile, someone telling you you're doing a great job or you're trustworthy, or you're a nice person, or even merely cooperating with somebody. All of these social 'reinforcers' are abstract but show similar activity in the reward centers of the brain. This suggests that, perhaps, if you're getting positive feedback in social media—'likes' and shares and retweets—it's a positive 'reinforcer' of using social media, and one that allows you to a.) get the positive effects of it, and b.) return to it, seeking out more social reinforcement."

Posts expressing sadness or anger may not get as many likes as positive emotions, unless others in the community also feel the same sense of outrage or sadness.

But after I had carefully crafted this online presence that would find the right kind of response, I started to wonder: Was anything online actually mine or protected? What are the copyright laws around my creative content on social media? Are all of my fractured and scattered tweets and posts property of the networks? What if a sexy selfie falls into the wrong hands, as in the case of revenge porn? On the Internet, copyright is a murky territory. Remix culture rules and fair use sometimes works. But social media sites take little responsibility for what people post, offering a limited license to content. When the digital content is of a sexual nature—such as nudes or sexts—questions of consent become intertwined with trust much as they do offline.

Know thy selfie rights

The selfie shooter is the copyright holder of a selfie. But what if the selfie shooter is a monkey, not a human being?

Nature photographer David Slater recently settled in the now infamous "monkey selfie" court case brought against him by PETA on behalf of Naruto, a crested macaque in Indonesia. Slater, whose company Wildlife Personalities, Ltd., used Naruto's image in the 2014 book *Wildlife Personalities* (created with self-publishing company Blurb), agreed to donate 25% of future revenue made off of Naruto's images to charities that protect crested macaques in Indonesia. PETA argued that Naruto the monkey owned the copyright, and that by publishing it without Naruto's permission, Slater and his company had infringed upon it. The case caught attention of people nationwide because of the implications that it raised through a monkey's accidental selfie.

The monkey selfie case was first brought up by People for the Ethical Treatment of Animals in 2015, suing on behalf of the monkey, seeking to secure copyrights and thus financial control to Naruto. U.S. District Judge William Orrick ruled in favor of Slater last year, stating that "while Congress and the president can extend the protection of law to animals as well as humans, there is no indication that they did so in the Copyright Act." But PETA appealed, taking the case to the San Francisco-based U.S. 9th Circuit Court of Appeals. Andrew J. Dhuey, Slater's attorney, did not comment on how much money the monkey selfies had already generated.

Despite the ensuing selfie copyright nightmare, the story of Naruto and David Slater the nature photographer began rather idyllically in 2011, when Slater was in Indonesia photographing crested macaques in Indonesia.

The story of the selfie also began like many selfies do: By accident, randomly, and for fun. After gaining the trust of the monkeys, one of them, Naruto, swiped Slater's camera and started taking selfies.

As any of us do when taking selfies, we do not take just one or two or three—we take many, until the best one surfaces. Maybe that one perfect selfie is even great. Taking selfies is hard. Naruto took many selfies, but only one went viral.

The monkey's selfie-taking turned Slater into a known photographer.

PETA took Slater to court, arguing that there's nothing in U.S. federal copyright law that limited copyright protection to human beings. PETA lost a lower court ruling, which a federal judge ruled that the monkey did not own rights to the image because he is an animal and not a human. But after that, PETA appealed and took it to the 9th Circuit Court of Appeals in San Francisco. Crested macaque are critically endangered, and any damages were to benefit Naruto, his family, and their habitat.

But oddly, there was another element of this selfie aside from the assumed copyright that was up for debate. Because the selfie-shooter is the copyright owner of the image, originally the U.S. Copyright Office considered this work in the public domain. They accepted that the monkey was the creator of the selfie, not the nature photographer David Slater, but they did not originally grant copyright to the monkey.

Others begged to differ. The picture is "property of the macaque, whose name is Naruto. And Slater owes Naruto some money," wrote Jordan Weissmann for SLATE. In the motion by Slater's lawyer, asking to dismiss the suit, the introduction began like this: "A monkey, an animal-rights organization and a primatologist walk into federal court to sue for infringement of the monkey's claimed copyright. What seems like the setup for a punchline is really happening."

In any case, Slater's lawyer argued that his company, Wildlife Personalities Ltd., owned worldwide commercial copyrights to all of the images, thus nullifying this case. His lawyer argued that "monkey see, monkey sue" should not hold up in court.

The arguments were pretty fascinating and certainly went well beyond the selfie itself(ie), which is the purpose of my book too—to provide context for the selfie, rather than literally take the selfie at face value.

Angela Dunning, an attorney for Blurb, the self-publishing site that published Slater's book, argued that PETA, not Naruto the monkey, would benefit from the work because, well, he is a monkey and they are an organization run by humans.

But it did not matter, because Slater lost. In this case, a selfie was used as a way to decide that animals have the same copyrights as humans, which could set an interesting precedent for any self-respecting dog that selfies and becomes a viral celebrity.

As Jeffrey S. Kerr, Esq, writes for *Alternet*, this case could also serve as a harbinger of the versatile ways that PETA as an organization can fight on behalf of animal rights:

"While PETA's monkey selfie lawsuit focused on one primate, Naruto, its aim is now more far-reaching. As long-held traditions and notions fall by the wayside—animal circuses, for example, are being relegated to the dustbin of history—there's no doubt that granting animals fundamental rights is the next step in our cultural and ethical evolution."

Yet in this case, selfie copyright shifted because of a case brought against a photographer by an outside organization. In other words, thanks to some random selfies shot by a monkey in Indonesia, an endangered species will have a bit more funding, albeit at the expense of a random freelance photographer.

Copyright Matters

When I reached out to David Lizerbram, a San Diego–based lawyer who specializes in social media and entertainment law, he had a lot to say about copyright law as it applies to social media.

The first question I asked him felt pretty basic, but I also wanted to spell it out in plain terms: How does placing your thoughts, ideas, or images on social media change the copyright on those things? What belongs to the network, and what belongs to you?

"I wouldn't say that putting a picture that you've taken on a social media platform changes the copyright," said Lizerbram. "You still own the copyright of a selfie that you took—a selfie that you took is redundant, right? By putting it on Instagram, you have not sold the copyright, you have not lost the copyright by putting it on Instagram or Facebook or whatever. You haven't given it away, you haven't made it public domain so that copyright no longer applies. Instead you have hosted it and are agreeing to the terms of a contract, which is in the site's terms of use, which includes a limited license."

Curious to get the exact information about these types of limited licenses, I turned to the obvious places where I'd easily find them: Facebook, Twitter, Instagram, and Snapchat's Terms of Service agreements (ToS), as they relate to copyright. On Instagram's terms of use, in #8 of the Basic Terms, it states:

8. You are solely responsible for your conduct and any data, text, files, information, usernames, images, graphics, photos, profiles, audio and video clips, sounds, musical works, works of authorship, applications, links and other content or materials (collectively, "Content") that you submit, post or display on or via the Service.[2]

OK, so that's pretty straightforward: You are responsible for your own content, and the social media platform will not be held accountable. What about the rights of that content, however? In the Rights section on Instagram, the service states:

Instagram does not claim ownership of any Content that you post on or through the Service. Instead, you hereby grant to Instagram a non-exclusive, fully paid and royalty-free, transferable, sub-licensable, worldwide license to use the Content that you post on or through the Service, subject to the Service's Privacy Policy, available here http://instagram.com/legal/privacy/, including but not limited to sections 3 ("Sharing of Your Information"), 4 ("How We Store Your Information"), and 5 ("Your Choices About Your Information"). You can choose who can view your Content and activities, including your photos, as described in the Privacy Policy.

In nonjargon terms, this means that Instagram does not literally own your content, but they nearly practically do—instead, by posting to their site, you grant them a license to use it in practically any way they see fit, and for any promotional purposes they would like. You agree to this by signing up for the service. They don't need to pay you or even let you know if the content is being used elsewhere. The exchange for a free service such as Facebook or Instagram, of course, is that you pay for it with your data, allowing the network to use it however they want and for whatever advertisements.

Other areas of the Rights section describe how the service is "supported by advertising revenue and may display advertisements and promotions," and of course those may be created with your content. Instagram doesn't have to let you know about any of this. They can also update this agreement whenever they want.

"Typically what that looks like is that you, by posting the image, you are typically giving the site a license which allows them to republish it across any media they are engaged in," said Lizerbram. "So, you are giving permission for that site to reproduce the image across whatever sort of other sites they are in partnership with. You are also typically giving permission for other users to repost, share, retweet, whatever the term is in that site."

In posting content to social media, you're also telling the network that this is original content. Rarely is that true, however. Memes, for example, are not original content, but people repost them all of the time. These social media rules of the road should make users even more wary, especially if they're resharing a popular meme. But do they?

"When it comes to social media copying, I would very strongly encourage Internet users to consider an ethics of appropriation before they try to figure out if something is legal," said artist Stacia Yeapanis, whose artwork often uses copyrighted content from mass media, which is made possible through fair use. "Is copying someone else's image going to harm another person in some way—emotionally or psychologically? Copyright law doesn't address this, but we should ask ourselves if our borrowing will have a negative impact on other people."

The most shocking thing, however, is that any of us could get in trouble for retweeting a meme. A MEME! Can you believe it?!

In a post that Mr. Lizerbram wrote on his blog called "Rules for Using Images Online,"[3] he irons out some true/false assumptions about image use. Not only can people online not use images that everyone else is using, but this also applies to memes.

"Memes, no matter how popular, are based on someone else's copyright. You can get in legal trouble for using a meme on your website or in your social media channels."

This seems insane, however, considering the very nature of social media and meme culture—that is, the idea of tracking down and notifying the person or company who holds the original copyright, and then going through and seeing who has retweeted or reposted or reshared an image that already has already gone viral. But it does happen.

"If you use any copyrighted material without express written permission from the creator, you could be sued or receive a Cease and Desist letter from a copyright holder," said Yeapanis. "The likelihood of that happening really depends on the condition under which the work is copied and often, whether the copyright holder thinks they can get any licensing money from you. So an individual posting a meme on their Facebook page is less likely to be singled out than a blog that earns advertising money. But then, there are copyright trolls, whose entire business model is based on buying up licenses and patents for the purpose of going after copyright infringers to extort money from them because most individuals don't have the money to fight a court battle over a meme or an online video."

The selfie or other content posted sometimes are original copyright, however.

Artist Jasmine Nyende has picked up modeling gigs because of her extensive selfie posting, which is part of her performance art practice. Brands and companies find her based on her Internet presence. I learned about this when I interviewed her for a story in *LA Weekly* about a performance piece she did about the Leimert Park neighborhood and deleted social media statuses at the art fair Art Contemporary Los Angeles 2017.[4]

Through Nyende's modeling, she's able to support herself and her creative practice.

Because of the politicized nature of her performance art, however, she can't necessarily take every paying gig that comes her way.

"I've had to turn down modeling gigs because I'm just like, I'm not going to model for that brand in relation to my art practice. And I'm gonna stick to my own personal politics which is linked to my own art practice. It's kind of impossible for me to divorce those two," she said.

When I asked her about specific brands, she didn't feel it was necessary to give them more social capital, so we didn't keep talking about that. Negotiating her own personal politics in relation to earning off her own self image wouldn't be as complicated if, of course, it wasn't her face and body in it. Earning off of one's self-image isn't necessarily a goal, but it can happen.

Appropriating selfies to call out shameful behaviors

I remember talking to a particularly creepy guy on Tinder. The conversation started out in a normal way—"Hey, how's your day," "What are you up to," etc.—but then it got gross. I didn't respond for a couple of days, probably because I wasn't interested (#cantremember #toomanyTinds), but then he came back with the question of "What are you looking for on here?" which was followed by something dickish and anti-Semitic. Before unmatching the shithead, I did as any twenty-first-century lady would and screengrabbed that conversation, and sent it to a friend.

The content in question is an exchange between me and said random dude on Tinder, and the purpose of my screengrab was noncommercial and intended for social commentary to my friend, sent via text. If I decided to publish this on a blog intended to satirize dumb guys on Tinder, I'd technically be protected under fair use, which determines if creative content is liable.[5] With the rise of screengrab culture on dating apps and text messages, anyone with access to the Internet and an idea for a single-concept Tumblr or Instagram can easily put together a series of images that point out these incidents. It's a real rude awakening for those who get caught being shitbags. They can be easily and quickly exposed through screengrabs of their profile pics, which are often selfies, and the content of their conversations.

Some of the most hilarious single-concept Tumblrs and Instagrams on the Internet wouldn't exist if it weren't for the ability to screengrab. Here I am thinking of Tumblrs made in reaction to Tinder culture, specifically those that call out creepy guys who don't respect women, either through sexist/racist/fatphobic/homophobic/etc. attitudes, violence, or who just throw out what is now referred to as "locker room talk" from fuckboys (often referred to as "fuckbois"), a term that the glorious Internet publication HuffPo defines as "a (usually straight, white) dude embodying something akin to the 'man whore' label, mashed up with some 'basic' qualities and a light-to-heavy sprinkling of misogyny."[6]

Instagram accounts and Tumblrs that compile screengrabs of men acting like this on dating apps only exist because of screengrab/fair use culture. These accounts ask for submissions from people who have experienced this douchery.[7] It's both a direct call out, and a darkly humorous satirical shout-out to all the women who have experienced this bullshit.

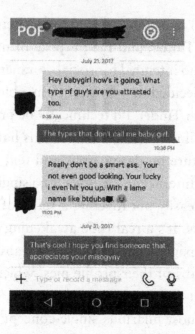

Courtesy of Alexandra Tweten.

One such example is the Instagram account @bye_felipe, which was created by Alexandra Tweten in order to "document and draw attention to the hostility and abuse women face simply for telling a man 'no.'"[8] Every convo posted there deserves to be seen and called out—the violence in each of them reinforces what it means to be a woman living in rape culture. This kind of abusive behavior happens in the physical world, not just on the Internet—it's all real life! The existence of these Tumblrs and Instagrams brings to light ongoing systemic sexism—the phenomena of when women don't respond to guys or just tell them no, they lash out with threats of violence or death.

Rather than just laughing at how creepy, assumptive, and disturbing most of these messages seemed to be, I began to wonder about the legalities of even sharing these online in the first place, and the risk inherent in doing so even if these screengrabs technically fell under "fair use."

In the Tinder Terms of Use, it's funny to note that one of the prohibited activities that users sign up for and agree to, under section 11 of the app, is to not "'stalk' or otherwise harass any person."[9] Had Tweten ever been sued because of screengrabbed content on her @byefelipe account?

"I have never encountered anyone claiming copyright infringement (yet)," Tweten told me via email. Furthermore, these types of projects end up being both commentary and parody, both of which fall under fair use.

Courtesy of Alexandra Tweten.

"Most of this seems like fair use," she said. "Tinder probably just doesn't care enough to go after the sites you linked to. If Tinder doesn't make an issue of it, then there's nothing stopping them from posting the content."

Other questions loom, though: Will the guys learn from this? Or is this just a way to call out misogyny, and raise awareness, and find community with others online who have experienced this? I wanted to know if any of the abusive guys on here learned from their behavior, or if they were just mad that they got caught. Said Tweten:

> One guy in particular that I can think of had a really bad submission and people found him and started emailing his mom and sister. I got an email from his sister saying that she was taking care of it (him being a shithead) and to please remove the post because people were harassing their family. My intention isn't to harass peoples' families, but I think it is helpful if they can become aware of what the guy is doing and try to help him or get him therapy or something.

But did any guys come forward and submit their own thoughts about the Instagram account? In fact, a few did—and these are the ones that felt remorse about what they saw. Tweten sent me both of these, and while the second one is a bit long, it felt important to include both. Here's the first one:

> I don't have a submission, because I am a dude. I just personally want to say I apologize for my entire gender. There is no explanation or reason dudes should be this way. Sites like these entertain me and make me sad at the same time. Hopefully some guy sees this and figures out not to be like this. so thank you.

And here is the second one, typos included:

> Hi,
> I'm sending this message to thank you for your Instagram profile. I admit I'm guilty of the wrongdoing -being abusive when ignored-. I've always knew inside of me that it was wrong

and shouldn't happen, but I've always allowed that asshole in me to take control and lead my actions.

Until I browsed through your posts.. seeing it as an outsider -seeing someone else doing it-, I know now how low I was. It feels awful to know that I was doing this to a woman just because she wouldn't reply or when I didn't like their replies.

I know there are women with issues, and maybe ignoring guys make them feel better about themselves or something, but I should have learned that this is THEIR issue, THEIR problem, and it doesn't give me any right to abuse or be mean to them.

I should have learned long ago to simply.. move on, unmatch and continue, just look forward to the next one.

I know now that abusing a woman -no matter how much she deserves it-, will only make less of a man of me.

Again, thank you for your profile. I'm sorry I'm sending this from an alias email, but my remorse is genuine, and I will work on whatever I have to work on to be a good man, a better man.

Thank you, and you will meet the person who will love and appreciate you just the way you are, and you both will sit together and laugh at other abusive assholes.

Peace,,,

Yeah, peace out, dude. Hope you undouche yourself one online date at a time.

Elsewhere on the Internet, Tumblrs like Tinder in Brooklyn exist purely to parody the overly artsiness of weirdos in Brooklyn. It is both a way of using other peoples' selfies for social commentary, and something that definitely wouldn't exist without screen-grab culture/fair use. Tinder in Brooklyn collects profiles of guys found in Brooklyn, like someone with a parrot on his shoulder, or a dude named BONE standing next to a giant rooster with the words "God Bless America" tattooed onto the rooster's side.[10] These types of Tumblrs aren't for calling out, but for just poking fun at the types of "eccentric" guys you might find in Brooklyn.

I came across Tinder in Brooklyn while sitting at Café Tropical in LA's Silver Lake neighborhood, waiting for my BFF Che. I found myself simultaneously watching people walk in and stroll up to the counter and order Cuban coffee while scrolling through this very Tumblr. The experience of switching back and forth from people on a screen to an in-person scene is overly stimulating, and after a while I started to conflate the two worlds in my mind. That guy who walks into the café starts to look like someone I just saw on Tinder. But are they actually, or am I just imagining that and slowly losing my mind? I'm not even in Brooklyn, but half the people in this LA café are probably from New York anyway. I start wondering if any of the guys on Tinder have been screengrabbed and blasted out onto the Internet and, if they were, would they care?

Those shots of the Tinder guys in Brooklyn were all just curated by someone named Lindsay, who says in her bio, "This is what has become of my life." Other Tumblrs like this, such as Male Feminists of Tinder, a love letter to male feminists and a gentle parody of dudes who say respectful things about women in their bios, offer far more flattering screengrabs.[11] That is, if you are into feminist dudes.

All of these Tumblrs serve their own purposes, but like the generally ambiguous terms of service and fair use of selfie images and other content on the Internet that can be used for satire, parody, commentary, or other noncommercial means, you may literally never know if someone has grabbed your image and 'grammed it. People don't usually think about that when they're hitting "post." What you don't know won't hurt you, until it does. So, there is always a risk in using these types of dating apps.

Screengrab opportunities can do more than just call out sex-ist bros on Tinder. Sometimes the issue at hand is inappropriate behavior at the site of mass murder.

The project YOLOCAUST is further proof that apparently people on the Internet can learn from their awkward selfie-ing behavior, or at least realize when someone else is exhibiting behavior that they wouldn't want to mirror themselves.[12] Israeli-German writer and satirist Shahak Shapira noticed the disturbing trend of people taking selfies at the Holocaust Memorial to the Murdered Jews of Europe in Berlin. Rather than taking a moment to contemplate, feel horrified by, or acknowledge that mass geno-cide took place here not even one hundred years ago under the dictates of a power-obsessed racist, adults were standing around taking smiling selfies at the site.

Disgusted by this behavior, Shapira appropriated twelve of the selfies, manipulating the background of each by photoshopping in images of Nazi crimes. Like a pile of dead bodies of people that had starved to death—with that same original smiling selfie in the foreground. No longer did the selfie at the Holocaust Memorial feel so cheerful. The selfie-takers noticed what happened to their images, and they felt shame, realizing that the selfie-ing was actu-ally horrifyingly disrespectful.

Luckily, there was a way out. People who took these selfies could email Shapiro and ask that they become "undouched"—to do so, they had to apologize and understand why taking these sel-fies at the Holocaust Memorial was disrespectful. This is different than dehumanizing them, screengrabbing their behavior and post-ing it online, or just calling them out in a blog post without any follow-up. YOLOCAUST asks them to recognize what they did, and do the work to correct their behaviors and right their wrongs.

The project went viral, and every single one of the people whose photos he used noticed that they were there and wrote to apologize for what they had done. Shapira then redid the home-page of his YOLOCAUST Project, Yolocaust.de, with a note in English and German explaining the breadth of the project, that it went viral, was visited by more than 2.5 million people, and reached all twelve people whose selfies were present. "Almost all of them understood the message, apologized, and decided to remove their selfies from their personal Facebook and Instagram profiles," Shapira wrote.

The project not only raised awareness about why this act was disrespectful, but it also allowed the person who took the photo to then remove it and realize what they were really saying when they took a selfie at the Holocaust Memorial. Since these selfies weren't screengrabs, the original creator—the one who owned the copyright—still had control over what they could do with it. Similar to the Tinder projects, this type of situation couldn't have happened without the opportunity to reuse selfie images within the fair use context of noncommercial parody/satire.

Contextualizing the clit pic

One of my favorite paintings, Courbet's *Origin of the World* (1866), is a painting of a nude woman's pussy.[13] Literally, it is just her hairy vagina, and it's gorgeous! It is somewhat anonymous, however—there is no name attributed to the model, and all credit goes to the painter, Courbet. She was his model. His work of art is of course considered "genius" because it is yet another dude painting a woman, capturing her image, and presenting her to the world. It is in fact exactly in line with what John Berger describes as "men look-ing at women" that he describes in his book *Ways of Seeing*. This line is especially resonant: "You painted a naked woman because you enjoyed looking at her, put a mirror in her hand and you called the painting 'Vanity,' thus morally condemning the woman whose nakedness you had depicted for your own pleasure."

In other words, it's the same logic that determines standards of beauty. A woman exists as the object of male desire.

Courbet's painting made me think of new media/Internet artist Ann Hirsch's project *horny lil feminist*, which includes video of her vagina. I was struck by her comparison of the body online today in relation to pornography; much of selfie culture is both compared to pornography and critiqued for appearing somewhat like porn. When asked to describe the project *horny lil feminist* for VICE i-D, Ann notes that it is a portrait of being a woman on the Internet today, but the big difference in how images of women are conceptualized today comes down to how women are presented in pornography.[14] When asked the question "how does showing an image of your vagina fall in with that goal?" she said: "I constantly deal with censorship issues, and it's so frustrating. The only images [of naked women] that are allowed on the Internet are pornographic. It's really difficult for a regular person to show themselves if they want to."

The history of art very much follows the same visual parallels as the history of (straight) pornography: Men objectifying and sexualizing women for the male gaze. Women taking self-portraits or selfies, capturing and objectifying themselves, is a threat to the patriarchal order, of men determining how women should look. This is cultural misogyny in a nutshell. That is, culturally it's somewhat okay for men to idealize and portray a woman nude—but when she takes back the gaze and shines the lens on herself, she is painted as narcissistic by men who want to retain control of the gaze. So, that same logic is applied to women who selfie by men who do not want to relinquish that image control. This is inherently sexist. Women should be able to selfie without judgment. Though at the same time, the selfie stands as a mode of self-objectifying and the notion that being seen requires the validation of onlookers. Ultimately, in selfie culture we are complicit in policing one another's bodies and images.

This whole incident made me think of revenge porn, which is defined as "the sexually explicit portrayal of one or more people that is distributed without their consent via any medium."[15] I have not heard of a case that's taken place between women—at least, not one that has been reported. Revenge porn, which has been sensationalized and reported on plenty, seems like a straight person thing—mostly, a clearly violent and sexually aggressive act that men use to harm the women who have hurt their feelings. Sad!

Revenge porn is rape culture

"Idiot." "Dumb girl." "Moron." These are some of the insults you're likely to hear if you mention that a woman sent nudes to a guy who is now her ex. Except those words are almost always directed at the women who provided the nudes, not the men who exploited them, posting these private images online. And within the context of systemic cultural sexism, there's always an implication that when something bad happens to a sext or a nude, it's the woman's fault.

When it comes to revenge porn, there's always a level of implied "you should've known better." Like saying it's your fault if you're a woman and you got raped, which is absolutely not true. The same applies to the female nude, sent from one person to another, that is publically posted as an act of revenge. This is an extension of rape culture, a term that was coined by feminists in the United States in the 1970s. According to Women Against Violence Against Women (WAVAW), the term "rape culture" was "designed to show the ways in which society blamed victims of sexual assault and normalized male sexual violence."[16] Rape culture includes any advertising campaigns that make a joke out of rape, news outlets taking pity on the "nice young man" whose future was somehow ruined by the woman he raped rather than focusing on the rape survivor, and how her life was literally ruined, describing women as objects, etc., and forcing men to take responsibility for the violence they perpetuate against women. An oft-cited example is a Dolce & Gabbana ad where a male model is pinning a woman down while three other guys look on, heavily suggesting and normalizing a gang rape scenario.[17]

Revenge porn is a virtual form of rape. The stories I encountered describe revenge porn as something that happens in hetero couples. This suggests a virtual form of rape culture, a result of systemic sexism. Women sending men nudes of themselves—which are of course a form of selfie—because they're an exchange of intimacy and pleasure is akin to personalized pornography. But it's also intimate. People who perpetrate revenge porn do so because they feel humiliated, so they in turn wrongfully want to humiliate.

In December 2016, the *New Yorker* ran an in-depth story about a lawyer who represents revenge porn cases. Her name is Carrie Goldberg and she is pioneering the legal field of sexual privacy.[18] Her aim is to use the law to help those who have experienced virtual rape through hacking, leaks, revenge porn, and other instances of attacks online.

Taking just one example of revenge porn, Margaret Talbot writes for the *New Yorker*:

> Like a lot of young men these days, he [Christopher Morcos] asked Norma to send him explicit selfies, and, like a lot of young women, she did. She made him promise that he would

keep the pictures to himself. He assured her that he had hidden them on an app with a secure password, and that in any case he would never circulate them. Once in a while, however, he made a joke about doing just that. Norma, a student at the Fashion Institute of Technology who lives with her parents, never laughed in response; she warned him that if he did she'd take him to court.

After they broke up, Talbot explains in her story, the guy, Morcos, hit Norma up with texts, trying to talk with her even though she was clearly moving on. He threatened to post the pics she sent—and eventually, he did. From there, the piece gets pretty hairy, akin to a teenage horror story for the twenty-first century. Norma receives a message from a stranger who said he saw her on PornHub, a popular X-rated site. He had posted eight images of her, and included her first and last name, her phone number, and a note saying that she was asking people to contact her for oral sex. None of this was true. But all her information was up there. It had been posted by someone she used to trust.

In this instance, it didn't matter that Norma held the copyright to those images. (Anyone who takes the photo owns the copyright.) It was all too late for that. Instead, laws required to take on revenge porn cases like these have to do with invasion of privacy. When Norma took Morcos to court, he was charged with "invasion of privacy in the third degree," which in New Jersey is known as "the revenge porn law."[19] The statute focuses on someone who distributes images that they are not licensed or privileged; that is, there is no consent to this type of distribution. The element of "upskirting" was added to this law in March 2016, which "occurs when a person is filmed or photographed underneath their clothing without their consent."[20]

Revenge porn exists because embittered exes—mostly men, but some women too—drop their exes' nudes on sites like myex.com, in an attempt to get some sort of revenge for their broken hearts, or just a sick sense of satisfaction through someone else's inevitable suffering after they discover these images posted to the Internet. What's worse is that taking down images like these from a variety of sites is a full time job, and not every site will comply with takedown requests.

Talbot writes that the "statute makes it a crime for a person who knows that he is not licensed or privileged to do so" to nonetheless disclose "any photograph, film, videotape, recording or any other reproduction of the image of another person whose intimate parts are exposed or who is engaged in an act of sexual penetration or sexual contact, unless that person has consented to such disclosure." The types of statutes are more popularly known as "nonconsensual-porn laws," and they exist in New Jersey, the District of Columbia, and thirty-three other states. Revenge porn may be the more common term, but according to University of Miami law professor Mary Anne Franks, the correct term is nonconsensual pornography.

"That means taking someone's private, nude, or sexual photos and distributing them without the subject's consent," writes Mary Emily O'Hara for the Internet news publication *Daily Dot*.[21] "It's a fairly new crime, but one with the potential to absolutely devastate the lives of its victims in an age in which online material can reach millions of viewers within minutes."

In 2016, at the federal level, US Representative Jackie Speier (D-Calif.) put forth the Intimate Privacy Protection Act, which received bipartisan support from "at least four other members of the House as well as Internet companies Twitter and Facebook, among others."[22] This bill would make it illegal to both distribute or profit from revenge porn; violators would face up to five years behind bars. As noted above, thirty-four states plus the District of Columbia already have revenge porn legislation; the IPPA would "allow federal prosecutors to pursue charges against individuals accused of knowingly distributing sexually explicit material 'with reckless regard for the victim's lack of consent.'"[23] The bill would provide protection for third-party websites and content providers where revenge porn is shared, ultimately not holding tech companies accountable. But sites that promote such content would be charged.

The ACLU chimed in, making some amendment suggestions to the law. Lee Rowland, staff attorney for the ACLU, told *Buzz-Feed News* that "a federal revenge porn law that is too broad might wrongfully criminalize activity that is protected by the First Amendment."[24] He noted that a federal law "should apply to people who 'maliciously and intentionally invade another person's privacy,' which would create a distinction between individuals trafficking in revenge porn and 'anyone who shares nudity without first getting a permission slip.'"

Carrie Goldberg, the revenge porn lawyer, took on the case Norma's case against Christopher Morcos. As a lawyer, she wanted to make sure that her clients do not feel ashamed for sending nudes.

Some would argue that those who "value their privacy" should never send nudes in the first place—but that same type of argument could be extended into the idea that you should never have an online presence or really share anything through digital means, ever. It doesn't make sense, it's not realistic for this day and age, and it's also wrong. But after getting burned like this, would the sender think to send them again? Could digital trust be rebuilt or reimagined with someone new, or is this a nightmare that needn't be risked again? In Norma's case, she felt she would never send a nude again.

In another case, also from December 2016 reported by *Fusion*, a thirty-one-year-old guy named Benjamin J. Barber, who had been convicted of revenge porn in the state of Oregon, attempted to defend himself on a local TV station.[25] His attempts at defending his actions failed. Not only did he try to say that revenge porn laws were "unconstitutional," he also seemed to think that he had a right to post content for which he didn't own the copyright. Sergeant Bob Ray with the Washington County Sheriff's Office took down Barber's weak argument, stating:

"If you use the Internet with the intent to harass or embarrass or basically demean someone, and there is sexually explicit material, and you can identify the other person who has not given their consent, that's essentially the threshold," he said. "If a person does that, they are essentially violating the law. Even just posting it on Facebook. Yes, even if the video was taken consensually."

There's nothing wrong with taking and sending nudes, sexting, or other types of digital foreplay. To send is to consent to someone else seeing that image. The threat is not a digital one so much as it is a personal one—who is this recipient, and can you trust that them with that image?

A limited licensing scenario from hell

Throughout this chapter, I've spent a lot of time talking about images that were either nonconsensually shared, or meant for only a specific audience. But there are images that anyone online can license or outright purchase. As Lizerbram explains in his blog post about the rules of image use online:

If you want to use an image, you have two options. First, you can buy the copyright. This usually applies when the owner of the image is an individual and the image isn't very famous or valuable. Second, and more commonly, you can license the copyright. This means you enter into a contract where you pay for the right to use the image. This is how stock photo websites like iStock operate.[26]

Naturally, the risk in putting an image onto one of these licensing sites is that anyone anywhere can license it and use it as they please. We hope for the best, and prepare for the worst.

Now imagine this: You take a portrait of you and others at your workplace, and then that image ends up being bought not only by a political candidate you dislike, but by the absolute worst possible candidate ever. Sure, licensing agreements were available to people who didn't 100 percent agree with your political views, but you never thought they'd end up with, say, Donald Trump! Now imagine your ad being seen by friends, family members, and others in your community as a symbol of Trump supporting workers.

That whole scenario actually happened to Chicago-based artists Ellen and Dave Greene when they posted an image of their then-business crew to the Internet under a limited license. The black-and-white photo showed them in their metal shop, Iron & Wire, wearing coats and looking tough. They were workers. Companies, advertising agencies, and other organizations could license the image for a fee through a stock footage site.

Before long, the Greenes noticed that their image was being used by a conservative super PAC, Rebuilding America Now. In fact, it was placed in an ad for Trump, focusing on "American workers" and "Making America Great Again." Their image ended up on a pro-Trump website leading up to the 2016 election, yet they were very much against DJT. Given the license they agreed to when they put the photo up, how could this have happened?

"From what I understand the stock video footage was used beyond its limited copyright," Ellen Greene told me via email. "It was available for purchase via different sites and we signed a model release form—we knew that it could be used in small local campaigns or in adverts or websites. Its national dissemination in a super PAC-funded ad was not part of the deal. However that is part of the problem when you are a part of stock footage in the Internet age—it can be used as needed by whomever and it is very hard to claim copyright or to enforce it."

The pro-Trump website TruthFeed.com used their image as the still frame.[27] This wasn't something that they agreed with at all. That same image had also been used by a campaign they actually did agree with—a man running for office in Portland, Oregon, asked if he could use this same image, and they decided he was a candidate they wanted to support.

"People are working hard . . . and making this country great. And upsetting relationships with other countries and inciting hate and being, frankly, unpatriotic and harassing a veteran's family who's lost a child is not the character that I want to support," Dave Greene told *DNA Info Chicago* when asked about how the image ended up on a Trump site.[28] Even though the Rebuilding America Now super PAC violated the licensing agreement, taking them on seemed like a bigger task than the Greenes were ready for.

What is there to do next? Post the whole story to social media. Get media outlets to write the real story of what happened. Is it reasonable to go back to the image-licensing site and tell them to take this down—if there's even a way to do that? Is this worth pursuing in court? In this case, reading the terms of the license and knowing copyright law simply didn't make a difference.

"We did not follow through with any litigation knowing full well that it would be futile," said Ellen Greene. "So we just cringed and it is a part of a strange history that our faces will always be associated with."

Jillian Mayer's 400 Nudes

Miami/LA/NYC-based Jillian Mayer comments on the ways technology affects us physically and emotionally. In her project *400 Nudes*, she locates four hundred nude selfies from around the Internet, including some from revenge porn sites, and photoshops her face onto them. Some are seamless, while others were obviously not of a body that belongs to her. For example, a blonde girl wearing a knit cap, mittens, and a matching colorful scarf low on her waist so as to just cover her crotch doesn't look right with Mayer's face masked into it. This collection of images was shown at the Musée d'art contemporain de Montréal in 2014, and received mixed reviews.

In making art out of actual revenge porn, Mayer further participates in the sharing and repurposing of intimate images that were never meant to be seen publicly. Within selfie culture, however, there is always an implied potential publicness, that this image could be shared. Selfies are taken with that awareness in mind. As an artist, is Mayer given leeway to use these images for the purposes of social commentary?

Mayer is both empathic to the women who originally shared these images, and fascinated by the images themselves. There is a certain sadness in all of these images. They are all evidence of betrayal. Once posted to the Internet, they join the glut of bodies as digital detritus or trash. In order for these images to be removed from the Internet, the girl whose nude was shared would have to hire a lawyer who would then issue a Cease and Desist. It's doubtful of how many would actually take such legal action.

Out of respect for the women whose bodies Mayer used in her work—whose bodies were posted on the Internet without their consent, for the purpose of humiliating and emotionally, physically, and sexually scarring them possibly forever—I have chosen not to include images of her artwork in my book. On a personal level, I wish that the girls could get their images off the Internet.

In an attempt to further empathize with those who were betrayed, Mayer photoshops her head onto all of the bodies. In this way, she somewhat anonymizes them; that is, she doesn't directly use these appropriated images for her own work. This work also becomes commentary on visual oversaturation. In an ideal world, nudes would eventually become destigmatized, and guys wouldn't violate the women who sent nudes for their own pleasure.

"I started doing a lot of reading about [nudes] and I found a website giving tips to young girls for taking nude selfies," Mayer tells the *Huffington Post*. "The tip that I found most interesting was to not show your face. Basically, that you should strip your nude body of its identity and send it to someone you want to sexualize you. I thought that's interesting and funny but also really terrible. Obviously they're trying to protect young girls with this article, but it's also preparing them for the fact that they will be betrayed."[29]

The original images that Mayer appropriates all included the womens' faces. In an attempt to focus on the sexualization, she gets rid of their faces and puts hers on, almost looking clownish—or using her face as a mask, as a way to hide or even protect them.

The same year that Mayer's project came out, the iCloud celebrity hack happened, involving Jennifer Lawrence, Ariana Grande, Selena Gomez, Kate Upton, and others. The perpetrator was Ryan Collins, thirty-six, of Lancaster, Pennsylvania, who "gained illegal access to at least 50 Apple iCloud accounts and 72 Google Gmail accounts, most belonging to Hollywood celebs," according to reports from *Variety*.[30] In this case of revenge porn focused on celebrities, the motivation wasn't a vengeful and crazy ex. It was about access to the object of desire, about having control of nudes that had more sexual currency, because they were the most recognizable celebrity bodies.

Whether a nude is consensually shared to someone else or never meant to be seen, it isn't intended for public viewing on the Internet. Nudes that are either posted or leaked and then shared humiliate the person in the image, regardless of whether or not they are public figures. Despite the fact that the person who takes a nude selfie is the copyright owner of the image, the transmission of that image to the intended recipient is an act of consensual sharing. Like any image, sext, or screengrabbed digital exchange, it could end up anywhere, seen by anyone. Consent is sexy. Sharing without asking is not caring.

Chapter 4

The 24/7 Selfie News Cycle

THE MAINSTREAM MEDIA NARRATIVES THAT surround selfies often focus on young women and how they look. After all, Kim Kardashian is the selfie queen, and everything she does revolves around her self-presentation. This is uncomfortable because young women are simultaneously told that their self-worth depends on their appearance, but then they are referred to as "vain" and "narcissistic" if they spend too much time taking and posting selfies, which are all about appearance. In this world of double-edged selfie swords, what's a girl to do? It's hard to resist the constant availability to this instantaneous mirror that offers attention or validation from peers, crushes, friends, whomever. Constant social media reflection from others can be affirming in these moments, or just recognition that *yes, someone else sees you*. To crave this isn't wrong or even unusual; it's human nature.

Amid the run-up to the 2016 election, a selfie image set the Internet ablaze. It was a photograph of hundreds of young women turning their backs to Hillary Clinton so that they could get a selfie with her. The image was taken by Barbara Kinney, Hillary Clinton's personal campaign photographer, and tweeted by Victor Ng, a designer, photographer, and Internet person for her campaign.[1] In this image, we see only a metal railing separating Hillary Clinton, who stands on a black box and is wearing a blue pantsuit, from a huge crowd of women. Their backs are turned to Clinton; they are holding up smartphones and selfie-ing hard. They were just snagging their moment with her—literally saying that they were WITH HER (#imwithher). She fondly waved on, posing for hundreds of photos on tiny screens that she might only see if they were tagged #HillaryClinton, #ImWithher or @hillary-clinton, and she searched on Twitter, Instagram, or Facebook. Obviously Hillary Clinton—aka #chillarybae, as I referred to her on my Facebook during the run-up to the 2016 election—had better things to do.

Clinton with selfie-ing women. Photo by Barbara Kinney /
Hillary for America. Tweeted by Victor Ng.

In the selfie 24/7 news cycle, the image became separated from its original context on the campaign trail, getting recontextualized as yet another example of how a crowd of women taking selfies are portrayed as self-absorbed, apathetic, and would rather selfie the moment instead of just being there. How easy it is to spin this into the desire of "all young women to constantly selfie" narrative, which quickly becomes the target of criticism. It's an easy headline and a familiar, sexist selfie narrative that's been repeated thousands of times online. But in this case, it was very far from the reality of that selfie opportunity.

The intrinsic sexism inherent in the blanket statement that "women are selfie-obsessed" is ignored. Time and again, the urge to selfie is instead blamed on "the kids today" —*insert actual eye roll here*—with an implication that women are the most selfie-obsessed. In one such piece for CNET, writer Chris Matyszczyk writes a boring and short-sighted take on the selfie, replete with obnoxious headline: "Astonishing pic of Hillary Clinton shows what we've become."[2] Written in letter form, he writes a plealike article to the reader, emphasizing the utter banality of women selfie-ing with Clinton. He doesn't directly address women in the story, though that is implied because the photograph is of women selfie-ing. He writes: "We need to attach ourselves to your fame, so that we can post the resulting picture to Twitter, Facebook and Snapchat. That way, we achieve our own sort of mini-fame. Which could be the maximal fame we ever attain."

Um, yeah right. That selfie is probably going to a girl's Instagram, and it'll be seen by her friends and maybe family, and everyone will be excited that she selfie-d with Hillary and that's great. This type of selfie is not unlike taking a photograph with a celebrity, or asking someone famous for their autograph. It's the same behavior, just with a different tool: the smartphone. And not every person who selfies with a celebrity is fame-obsessed, as the author implies.

Ultimately, this article attempts to both bemoan the selfie generation while also presenting a "holier-than-thou" argument masked in misogyny. The best part here is that the headline is crafted so that he gets the rewards of clickbait. In this narrative, selfie-ing is framed as a pathetic practice performed only by women for attention, rather than a practice deeply rooted in adolescence and celebrity culture that capitalizes on attention as power.

The critique of this image was immediately that women just wanted to selfie, and they would rather get a pic with Clinton than hear her speak. But something was definitely missing. After the article was published, someone noticed that actually, this wasn't a random crazy selfie-ing pic. This was a photo op that Clinton invited. No one spontaneously turned away from her to get that image. And how else would anyone get a photo with her in this type of situation than to take a selfie?

Whereas the other candidate was touting "locker room talk" and normalizing violence against women, the critique of young women selfie-ing with Hillary Clinton, who could've potentially been the first female president, was viewed through the lens of young people—nay, women!—just wanting to sit around and navel-gaze.

"Selfies are influential and geezers can call selfiers as narcissistic as they want without realizing their complicit behavior: ironically, the antiselfie journalists are riding on the backs of selfiers, clearly for the same click bait (unoriginal at that) that the selfies are vying for," said Janna Avner, an LA-based artist whose work deals with artificial intelligence. "Others who are not on social media get pissed about selfie culture probably because they have no creative outlet of their own. They literally have NO social capital online, or in the world, and are unwilling to adapt and evolve to new technologies to seek the recognition they want, because everyone does want recognition at some point or another. They can't see how to benefit from the tools at hand the same way selfie users might."

Also, hello, this was a *photo op*! This happens with any public figure at a promotional event. Here are a few facts about this selfie that most writers who quickly condemned this viral pic sadly missed out on, or just overlooked because it was just too hard to resist a knee-jerk, judgmental reaction.

1. **Hillary Clinton invited the selfie.** She understands that an image of her posted by a smart young woman will do more to sway friends to vote for her than what she says possibly could. The selfie is powerful. We are living in the age of social news, media, recommendations, and homophily, or the idea that "birds of a feather flock together." And though friends have always influenced friends, now it's even faster via social media. An update to this CNET article hours later completely changed its meaning: "Update, 8:20 a.m. PT September 26: Information added that the candidate invited the selfies." Similar reports surfaced elsewhere. "[Photographer Barbara] Kinney said Clinton stood up on the podium and said, 'Okay everybody, turn around and we'll do a group selfie,' before making the staffer standing next to her move out of the way so each side of the room could take an aesthetically pleasing photo," writes Nicole Gallucci for *Mashable*. Clinton became so used to people wanting selfies after her speeches that she would just grab cameras and start taking pictures of herself for them. "It's kind of funny," said Kinney.[3] Hello and duh—Hillary knew what millennials wanted!

2. **It is easier and faster to sequester a short few minutes of selfie-taking than going one-by-one getting a nonselfie photo with every person.** Doing the latter actually would take away from the time that Clinton had to speak with people. The selfie is far more time-efficient and effective, allowing Ms. Clinton to get back to her campaigning.

3. **The selfie offers a feeling of instant connection with the celebrity, and recognition from peers.** Speed is everything. Everyone who took a selfie could feel like they #connected with her, and each woman got an image to prove it. A girl with dyed reddish hair and glasses wearing a blue sleeveless blouse held up her white iPhone and snapped. Two ladies with flowing blonde hair and big neon green shirts that say, "What are you going to do about it?" on the backs gazed into their smartphones. Countless other women did the same thing, capturing an image of themselves with Clinton. And then they had an image to prove that this actually happened, and it's all very exciting.

4. **The people in this photo are practically all young women, and we have no idea who they are.** In tweeting this image, it becomes iconic of Hillary Clinton's 2016 presidential campaign. Taken out of its context as a planned photo op on the campaign trail, it can easily be read as a crazy moment of women wanting to selfie with Clinton rather than hear her speak. Viewers generalize based on how these people look, their gender, their race, their implied socioeconomic status, etc. Who are these people that are selfie-ing? They become part of the selfie-as-meme, identifiable only through their act of selfie-ing.

5. **While this powerful image of women supporting and celebrating the first female president circulates around the web and is labeled as narcissistic by some white guy in Silicon Valley, her opponent's narcissism, sexism, racism, anti-immigration, Islamophobia, and inability to hold his tongue on Twitter are written off as entertainment, examined as worthy pathology (i.e. everyone wants to diagnose him), and normalizing of violence against minorities.** Instead, the underlying shame of women taking selfies with other

women is perpetuated through critiques of this photo, rather than taking a moment to celebrate that women are gathered to hear another female political candidate. And in the meantime, Trump was out there openly harassing women. But sadly, his harassment of women mattered less to voters.

6. **This is not the only selfie with Hillary Clinton.** Obviously she has taken plenty with all types of people. Just google "Hillary Clinton selfie" and you'll find a great picture of her with Kim Kardashian West and Kanye West. While the selfie with Clinton was also an endorsement of her, Kim Kardashian West's selfie with Hillary was not. It was purely promotional for Kim, as she does. She tweeted a selfie of her with Kanye and Hillary Clinton.[4] Sure, she may have hashtagged it #Hillaryforpresident in order to add to the hashtag and brand herself in that moment, but Kim didn't officially endorse her. Instead, she just posted this crafted selfie, letting everyone know that it happened, that she got a good selfie. In Kim K's world, selfies are about her own brand.

I made another curious observation: In a sea of women selfie-ing, there is one man who stands there looking straight at Mrs. Clinton, not photographing the moment, while everyone else has turned around and selfie-d with her. He was the lone individual who preferred not to document this moment. Given a photo opportunity, he decided against it. In fact, when you think about it, that's actually way stranger.

In short, reactions to this picture of women taking a selfie with Clinton were careless. It's not about the selfie, but the bigger picture and how we got to this place that once again becomes a conversation about young women and selfies, about people wanting to document moments that they deem important, and about the vast accessibility of smartphone cameras and peoples' desire to participate on social media with their friends. Or just to take a freakin' photo with a historic political candidate.

Not everyone got it wrong, however. In his well-considered op-ed for the *Guardian*, Jonathan Jones recontextualized the outrage and outright shaming that the Hillary selfie conjured amongst readers. THOSE TAKING SELFIES WITH HILLARY CLINTON AREN'T NARCISSISTS—BUT OUR BEST HOPE, his headline reads.[5] Instead, he compared the nature of selfies to self-portraiture in art history, much like I did in my ongoing selfie column for *Hyperallergic*,[6] which considered the selfie in its earlier iterations. Jones writes:

> Taking a selfie has now become the natural way for many people to mark important events, from dates to nights out to weddings—why not great political moments as well? Traditionally, portraits were painted of rulers and leaders at weighty historical moments. Velázquez's masterpiece, "The Surrender of Breda," and Titian's portrait of Phillip II offering his son as a sacrifice for victory at the Battle of Lepanto use all the resources of oil painting to portray people in history. Perhaps what these women are doing is the democratic equivalent—they are expressing their sense of history with the resources they hold in their hands: their phones.

As the above example shows, the media's perpetuation of the selfie as a "self-indulgent indicator of our times" is short-sighted and, often an indication of lazy journalism filled with biased, overeditorialized "news."[7]

The selfie in and of itself(ie) complicates ideas of likability and honesty, opinion and objectivity, vulnerability and publicity. As a cultural phenomenon, it falls in line with celebrity culture, adolescence, validation, and being seen moreso than a "real" portrayal of life. So it is no wonder that writers—particularly online where social media makes for a more emotionally charged, eager-to-click readership—have categorized the slippery-seeming selfie as news in and of itself. The old-school critiques of the selfie generation don't take into account that the selfiers are actually just using their phones in the most basic way possible, and that way is toward crafting a narrative.

Of course, any place/time/space/location is an opportunity to selfie. In turn, the coverage of the selfie trend has become less about examining them within the context of online-offline fluidity, and more about describing them as disassociating or disconnecting from the physical world, aka the "real world." The Internet is "real" in the sense that we have experiences there. In this duality of "real" (physical world) and "not real" (Internet), however, there's an implied assumption that the Internet doesn't influence people and isn't real life, which is completely untrue. If anything, the social media space during the election started to feel even more "real" than anything else, driving the narrative of each candidate.

"The Internet influences people," said Avner. "Henceforth, selfies do the same, as informative content presented in any other format online might."

Selfies at the edge: EXTREME SELFIES!!!

The selfie has material consequences. It does not just exist in a virtual space separate from the "real world." Aside from the presidential debacle, the most popularized viral selfie stories focus on selfies at the edges of extreme situations, typically encompassing thrill-seeking, death, survival, or life-saving moments, or are about being seen with celebs. Sometimes, what happens when someone takes a selfie actually changes the course of their life.

It's astounding and fascinating that everyday citizen photography has gotten to this point, where people will actually document these types of moments on their own—not to mention videocams of police violence. In the case of Keith Scott's fatal shooting in Charlotte, North Carolina, his wife documented the entire event while also managing to pay attention to the tragedy unfolding in front of her.[8] We saw the same action in the fatal shooting of Philando Castile. In the St. Paul suburb of St. Anthony, Minnesota, on July 6, 2016, Officer Jeronimo Yanez was freaking out after shooting Castile while Castile's girlfriend, Diamond Reynolds, took out her phone and started a Facebook Live stream of the aftermath. In this way, the selfie is not just about turning the camera on oneself—it is about knowing when to take it out, turn it the other way, and tell the world. Otherwise this moment will go unseen.

Selfie videos of police violence differ from extreme selfies, mundane mirror selfies, webcam selfies, and bathroom selfies. Though the selfie as a form permeates our lives, the meaning of the selfie varies with every context.

But now to extreme selfies: These are captivating images that show people risking their lives for a selfie. A selfie-d stunt can become a meme if it goes viral. In the risk-taking selfie genre, this becomes a one-up game, to see who can do it better, who can get more likes, and how fun things can get before they become scary. The extreme selfie is a version of teen risk-taking behavior, forever replicable and easily influencing others, making them want to copy and share their own version. The more attention, the better.

And in fact, the selfie that results in death has become so noticeable that it got its own name: killfie.[9] According to a study, "Me, Myself and My Killfie: Characterizing and Preventing Selfie Deaths," by a team of researchers from the United States and India, there have been 127 selfie-related deaths since March 2014, shortly after the trend tipped.[10] Men made up 75.5 percent of those killfies. The study isn't peer-reviewed, but it does have some thorough data. Apparently, India has the highest number of selfie casualties, at seventy-six total, with Pakistan at nine and the United States following with eight. Of the selfie-related deaths in India, fifteen of those were taken on train tracks, because apparently young couples like to take risqué pics there.

Example A: Selfie-ing and texting while driving

An extreme selfie occurred in April 2014, when a woman named Courtney Ann Sanford posted "The happy song makes me so HAPPY!" to Facebook just moments before hitting a truck head-on and dying immediately.[11] Sanford veered into oncoming traffic because she was texting and driving. In following up on this story, investigators also noticed that she had been taking and posting selfies as she drove.

The world will never know why Sanford was so busy on social media that morning. Was she feeling a need to connect with others, having a hard time on her own in the morning? Maybe she'd meant to post a cute selfie before heading to work but had forgotten, and then tried to make up for lost time while driving, which is not a good time to post anything, let alone text—plus it is illegal to text and drive.[12] We'll never know what went through her head that morning.[13]

For the selfie generation, one mirror is never enough. Social media posts offer immediate approval, validation, and affirmation from not just one person, but many. The responses from others offer not just one head nod, but many; it is the difference between one person offering a high-five and twenty-five people offering a snap even though that snap is less directed, more random, and completely fleeting aside from its quantifiable nature. In other words, twenty-five tiny snap reflections could mean more than a single high-five and congratulations. Who doesn't want more immediate rewards?

We don't know if that's what Ms. Sanford was looking for as she drove while posting selfies and status updates, but it's quite possible that she was bored and alone and looking to connect. After all, Facebook and all social media purport to offer this moment of #connection through sharing.

This event became instant news fodder. Death by selfie was the news angle. But certainly, someone putting on makeup while driving, talking on the phone, or doing anything else distracting could cause an accident. But that wouldn't make for an interesting, sensationalizing headline like "Selfie-ing actually kills." Seriously, though, don't text and drive.

Example B: Daredevil teen selfies

A teenager posting a selfie of something thrilling is another hot topic for selfie sensationalizing stories. It's also easily condemned. With daredevil teen selfies, it's possible to carry out something completely risky without consulting anyone else; all you need is a smartphone, knowledge of your best angles, and an impulse. If there's no selfie to show for the feat, it's like it never happened. The selfie presents evidence that it occurred, that the tree did fall in the forest even if no one was there to see it.

Teens Daniel Lau, Andrew Tso, and Airin S. captured an extreme selfie video using a selfie stick tool and wide-angle lens of themselves at a height of 1,135 feet above the ground, atop one of Hong Kong's tallest skyscrapers. In an online attention culture, this daredevil video wins. It went totally viral! Score. This was a high-risk selfie.

When articles about this selfie video first started coming out, the video had around 515 thousand views. As I write this book, the video has nearly 3.4 million views on YouTube.[14] In the video, Lau gracefully glides his selfie stick, offering a casual pan of the city from high up above; his companions eat bananas, smiling, as if they're just hanging out at the park having a picnic. Everyone appears to be calm. Though the selfie stick served as a way for Lau to document this feat, it would be more interesting to find out if this sort of stunt was typical for Lau. No one died—at least, not in this shot. In this moment, the teen daredevil succeeded, evidence of pulling off a high-risk selfie, and looking so cool all along. The selfie turned them into viral Internet celebs.

Selfies like this come off as fearless. Teens grow up with the Internet always by their side, and adolescence is a time of risk-taking and proving one's social identity. I could imagine how Lau's friends might want to copy what he did. Or not. Or maybe everyone in his high school thought he was batshit. The fear that parents have about videos like this, of course, is that kids are easily influenced, and they will want to copy the act in this video. And this could be true, given that content that is extremely liked or shared is more likely to trigger the rewards section of the brain.

"[As a parent], you're always told to monitor who your kids' friends are, etc., but in this day and age, it's not just the kids that they're hanging out with at school or the kids they're going to bring home, it's also that they're exposed to a much wider range of influence by all of the people that they are friends with or following in any of these social medias, which is a bit scary," said Mirella Dapretto, a professor of psychiatry and biobehavioral sciences at UCLA. "I want to stress that I am not one of those people who thinks social media is *bad*—because it could also work for the good. Your kid could be influenced by people that are doing good things as well."

But in any case, there are plenty of other high-risk selfies to choose from that offer seemingly fear-defying feats that could be replicable by the average teenager. A YouTube video on the channel Keepin' it Karl named "25 Most Dangerous Selfies Ever!"[15] offers a glimpse into some high-risk selfies, like selfies at the summit of Mount Everest, from space, while a speeding train approaches, at the top of the 124-foot-tall Christ the Redeemer statue in Rio de Janeiro, with a wild bear in the background, or while being lit on fire. A couple of selfies capturing great white sharks approaching have been reported as fakes. Apparently these are the easiest types of selfies to make up.

These types of high-risk selfies always come with a very short window of actual shooting time. Such momentary high risks for seemingly brief-lived viral success are arguably less creative than risk-takers of the past, who had to plan both their stunt and the documentation of it, requiring more intense stunts that were both timely and timeless, rather than just of the Internet moment. High-risk selfie-shooters of the present day become viral Internet sensations, sending traffic to their Twitter and YouTube channels. Yet despite their feats, these people are often casually written off as narcissists. The more extreme the selfie, the more attention and virality it will garner from onlookers. It's the same thing that stunt people have always done, except now it's more amateur and with a broader audience.

Nevertheless, headlines with the word "selfie" in them tend to be sensational. In 2015, the Russian government began handing out pamphlets advocating for people to take "safe selfies." "A cool selfie can cost you your life," the interior ministry states in a brochure.[16] Indeed, it could—but for those determined to take a high-risk selfie, it doesn't matter.

Faking the extreme selfie: Obviously, photographs lie and attention wins

Fake is the new real. Photographs lie, and so do selfies. If you're looking for truth, you won't find it in selfies, which embody a careful mixture of emotional vulnerability and absolute posting for publicity's sake. Selfie enough and you will know what works on social media. The extreme selfie and the survival selfie are types of selfies that hit the mark between vulnerability and publicity. They even don't have to document any actual events to garner a response. The only thing they have to do is get the viewer to believe, to draw them into the narrative. And in the land of selfiedom, the image that gets the most attention wins.

Case in point: In early August 2014, an image of a man taking a selfie while a great white shark swam behind him began circulating around the web. The website *World News Daily Report* ran an Internet-attention-getting headline: MAN TAKES SELFIE MOMENTS BEFORE DEADLY SHARK ATTACK.[17] The story was about a man who lost his life hours after getting married because he decided to go swimming and encountered a shark!!!! The article read like plot twists from a soap opera. It seemed rather *uncanny* that while this man died, most likely eaten by the shark, his photo *somehow* became available online immediately after he died. #HowFishy! But for an Internet public that was already divided about their #selfiefeelings and looking for the next story, this was just more evidence for the case that, *truly,* people risked their lives to capture the perfect image and *what kind of a world are we living in people, I mean seriously?!*

On August 8, 2014, Pete Wentz, drummer for the band Fall Out Boy, tweeted the *World News Daily Report* article with the words "Rest In Pete" and a link to the story.[18] He was quickly identified as that guy in the killer shark image—not some thirty-four-year-old insurance salesman from Portland named James Crowlett as the article claimed. And Pete was definitely still alive. It was all a publicity stunt! For anyone who took a closer look at this Internet newspaper, they would have seen that it was a spoof site. This shark selfie was a photoshopped selfie-before-death joke and the Internet fell for it. This parody article, aka "fake news" story, went viral, scoring nearly one hundred thousand shares on Facebook. This perfectly crafted selfie hit a sweet spot.

This wasn't the only selfie with a great white shark, which indicated that many people were thinking of this idea at the same time. Similar-looking and seemingly "real" great white shark selfies surfaced, such as one taken by seventeen-year-old Alex Hayes, an Instagram-famous teenager in Australia.

His feed is filled with sun-soaked photos of him surfing or hanging out on picturesque beaches and generally looking adorable. Because he does post branded content, some of his posts are sponsored, making his social media part of an actual earning gig. This fake shark photo was what made him more known on IG, both to the Australian public and the world in June 2015. A hoax selfie may tell a thousand words—but it is also currency for gaining new followers. Ultimately, the image served as marketing for Hayes' social media brand. Here's how he staged it.

Hayes had been out surfing and then took a selfie with the water as his backdrop; later, he photoshopped in a great white shark lurking just below the surface of the water. The photo made the rounds, easily convincing people that the young surfer was in danger, risking taking a selfie even though he could've been killed by a shark! People left concerned comments on the teenager's Instagram. Later, it turned out that this image was just manipulated. Likely, commentators would feel duped—they leant their empathy to something that never actually happened, and felt for a guy who wasn't ever actually in danger of death by shark. The joke is on the empathetic viewer.

Another more obvious great white shark selfie shows a chubby white man wearing a pair of black Speedo goggles, grinning at the camera and showing only his top gums while a great white shark comes up behind him. The shark also seems to be smiling, its pointed teeth very visible in its open mouth. The two subjects appear so close in this camera, it looks as if they staged this shot together—could this be a true collaboration between man and cold-blooded killer fish?[19] Though this image didn't fool the Internet as easily, it was still lumped into YouTube videos about extreme selfies by seemingly idiotic people, further evidence of just how gullible people are on the web, especially when the image involves a death-defying risk.

Men posted all of these extreme great white shark selfies. What significance could that have? I got in touch with Rob Horning, an editor at *Real Life* magazine and *New Inquiry*, to talk more about the extreme selfie, why only men posted them, and the selfie's relationship to "authenticity."

"I think selfies are the safest content to post on social media, especially for men, who are rarely accused of being narcissistic and self-obsessed," said Horning. "Selfies don't imply a desire to communicate anything but the poster's continued existence; they are not typically political or argumentative, they are not like sharing links to articles or whatever. They are a way to stay present on social networks, which demand regular posting, without the trouble of having to stake a position on anything other than wanting to be noticed and acknowledged."

The staged vulnerability in extreme selfies casts the selfie taker as the hero of their own selfie narrative, as a character who has continued to capture attention and garner a response. In this sense they reveal a different truth about 'who we are' and how we want to be seen by using the possibilities afforded by photo-editing, manipulation, stickers, captions, etc., etc., etc. All selfies are in this sense aspirational, and that is especially obvious when you photoshop yourself into a picture with a shark and claim to have escaped."

Survival selfies are another category of selfie that will get a specific type of attention. The onlooker will feel a sense of relief that the person survived, and conclude that this person was brave.

Ferdinand Puentes was on a flight off the coast of Hawaii in December 2013 when he heard beeps and sirens followed by a loud bang. His Makani Kai Air flight was going down fast. So Puentes did what any self-surveilling passenger would do: He threw on his GoPro camera and captured the flight spiraling down. And then, after he was floating in the water wearing a life jacket, he took a selfie with the airplane remains in the background. Some would call this a survival selfie as attention; others would call it a wild and heroic documentary. And still others would refer to it as selfie journalism or citizen journalism. Regardless, Puentes survived, and his survival selfie received validation. He could now present himself in a new way for others and to himself.

"Selfies are not meant to be passport photos," said Horning. "They are meant to broaden the possibilities for what sort of self you are to yourself and your friends."

The kids today are going to hell
and they're selfie-ing all the way there

Adolescence is a period of life in which there is a heightened focus on the self; the selfie becomes a natural outgrowth for this awkward developmental period, a way to self-surveil at a time when teens are attempting to find themselves within their social milieu. Instead of recognizing adolescence for what it is, and realizing that every generation of young people receives the same sort of criticism, the cultural memory tends to immediately forget what just happened to a recent generation of teenagers, only to be reignited by the successive generation of teenagers who exhibit the usual adolescent behavior.

Jason Feifer, a former *Fast Company* editor and current editor in chief at *Entrepreneur* magazine, happened to pick up on a few of the more confusing types of selfies created by young people, compiling them on three selfie Tumblrs: Selfies at Serious Places, Selfies at Funerals, and Selfies with Homeless People.[20] While all three Tumblrs offered an idea of the visual communication that young people were using, the funeral selfies Tumblr blew up the Internet. Meanwhile, selfies with homeless people just felt morally reprehensible to anyone who has half a heart and/or compassion for the homeless. Seriously, if you selfie like this there is something wrong with you.

Funeral selfies and selfies at serious places appeared more complex, mostly because of the wide range of emotions that these selfies captured. They blur the lines of public and private.

Naturally, Feifer's Tumblrs fascinated adults too, and the Internet couldn't wait to gobble them up. In a content-hungry Internet media landscape, all of these simple Tumblrs were easy to write about, reshare, and comment on with moralizing tones. In turn, Feifer became a sort of expert on these types of selfies.

"The first one, Selfies at Serious Places, was a more abstract idea, but it started because my wife and I were on vacation in Europe and noticed people taking selfies at the Berlin Wall, which doesn't hold enough of its original sad representation to feel uncomfortable taking a smiling selfie in front of it," he said. "Then a few days later we were in front of the Anne Frank house, which very much does maintain that sad symbolism, and people were still taking selfies in front of it. And that's when I was like, 'This is happening, this is a thing.'"

The common assumption that selfies are wrong, bad, or just rude could've easily been gleaned from this observation, but that's not what Feifer thought when he started noticing the abundance of selfie-taking opportunities. As a journalist, he approached the selfie with curiosity.

"I never looked at it in a moralizing way," he said. "I wasn't even upset that people were doing it. I didn't create the Tumblr to channel any ill will toward these people. I just made it because I thought it was interesting that this was a thing that people were doing and I thought that when polled together in a critical mass it just said something, and I didn't want to say what that thing was."

Essentially, through creating Tumblrs with these themed selfies, he turned each category of selfie into meme. All three of the Tumblr designs he used were pretty basic-looking layouts. The backgrounds are a clean white, and the fonts are all in some form of serif typeface. Each Tumblr is brief, only a few pages, and offers examples of the hashtagged meme.

After Feifer noticed that this was in fact a thing and created the Tumblr Selfies at Serious Places, he began searching around for other selfie trends. Eventually he stumbled upon #funeralselfies after doing some searching on social media. The idea for Selfies at Funerals came about very casually after a conversation with some friends at a bar, who suggested he create a new Tumblr devoted only to that selfie category.

"Selfies at funerals connected with people the most for all sorts of reasons," said Feifer. In time, Feifer told me that he became a sort of "selfie spokesperson or selfie whisperer."

"The conclusion that I came to was that there is nothing wrong with this because there is no ill intent behind it," he said. "I think that what we are seeing is a language that people over the age of eighteen just don't speak. It is a visual language. Instead of me, a teenager, describing how I feel in words, I may not have the capacity to do that very well because not everyone is a great writer and certainly not every teenager is a great writer. So just taking a photo and posting it is a far more efficient means of communication. Although it was posted on social media for everybody to see, people don't think of social networks that way. Unless you're a journalist on Twitter, you don't assume that everyone is seeing your thing. You just assume that your private network is seeing your thing. And then they understand the context in which it's being seen."

The funeral selfies created moral outrage from a variety of media sources, taking aim at teenagers and their "self-absorption" and narcissistic ways. Sure, adolescence is a time for intense focus on the self, but social media is also just where teenagers socialize, showing off to their friends in the spaces where they are all hanging out. Teenagers weren't trying to give adults a chance to see, but unless the accounts were private, the posts were entirely public and searchable.

But photographs referencing death aren't anything new, either. Victorian postmortem photographs documented the dead. Or rather, shutter speeds were so slow that the only good time to get a photograph of someone was when they were dead, and before they were buried. Now shutter speeds are rapid and sharing is as immediate as can be, and sharing is considered social. So the kids today, they're being social in spaces where their friends are hanging out. And some of those spaces are online.

"I feel like what I stirred up was a generational clash more than it was any kind of unearthing of a particular kind of disrespect from a generation, which I really don't believe in," said Feifer. "I don't believe that millennial or Gen Z—I firmly don't believe that they think, act, or function any different than any previous generation, it's just that they have technology [that previous generations did not]."

The Tumblr spawned a variety of articles about funeral selfies, from defense of selfies at funerals to stories bemoaning teens' lack of social etiquette. The polarization of this led to further confusion about what was actually acceptable online when one is mourning loss of life, and also just being a teenager out in the world sharing with friends. How do kids socialize so differently today than they did before?

Another one of the selfies that ended up on SelfiesAt SeriousPlaces.tumblr.com was then-twenty-year-old Jake Fletcher's selfie at Chernobyl. The photo was taken on June 5, 2013, at the site of Nuclear Reactor 4, Chernobyl Nuclear Power Plant, and hashtagged with #chernobyl. At the time of the photo, the New Safe Confinement, an arch-shaped steel structure to protect the damaged nuclear reactor, had not yet been completed.

#chernobyl. Courtesy of Jake Fletcher.

Feifer noticed this selfie and added it to his Tumblr. Jake saw that it had gotten picked up, and he wrote to Feifer clarifying why he took the selfie. He didn't request that it be taken down, however. Rather, he wanted to explain that it was not a reckless, narcissistic selfie as many on the Internet assumed it was, and he asked that his response be posted with the image. He clarified how truly aware he was of the significance of selfie-ing at Chernobyl, where the world's worst nuclear power plant disaster occurred on April 26, 1986, when thirty-two people died and many more suffered radiation burns. He wanted to explain himself and his selfie.

As I'm sure you're aware, Chernobyl isn't Disneyland, in fact it's probably the furthest thing from it. You don't go to Chernobyl for fun, you go there to learn about the disaster and see the massive scale of the devastation for yourself. I was fascinated by what I had heard about the event—as I'm only 20 I wasn't around when the disaster unfolded, so keen to learn more I took it upon myself to go to Ukraine and visit the site. The first thing that strikes you is the bleak nature of the place, followed by the realisation of how fast people had to leave when you visited the abandoned villages. And then you get to the sarcophagus of the reactor. That expression on my face is meant to be shock, not some vacuous, feeble attempt at narcissistic irony. The shock of seeing the scene of the disaster I'd heard so much about. The shock of seeing how close the reactor is knowing that 27 years ago standing in the same spot would have killed you in mere minutes. And what was probably the most shocking thing for me was seeing how many people still work there. People imagine Chernobyl to be an empty wasteland, the reality is 5000 people are still working in and around the site. All these feelings culminate inside you and you're left numb and confused trying to take everything in. It was probably one of the most surreal experiences for me during my time on Earth, without question. I would encourage as many people to visit Chernobyl before October 2015 (the expected completion date of the dome which will replace the sarcophagus) to experience what I experienced. Until you visit the place you don't get a true scale of the events that happened back in April 1986. If you're in Kiev but unable to visit Chernobyl, the museum in Kiev is an unmissable, fitting tribute that is able to convey some reality of the events. I would certainly go back if I'm not now banned from entering Ukraine. Finally, I think some people have been quick to demonise myself and my picture. As I've already said, you don't go to Chernobyl for a party, and I'm quite proud that a photo of me taking in some culture, documenting my travels and learning about the world's worst nuclear disaster has gone viral. It makes a change from seeing the usual images of drunk British teenagers ruining a Mediterranean island by drinking too much alcohol and urinating/vomiting/fighting/having sex in the middle of the street. I hope that some people will now think about images like mine for just a bit longer before bemoaning that they show society's failures laid bare before them.

The last part of Jake's long explanation really stuck with me. Instead of knee-jerk reacting to any selfie like Jake's at a loaded historical site, labeling all the kids today as worthless narcissists, the viewers themselves could take a minute to wonder: What led that person to take a selfie in a place like Chernobyl, anyway?

The answer might be far more complex than you think.

It's been four years since that selfie. The dome was completed in November 2016. As of this writing, Jake is now twenty-four years old and lives in Manchester, UK. When I wrote to him, he told me that he still stands by that selfie he took. He also recognizes that not everyone is as contemplative when selfie-ing in a serious place.

"These days you see a lot of young people posting pictures in various places around the world just for a mere photo op—oblivious to any historical or cultural importance these places have—they're there just to say they were also there," he said.

Of course, you'd never know of the selfie-shooter's intentions unless you asked them or unless they told you. In that way, a selfie is more than just a "photo that says a thousand words." It says far more, depending on how the selfie shooter will describe the image, their intentions behind it, and why they decided to share it in the first place.

I did not come of age on social media, but I was on AOL Instant Messenger and in chat rooms as a teenager. I didn't do LiveJournal like my younger sister did; she wrote journal entries about her feelings and what was going on in her life, and formed online communities of people who read and engaged with her posts. I mostly wrote about my feelings on paper, in my room, alone. In both high school and college, I recall writing about funerals and death in my journal, likely accompanied by self-portraits that I took of my face to see for myself how I was feeling about what was happening. Since I'm a writer I wanted to think and write about all my feelings, but I realized that not everyone was like me. I did want to see how I was feeling rather than just feeling the feelings, however, so I took all these photos and vowed never to show anyone because they *were* just for me. But were I a teen today, would that still hold true? Maybe they'd be selfies I'd save to my phone and never post. Or maybe I would post them all, performing my experience for others.

"Selfies came to further symbolize this thing that people were accusing this young generation of doing," said Feifer. "And people like to be outraged and the media likes to serve—as a member of the media, I'm talking about the media in this ominous way— but it is true that a story that gets people on an emotional level is going to get people engaged. So this fit perfectly."

Was it necessary for the media to wax on and on about the loss of decency and the seeming disrespect for the dead that teens have when adults are publicly mourning death on social media all of the time? Oddly, it is socially acceptable to publicly mourn the death of a public figure or express grievances about a mass murder or bombing in some other part of the world via social media, but that's not so when teens share their feelings about personal loss a la funeral selfies.

In Kyle Chayka's article "Why Social Media Turns to Images to Help Us Cope With Tragedy" for *New York Magazine*, he discusses the nature of memes such as the bear hugging the state of California with the text "Pray for San Bernadino" after the tragic terrorist act at a senior center in San Bernadino County.[21] Similarly, after 130 people were shot and killed in Paris, Facebook flooded with French artist Jean Jullien's sketches of a peace symbol containing the Eiffel tower. These images represent a collective social mourning. They are impersonal, and show people collectively grieving offline and possibly with others while sharing their support and solidarity for those whose lives have been lost. The lack of individualization in such memes makes them feel selfless and detached from any one person's experience. They are safe in their sameness, lacking the vulnerability of the teen #funeralselfie that's meant just for their peers. A teenager posts a personal goodbye note to a loved one. A young man flexes his muscles in the mirror before he heads to a grandparent's funeral. Collective mourning memes come off as socially acceptable.

I asked Feifer if any other people he included on the Tumblrs wrote to him about their selfies in his Tumblrs. He told me that a few from the Selfies at Serious Places Tumblr decided to explain themselves. Their answers were legitimate and, like my *Hyperallergic* selfie column story about funeral selfies, considered the intentions, feelings, and context for each of the selfies rather than broadly generalizing about them.[22]

Adolescence is a rebellious time of life, but it's also just curious, raw, and emotional. If the act of mourning were not socially performative in nature, then certainly no one would post anything about loss at all. Yet it is cathartic to share, and when all the Internet is a stage and anyone who looks is an audience member, the performance is always available.

#aftersex selfie

The hashtag #aftersex started trending in early 2014. In a story for Nerve.com, Kate Hakala asks of the #aftersex shots: "It, like a lot of Instagram pics, is a private moment built for an audience. Is the #aftersex shot, taken to be shared, the new social cigarette?"[23]

I looked through these selfies, and TBH I thought many of them were hot. Of course, if the couple posting it didn't think they were sexy, they wouldn't have posted them at all. Many of the #aftersex selfies were rather artful in their execution; a nude man covering his dick, gazing into the mirror with a content, dreamy look poses in front of a woman who, standing behind him, wraps her arm around him, holds the phone, and shoots a picture into the mirror. Other #aftersex selfies show two people laying in bed, lovingly gazing at the camera, shirts off—but because of the Instagram rules, no nudity. The selfies are exhibitionist in nature, and they get attention.

"Certainly #aftersex shots are a brag, maybe they're an overshare, but they're also just another modern way—like viral proposal videos, like engagement photos—to publicly declare love," writes Hakala. "I'll watch that."

Love? Yea right—way to try and suggest that all sex is about love. For #aftersex selfies, I think it is far more accurate to say that the driving factors are lust and the thrill of attention from strangers. People who take #aftersex selfies are risk-takers and exhibitionists, and they get off on sharing that image—of who *could* see it, of who *might* notice. And for the writer who is writing about #aftersex selfies, it makes for a titillating headline.

Danny's Selfies

Another type of fascinating selfie that makes news has less to do with sexiness and more to do with sadness. Danny Bowman, nineteen, the subject of a 2014 story about selfie isolation and obsession, was easily exploited. As the British tabloid the *Mirror UK* puts it, the "teenager became so obsessed with taking the perfect selfie he tried to kill himself when he failed to do it."[24] This tale of extreme selfie-ing was perfect tabloid fodder and evidence of selfie-infused narcissism. But a deeper reading of the story suggests that this is not actually the case.

The details go like this: Danny Bowman spent ten hours per day taking up to two hundred selfies of himself with his iPhone. He had dropped out of school. He lost friends. His parents worried about him. He was completely lost in his selfie world, which was fueled by a desire to become a model. Truly, that is a troubling story! At the same time, his obsessive selfie-ing seemed to be less about an addiction to likes, and more so about OCD and body dysmorphia. Selfie-ing became a way for him to feel like he had control over his appearance because he controlled the camera, his angles, the light, and the outcome.

Achieving the perfect selfie was impossible, however, and control was an illusion.

"I finally realised I was never going to take a picture that made the craving go away and that was when I hit rock bottom," said Danny in the *Mirror UK*.

In this story, the selfie became the news angle again. Here, it was evidence of an addiction that is bigger than the selfie. But because he was photographing himself in an attempt to figure out how to become a model, what else could the narrative focus on than his selfies?

When viral selfies get read through sexism

Before the vast availability of the front-facing smartphone camera, the process of self-reflection was not assumed public by default. People were not constantly thinking about how their content was received by others, because it wasn't so instantaneously produced. For girls growing up today, this sort of self-objectification has become normalized yet girls are still being shamed for this even though at this point selfie-ing is a normal part of growing up. How did we get here?

It's a question that Elisa Kreisinger posed in "No Shame in a Selfie," episode 4 of her *Refinery29* podcast Strong Opinions Loosely Held. She focuses this episode on understanding the shaming effect of selfies, particularly as they affect young women.[25] She began the podcast with a few simple questions: *Why are young women drawn to the selfie, and why do we think it's okay to shame them for it? Are we narcissistic? Are we trying to find ourselves?*

Then she asked the big question, the one that perhaps anyone who has taken a selfie or some time to self-reflect has actually asked: *How do we find ourselves?* In an age of constant and instant communication of any thought that could be delivered to a friend via text or posted to social media, the question has actually become more complicated than ever before. *How do we find ourselves in an age that is so focused on the idea of the selfie, but has perhaps less interest in the self?* Well, the answer is obviously not through social media. But meanwhile, social media does shape perceptions of people.

Kreisinger points to one pertinent example of selfie-shaming that was targeted at young women. This story made its way around the Internet in fall 2015. "A group of sorority sisters were attending a baseball game," Kreisinger explained on the podcast.

"The announcers asked fans to take a selfie and use a hashtag to promote the game and its sponsor, T-Mobile." They did as any girls would, and took time to try and capture the perfect selfie by shooting many of the same poses over again, and trying out different angles and arrangements. The motivation for this was simple: Fans might see themselves reflected back on the big screen at a baseball game. It's not fifteen minutes of fame—it's about less than five seconds of attention. But still, exciting and makes someone feel like a celebrity within that context.

Rather than praise the girls for trying to put their best selfie forward, the commentary from the announcers went on with a completely mocking tone: "Do you have to make faces when you take selfies?" said one guy, and then the other chimed in, pretending that he was the sorority sister having some thoughts about the selfie. "That's the best one of the 300 photos that I've taken today!" he said, mocking her.

"The twelve women were sitting in the stands taking selfies for two minutes," explained Kreisinger. "For a sports event, this is a shockingly long time to hold a shot."

The shot was coming from these announcers, who were blatantly making fun of the girls. The twelve women stay onscreen as the commentary continues. 'Selfie with a churro, selfie with a selfie!' the announcers continued poking fun at the young women as they took selfies. The women were unaware of the on-air commentary until the video went viral. Then they saw themselves reflected back in this giant stadium mirror.

You can imagine their absolute mortification. After all, they were doing exactly what the sportscasters had asked them to do: *Look cute, take a selfie, hashtag it for the game to show support for the team, and post!* And after they'd done exactly that, after they followed seemingly innocuously, corporate-instructed, "correct" instructions on what to do and how to behave as young women at a sporting event, they became controversial selfie-ing figures in the media.

News reports later portrayed the story in a very different way. ABC7 News in San Francisco/Oakland/San Jose made it seem as if the sportscasters had caught the girls in the act, totally self-absorbed, painting yet another tale of "young women being more interested in taking selfies than watching the game."[26]

Like many other lazy media reports that forget to include all the facts about the event in question, this one did not mention that the girls were doing exactly what they had been told to do: take a selfie at the game, and hashtag it.

This reminds me of the stories that came out about the selfie with Hillary—look at all these girls selfie-ing and ruining their generation, rather than realizing that this was a photo op presented by Mrs. Clinton for the audience. In one fell swoop, the girls were shamed for doing exactly what they were told to do: take a selfie.

Chapter 5

Meta-Selfie Advertising, lol

A SELFIE IS AN ADVERTISEMENT. The shift from selfies as spontaneously posted images of the "now" to being obviously staged, hashtagged as necessary, and completely crafted happened almost as quickly as the mainstreamification of the selfie in 2013, when it was named word of the year by OxfordDictionaries.com.[1] The selfie existed previously, it just wasn't named as such. Before it had a name, the selfie resembled blurry webcam photos in peoples' bedrooms taken for MySpace profile pics, or awkward, fuzzy dumbphone pics that you took and then forgot about because you had a better camera for "real" photos. The first recorded use of the word "selfie," however, popped up in an Australian online forum in 2002, posted by some wasted dude:

> Um, drunk at a mates 21st, I tripped ofer [sic] and landed lip
> first (with front teeth coming a very close second) on a set of

steps. I had a hole about 1cm long right through my bottom lip. And sorry about the focus, it was a selfie.[2]

Fast forward eleven years and the selfie returned. The selfie began its ascent in 2013.[3] Previously, a photo of oneself was just deemed a self-portrait, and it wasn't expected that it could be shared. But the selfie suggests a potential publicness. The selfie may have begun on social networks like MySpace and Friendster, but today it is a marketer's dream come true.

The selfie taker who posts their image is both complicit in the use of their selfie within the network's circulatory nature, and also happily providing free advertising for any product, place, or thing that they may be depicting and hashtagging. This circular nature creates a self-fulfilling advertisement prophecy of subject as both consumer and advertiser. Selfies become a form of personal branding, and branding for the companies pictured therein. In other countries, such as the Philippines and China, however, selfies function in different ways.

Western selfie self-advertising

Selfies that prop up moments of accomplishment, joy, or appear otherwise celebratory deliver messages of happiness, connectedness, and overall positivity about the person pictured. An individual feels great joy after purchasing a product—some new toothpaste, for example—and then decides that they love it so much, they want to tell their friends about it on social media. Rather than spread that feeling through word-of-mouth, however, they take a selfie with the toothpaste and post it to social media. Feel good about purchase, take picture with purchase, not-so-subtly encourage others to buy or celebrate the product. The selfie becomes an easy word-of-mouth advertisement without any effort from the company itself.

In other instances, everyday people are paid to be micro-advertisers by a company and can earn either money or freebies by posting about a product or company. The company BzzAgent, for example, asks people to sign up—those who sign up for these services generally have to have a social media following—and then the user is offered money or free products in exchange for advertising on their social media. Some posts may appear more raw and "authentic" because a person has fewer followers, for example. Some agencies require that posters hashtag with #GotIt-Free or a similar tag in order to show that yes, this is an advertisement, but not everyone feels that will do as well.

In a story for the *New Statesman*, Amelia Tait interviews Aron Vitos, a twenty-one-year-old student from Budapest who uses PostForRent, where micro-influencers can get connected to advertisers who will ask for products marketed on Instagram.[4] Wouldn't this inevitably lead to Vitos' followers distrusting his social media presence, simply because he is always posting about products? Maybe.

Vitos appears to be a pretty mainstream kind of guy, someone who loves big businesses such as H&M, Forbes, and Vodafone, and endorsing corporations on social media, so his posts likely don't appear very off-brand to followers. He does not always disclose that his posts are paid advertisements. "I think not using [them] creates a more authentic look of the post," he told *New Statesmen*. "When you have to tag the brand itself and add the hashtags the brand asked you to, people would already know it's an ad. I sometimes do it to clear my conscience but I don't think this has that much weight on the post."

We expect that the Kardashians endorsing something like Fit-Tea detox tea on their social media is clearly for promotional purposes—as social media celebrities, we expect that they're getting paid to sponsor products because they've made themselves into celebrities through reality TV and social media.[5] The regular person who is endorsing products on social media is, ultimately, emulating the Kardashians' mode of doing exactly the same thing.

Kendall Jenner took that one step further by co-opting activism that spreads through social media. (As we know from chapter 2, that's not how actual activism works. But in the Kardashians' social media advertising landscape, that doesn't matter.) In the ad, Jenner attempts to market herself as an "activist" by having an "authentic" experience—except she is only doing so for commercial gains.

Jenner appears as a protestor in a Pepsi ad, featuring other protestors clashing with police. In the ad, she hands a Pepsi to a police officer, who takes a sip and then stands down. A woman in a hijab photographs her, and the crowd cheers as suddenly everything is wonderful! Wait, what?! Apparently with a Pepsi in hand, the cops realize that actually, *it's all good.* Obviously, this would never happen to anyone who is actively participating in a protest, and is actually insulting to people who are working for social justice.

People spoke up on social media and elsewhere, like this especially poignant tweet from Bernice King, Dr. Martin Luther King Jr's daughter:

"If only Daddy would have known the power of #Pepsi."[6] Pepsi apologized and removed the ad.

The Kardashians are one thing, but when actual friends who don't appear to be micro-influencers and are in peoples' social networks start promoting a product or service, the line between social media "authenticity" and straight-up marketing gets hazy. Regardless, it's important to remember that the selfie, no matter what the purpose of it, is always an advertisement for whomever or whatever is pictured in the image, whether that's just a person in a bathroom or a person discussing a product or service. The selfie tows the line between vulnerability and publicity, capitalizing on the space in between. Thanks to social media, marketing to individuals on a hyperpersonalized level has become accessible, easy, and seemingly carefree. And always, the product is you.

Aside from the selfie as advertisement, after the selfie trend tipped in 2013, companies began using the selfie in campaigns as a way to #connect with millennial consumers. Or whatever. In order to do so, the company using the selfie has to buck the popular notion of selfies as narcissistic, and of millennials as the trash generation, lazy, addicted to their phones. Instead, in this context the selfie must just be seen as a way to #connect and be social, sharing with a niche "community"—aka, target audience, not actual community—over a product or consumer interest. This is a way to make people feel something about a product, or create a sense of intimacy between consumer and consumed, and to tell people that selfie-ing is a normalized and acceptable behavior within the context of surveillance culture, which ultimately assures that everything we are saying in earshot of our phones or posting to networks is being recorded. When the creepiness of this is reframed in the context of socializing, it's far more marketable.

Through participating in selfie-ing, the consumer is also offering up their personalized data to the social network. This included not just the data of their online purchases, sites visited, and links clicked, which is already being used to advertise, but also their selfies-as-endorsements of product or place. In advertising, selfie-ing is often presented as "carefree" and with an element of "fun" involved. It's an experience that can be easily commodified.

Aside from the selfie as personal branding, there are a number of ad campaigns that use the selfie to sell a product. Many other major brands have incorporated the selfie into their advertising campaigns, such as Heinz, United Airlines, National Geographic, Macy's, and DOVE. But as selfies became more normalized, the advertisements around them changed. Back in the earlier selfie days, circa 2013–2014, there was a more nuanced approach to the selfie in advertising, considering it in relation to the history of self-portraiture. By 2017, it was just a request to selfie with a product. The selfie advertisements from right after the trend tipped were more involved and nuanced, treating the idea of the selfie as something to ponder, as in the DOVE campaign, which questioned ways that women learned how to think about their appearances. By 2017, the selfie in advertising was very simple, often combining the product itself with a selfie "ask," like the quick Heinz campaign, which just solicits people to take a selfie with a bottle of Heinz ketchup.

In a 2014 advertisement for the Samsung NX mini mirror-less camera, famous artists like Frida Kahlo use the camera to create self-portraits that, at first glance, appeared to be selfies.[7] The ad reproduces scenes of famous artists creating their now famous self-portraits, replacing the original portrait with a slightly inauspicious selfie taken with the Samsung smartphone. Dürer takes a self-portrait while sitting in front of the window seen in his 1498 self-portrait that he painted at age twenty-six. In the two other selfie self-portrait examples, Frida poses in front of a garden, and Van Gogh is in front of a blue wall with swirls in it, looking serious. In fact, all the artists look serious in their self-portraits, something that is opposite of the selfie form's assumed silliness. The ad suggests that selfies are totally legitimate and much more like self-portraits than we may have previously assumed, and also draws parallels between the history of self-portraiture in art and today's means of taking a quick snapshot of your face. It suggests that the selfie is in fact just a self-portrait for the digital age, minus the effect of posting to the network.

A 2014 *National Geographic* ad campaign featured animals taking bathroom selfies, back when these were somewhat novel. A coy kangaroo captures itself in a solitary moment, standing in front of an ornate mirror and a sink covered in rose designs, echoing millions of #bathroomselfie and #elevatorselfie examples. In another, a gorilla poses confidently in front of a bathroom mirror that hangs on a wall of aqua-blue tiles. A lackadaisical koala chills in a wood-paneled elevator, sitting down and taking a selfie in the floor-to-ceiling mirror. The anthropomorphism of these animals creates a distancing effect from the human, who is usually the one taking selfies, allowing for a moment of reflection. One might ask themselves: *Why did I take that #bathroomselfie or #elevatorselfie?* Making public these spaces that are usually reserved for matters not visible—using the bathroom, spacing out in the elevator—is indicative of a shift toward sharing moments that one would normally not document.

In another 2014 selfie advertising campaign, DOVE attempted to take a more "authentic" approach to the selfie. They looked at how young women were selfie-ing, and asked how that was affecting how they perceived standards of beauty. This could have been a very fascinating conversation. DOVE located the selfie as a conversation starter about mother-daughter relationships, asking how taking selfies together could become a point of #connecting, and a way to bridge generations. DOVE appears as a conduit for these conversations, making this campaign appear to be more "do-gooder" than an attempt to sell product, when in fact it is using this seemingly benign approach to advertise its brand.

The ad begins with a young woman selfie-ing by herself in the middle of a field on an overcast afternoon. She seems pleased with her selfies. For her, she sees the selfie as a moment with herself, and a way for her to understand how she appears to others. DOVE doesn't let on whether or not she has shared that image to a network; if she did, the image would take on a very different effect, for she would be judged by her friends, peers, and followers alike, which is most of the selfie discourse. Instead, she doesn't post. There's an implied sincerity to this method of what seems to be solitary selfie-ing and not posting. As the ad continues, we see other girls reflecting on how media affects the ways that they understand themselves. "I think that a lot of girls compare themselves to what they see on TV and what they see in magazines and movies and videos. To fit in, you have to fit this mold," one girl explains. It comes off as candid rather than scripted, as if these really are just people having frank conversations about the world.

The DOVE campaign puts the focus on young women, telling them that they have the "power" to create new standards of beauty through selfie-ing. Except DOVE never discusses what happens when the selfies are posted to a network, which is where the socializing, shaming, self-esteem making and breaking, validation, and everything else take place for teenage girls. But in the world of this advertisement, apparently social media and selfies don't mix. So unless the girls in the DOVE ad became social media celebrities, they would not actually change beauty standards. But DOVE isn't suggesting that they become social media celebrities. Instead, the advertisement focuses on mother-daughter relationships.

It can *feel* empowering to take selfies, however, because it is a photo that offers an element of self-control. The false and idealistic DOVE ad tells women that they can change standards of beauty through selfie-ing, even though they don't have any type of social media status. It's supposed to be inspirational, but actually just feels out of touch. What makes this ad somewhat interesting, however, is the dialogue therein of girls talking about how they see themselves, and what they do and don't like about their appearances.[8] But DOVE fails to include how esteem is further shaped through social interactions on social media, where the girls' peers hang out.

The selfies in the DOVE ad seem to assume that the selfie is the same as a self-portrait, which it is not. Perhaps this ad campaign would have been more effective if it focused on the double standards of female self-portraiture, and why women are judged and judge themselves so harshly on their appearances and feel compelled to photograph themselves in the first place. Or what happens when a selfie is shared to a social network, and how that affects teenagers' self-esteem. Instead, it just merely skims and reflects back on the surface of today's selfie realities. At the end of the ad, the selfies are then hung in a makeshift art gallery, not on Instagram where they'd likely be found, or just left on the girls' phones. This bizarrely idealistic rendering of the selfie as a space for love, compassion, and intergenerational dialogue couldn't be further from the reality. But then again, at the end of the day this is an advertisement for DOVE, attempting to position it as some sort of benign company that supports women. (#corporatephilanthropy)

The selfie began shifting in 2015, becoming briefer and more hashtaggable. Macy's created a competition for a 2015 campaign, asking consumers to photograph "what America means to them" and then hashtagging that image with #AmericanSelfie. A United Airlines campaign from 2016 used Olympic athletes taking selfies at the airport with airline employees, ultimately just using the celebrity endorsement of a company or brand. A 2016 very tween Chick-fil-A advertisement that points to the fun of "youthful" selfie behavior and employs selfie-ing as an activity that teenage girls do together, as it's more popularly known. The Chick-fil-A One mobile app advertisement uses Internet-inspired slang like "idk" and "totes."[9] But a group selfie is really the catalyst for the action that takes place in this advertisement.

In the sixteen-second ad, two young girls are hanging out in a park—one is getting ready to order from the Chick-fil-A mobile app, and the other is just sitting there selfie-ing—when a Chick-fil-A employee runs up, confirms the order, takes a selfie with both of them using her phone, and then scampers off. The advertisement is so over-the-top in its enthusiastic dialogue and delight of selfie-ing that it actually comes across as a parody or just a camp version of taking a selfie. The selfie in this advertisement is used to attract a younger consumer, and potentially a more hip one, who is cool with the selfie and uses it as part of socializing through apps, as teenagers do.

In January 2017, comedian Josh Gondelman made fun of a Heinz selfie campaign. He tweeted a picture of a Heinz bottle that actually had the text "Selfie For Good: Take a Selfie & Heinz Donates."[10] What was going on in this campaign? Heinz had placed these bottles at participating restaurants. For every selfie that someone took with that Heinz bottle and then texted to the number on the bottle, Heinz would donate $1 to Stop Hunger Now.[11] For an additional share using the link in the text reply message, Heinz would donate another $0.57. In using this selfie, Heinz takes advantage of peoples' desire to selfie and also to be judged as "good" rather than narcissistic for participating in selfie-ing. That is, since the corporate entity of Heinz decided selfies could be used for good.

Josh Gondelman ✔
@joshgondelman

Thank goodness. Too many people have
gone ketchupless for too long.

4:30 PM - 30 Jan 2017

6 Retweets 85 Likes

Selfie-worthy street art is self-advertising

SOCIAL MEDIA IS SELLING YOUR SHIT. I see this spray-painted
onto the pavement at a heavily trafficked corner in the heart of
LA's Highland Park neighborhood. People step on and around it,
and sometimes pause to look at the graffiti. This marking bothers
me because, like most sidewalk graffiti, its message is clear and
inflammatory but offers no solutions. It's just a statement, and it's
something that we all already know.

This stencil was probably laid down onto the ground late
at night. I can picture the undercover graffiti artist wearing
a black hoodie, crouched over their stencil with this design
of a goblin/ghostlike character, pressing the nozzle down,

and releasing the paint onto the sidewalk. Inside this float-y character, passersby will also notice logos of Facebook and Snapchat.

Sarah T. Roberts
@ubiquity75

⊕ Follow   ⌄

"Social media is selling your shit." Echo Park, Los Angeles.

6:52 PM - 20 Sep 2016

#socialmediaissellingyourshit
Project by Blak Hat (@theblakhat)
Photo Credit: Sarah T. Roberts (@ubiquity75)
Location: Echo Park near Mohawk Bend,
a restaurant on Sunset Blvd

Through some Twitter sleuthing, I discovered that the artist who made it goes by the moniker Blak Hat (@theblakhat). Their mission is "deprogramming the collective mind." I've seen Blak Hat's graffiti all over Los Angeles, from Highland Park to Echo Park, further west to Mid-City, and way up in the Valley.[12] It's also gotten 'grammed and hashtagged with #socialmediaissellingyourshit.[13] Clearly, that's what the artist intended—and the message has come across loud and clear. And yes, social media *is* selling your shit, but that's only because *you* are using social media and it is a free service. Blak Hat's graffiti is perfect for Instagram and social media.

What a great anti-social media social media branding strategy. People passing it consider posting it to social media, offering up both free advertising to the artist and post, ironically muting his message altogether by sharing it to social media. The social media loop is self-perpetuating even if its message is anti-social media.

Street art like this reminds me of the ways that even public awareness-raising messages double as an artist's branding. In New York, a street artist who goes by the name of Hanksy[14]—another obvious play on the well-known artist Banksy—admitted in an interview with Utmost.us that good street art is also contingent on fast digestibility from quickly moving passersby. Said Hanksy in the story "Hanksy: The Next Viral Street Art Sensation" by Brian Redondo: "It's pop culture, the shareability of an image, the fact that it's out on the street. So not only are you touching art lovers or street art fans, you're also touching people that like stupid Internet jokes. People are gonna see this, take a picture of it, and they're going to share it with their friends."

A similar sensibility occurs in Los Angeles, where quite a few instances of street art seem like they were created only for selfie-ing. One such artwork is Dangerbird Records at the Silverlake Junction in Silverlake, where a wall-size yellow mural with zig-zaggy blue and purple shapes has been painted. Up top, the words "Stand Here and Think About Someone You Love" are painted over the colorful background, and two black outlines of arms with hands reaching up jut from the ground. Passersby can easily stand in between the hands and pose for a selfie or ask someone else to take a picture of them.[15]

Another super selfie-able image is the angel wings painted on a wall outside of St. Regis Wine & Liquor in Beverly Grove. How impossibly tempting is it to just stand there in the middle of them and selfie? (#howangelic) As *Thrillist* reports, they are part of Colette Miller's Global Angel Wings Project, which has been ongoing since 2012.[16] The artist paints these wings on walls as street art, which she says are there to "remind humanity, we can be the Angels of this Earth."[17] They are also a symbol of peace, as she describes it. The project began in the streets of downtown Los Angeles, the City of Angels, and has since been installed in cities around the world. In giving people an opportunity to selfie with her angel wings, Miller offers them a chance to step outside of their day. She is also promoting her work through other peoples' endorsements of it. So, whether the artist is trying to spread a message about social media using your data, or raise awareness through more of a do-gooder-type message, anyone who selfies with or just posts images of these is inadvertently marketing for the artist. In this way, artists are using the same techniques as corporations to spread the word about their art practice.

Comedians' jokes and the verbal selfie: Branding through tweets

I love comedian Kate Berlant's tweets. They are usually a phrase or a sentence, and they always have an assertive, yet very nonchalant tone. There's a swift delivery, as in her jokes. Each one reinforces her style of comedy and, ultimately, herself as a radical brand, espousing mostly progressive or Leftist politics. Though I've met Kate in person and seen her perform, and also interviewed her for several articles, I've also come to have an image of her in my mind based solely on her social media presence. Her tweets are so even-keeled and poignant in their messaging that it makes me feel like, perhaps, social media was made for Kate Berlant and comedians like her to present one-liner jokes. These are verbal selfies.

In an interview with Berlant that I did for *CRAVE Magazine*,[18] we candidly discussed her love of tweets: "Whereas Facebook feels like an utter trash can, Twitter feels like it has the means, a sense of productivity and actual communication and urgency, and obviously now more than ever Twitter is used as a survival mechanism, a way of truly mobilizing ideas and community," said Berlant. "And it can be fun. For comedy, there's an immediacy to it that's obviously very fun."

Here are a few of my favorite Kate Berlant tweets:

Contempt-orary art (June 21, 2017)[19]

Just bombed so hard I tried to recover by reciting a tweet (August 6, 2016)[20]

Actually I'M Terry Gross and THIS is Fresh Air (April 28, 2016)[21]

I wonder how many whites are meditating in their Sundance hotel rooms right now (Jan 22, 2016)[22]

Each time we hit "publish" on a social platform, we proclaim our thoughts, ideas, and feelings as part of our personal brand, whether or not that's what we intend to—it is a statement and a publication. It's not uncommon for a friend to talk about something they've posted or, even something they do IRL as very "on-brand" for them. If it's "off-brand," that's another way of saying "out of character." Except now it's not about referring to oneself as a character, it's about referring to oneself *as a brand*.

Selfie advertising in the supposedly selfiest country, the Philippines

Before companies started getting "woke" to the selfie fixation among Americans, and before Jeopardy killed the word "woke," advertisements coming out of Southeast Asia were already riding the selfie wave.[23] This makes perfect sense considering that a March 2014 article in *TIME Magazine* ranked Makati City and Pasig, Philippines, as two of the Selfie Capitals of the World.[24] Four of the top ten most selfie-ing cities were in Asia, in fact, with Petaling Jaya, Malaysia at number five; Cebu City, Phillipines at number nine; and George Town, Malaysia clocking in tenth. Why is the Phillipines such a selfie-centric country?

Dorothy R. Santos, a Bay Area-based Filipina-American writer, editor, curator, and educator whose research interests include new media, digital art, activism, artificial intelligence, and biotechnology, had a lot to say about the large number of selfies coming out of the Philippines. San Francisco-based Santos offered her queer Filipina-American approach to the ad.

"Selfies are pretty intergenerational in the Philippines," said Santos.[25] "In my family, my uncles and aunts take way more selfies than I do and I think it's because they want to acknowledge their existence and show their social networks their surroundings. I also think that the Filipino diaspora has a lot to do with why people share pictures and selfies constantly. It's a way of showing where you are and your positionality."

A 2014 McDonald's ad from the Philippines reflects these values of wanting to constantly be seen within social circles through

the use of selfie-ing. The ad played on the socialness of the selfie, suggesting that the selfie is not only fun and social, but that
stealth selfie-ing could even land you a cute date.[26] Even if you, as
a viewer, don't understand a word of Tagalog, it's obvious from
the advertisement that the selfie is portrayed as really cool.

In this ad, an older gentleman strolls into a McDonald's with
what appears to be a walking stick. His two friends, who just came
from the gym, notice it and mock him. But they're in for a serious
surprise. The older gentleman, who is wearing an old-fashioned
flat cap, suddenly whips his supposed "cane" into the air, slides
a smartphone onto it — surprise, it's a selfie stick! — and snaps a
selfie with his now-befuddled friends capturing all of their surprised looks. A woman at a nearby table notices his stealth move
and starts giggling. Soon he joins her and, together, they take flirty
selfies galore! The ad suggests that you should not judge a book
by its cover, and that selfies are social and hip for any generation.

The most unusual thing about this ad, however, is that it's
not targeting a millennial audience at all. Instead, it's about older
people who are portrayed as "young at heart," capturing a type
of youthfulness through the playful, front-facing lens coupled
with a spontaneity that's usually viewed as adolescent. So why
does this advertisement land with Filipino audiences?

Dr. Christian George C. Francisco, dean of the College of Liberal Arts and Communication at De La Salle University-Dasma-
rinas, Philippines, whose research focuses on popular language,
had some ideas about this advertisement.[27] He explained his
thoughts to me in a list:

1. Filipinos take selfie photos to showcase the current development about themselves.
2. Since selfie-ing has become a fad, some people do it for no
   reason at all. These are free riders of the popular culture.

3. Generally, Filipinos are one of the happiest people, as evidently seen on global surveys. They would like their friends, relatives, acquaintances, etc. to see them in their current situation/status.

4. Filipinos are generally relational. Culturally speaking, we would always like our relatives abroad to be informed of what's going on with us.

5. Selfie-ing is a reflection of the Filipino culture where most of the photos are seen as happy or with happy faces.

Based on these ideas, we can see why the Philippines McDonald's ad was so upbeat and social, focusing on a sharable, happy, social experience. This is ironic, given that the Philippines' brutal President Rodrigo Duterte, known as the "death squad" mayor, regularly endorses the killings of criminals and journalists, including mass executions.[28]

Unlike the American selfie advertisements, which focus more on self-imaging and how one appears to themselves and their friends, creating oneself as a brand, or often delusionally thinking about oneself as a social media celebrity, the Filipino ad focuses purely on the use of the selfie within a social context. This echoes prevailing cultural beliefs about the selfie as social. But if the selfie is decidedly a youth culture/ millennial phenomena, why would this ad feature an older Filipino man selfie-ing?

"Generally, the way selfie-ing was presented in the ad, we could say that technology works beyond boundaries of generation," said Dr. Francisco. "As evidently seen in the video, even if they are already old, with a hearing disability, they get to catch up with what the present time is giving them."

The gender dynamics in this advertisement, however, seemed odd. Did the older gentleman's selfie-ing win over the woman, or were the two of them already together? Did his selfie techniques suggest that he was "hip" and "with it," and ultimately had a youthful vibe that she found attractive?

"[The ad] has also shown adaptability, especially when the old man showcased his know-how to do selfie-ing," says Dr. Francisco. "Power and machismo images have been presented as well. This is when the old man boasted, through his actions, that he is more up-to-date than the other two. Machismo is when he sat down with an old lady, presumed to be his wife. In sum, power play may also be seen in a manner that he is more up-to-date and at the same time, he has a girl to date."

Certainly, this ad could also be a parody of the selfie since "many from the older generation would still abhor engaging with technology," as Dr. Francisco said. That's one approach to analyzing the ad. Santos read the selfie more as a way to be seen rather than as part of machismo or power dynamics.

"The McDonald's commercial is a fascinating take on the phenomenon of the selfie stick and the *lola* (grandmother) who ends up liking the older gentleman as opposed to the two older men who just finished working out," said Santos. "My gut reaction to the commercial was that it went back to the roots of making your presence known. I think the juxtaposition of selfie sticks and biometrics tech—the older guys' heart monitor watch or FitBit—within an establishment also brings to mind the disparity of classes, perhaps."

The Filipino McDonald's selfie ad offers some insight into how consumers view themselves and others within that specific market economy. Then again, the Philippines is also home to the only "selfie art" museum. That's right: Rather than go to an art museum and get yelled at for taking selfies with art, the exhibitions at the museum Art in Island[29] were created specifically so that people could take selfies *with* them. Indeed, the work of art isn't complete until *you*, the viewer, become a part of it—an actual participant. Taking a selfie with the artwork is optional, but it is arguably more fun than just getting someone to photograph you completing the scene. This creates an advertisement both of the cartoonish artwork, and the museum itself(ie).

For example, in Fragonard's painting *The Swing* (1767) at the Art in Island Museum, the viewer sees a white European woman wearing a pink dress on a swing. In midswing, she lets a male romantic interest see up her skirt while she simultaneously kicks off her shoe. This painting is recreated at the Art in Island Museum in Manila, and the viewer can actually pretend to catch her shoe rather than look at the scene from afar. If the viewer selfies while pretending to catch her shoe, they also become a part of the interaction rather than a passive viewer of it. This sort of whimsy would likely only be seen at a children's museum in the US, but in the Philippines it is culturally acceptable and fun for adults and kids alike.

"It doesn't surprise me that this type of venue was created and I think it goes back to wanting to be seen and heard, but in a playful and whimsical manner," said Santos. The art museum has a similar sensibility to the McDonald's advertisement: Both are about making selfie-ing into a fun and communal experience, rather than one that, as is seen in the prevailing American message about it, is about individual personal branding.

Beyond advertising: Chinese selfies / *zipai*

No cities in China made the *TIME* magazine selfie database, but that's because the research for that study was limited to Instagram, the image-only social network that Facebook purchased for $1 billion in April 2012.[30] As of the writing of this book, Facebook is still censored in China.[31] Weibo is the standard social media in China, often referred to as "China's Twitter." In China, the selfie has its own cultural implications, but unlike how it is seen in the US, the selfie, known as *zipai,* also functions within live streaming apps and as more than a brand; it is part of creating and living a virtual identity.

Meitu, a virtual anime identity app that launched in 2008, and others like Meiren Xiangji, provide functions that can enlarge eyes and whiten faces for the selfie, adhering to Chinese standards of beauty.[32] Fair skin is a standard, and women take photos to slim their faces as well, much like Kim K. Enlarged eyes signify a sense of youthful innocence, which is also admired. The actress Fan Bingbing is an ideal standard of beauty, considered *baifumei,* which means "pale, rich, and beautiful." White skin is also desirable; China has a huge whitening products industry. This is all embodied by Fan Bingbing: "The ultimate *baifumei* is actress Fan Bingbing, adored and emulated for her translucent white skin, large eyes and 'melon seed' (oval-shaped) face," writes Clare Kane in the article "What Selfies in America vs. China Can Tell Us About Beauty Standards" for *Mic.*[33] Furthermore, there is an emphasis on being cute over sexy.

"The functions on Photoshop-like apps lay users' beauty desires bare: The most popular Chinese beauty app, Meitu Xiuxiu, allows you to whiten your skin, slim your face and make your eyes impossibly huge," writes Kane.[34]

In an article for the *Washington Post* entitled "These viral selfie apps with 1 billion downloads are shaping China's start-up culture," Emily Rauhala brings up a few examples of the extremes on Meitu:

Zhu Tingting, a 24-year-old college senior from Nanjing, is among the fans who regularly attend Meitu events. She said, without irony, that Meitu changed her life. She spends about two hours a day taking selfies. 'Nowadays, when girls go out, it just means finding a place to take pictures and post them on social media,' she said. Wang Bei, a 33-year-old civil servant from Hebei province, said she appreciates the compliments she gets when she posts "beautified" selfies. "I wish I could live in the world of my Meitu phone forever."

Cameras, like Casio's *zipai shenqi*, which fans refer to as "godly tools for selfies," cost up to $1,000 USD and do the job of making peoples' faces more slender, whitening their skin, and enlarging their eyes much like the selfie apps do—except the camera offers a built-in solution.[35] In China, there is less of an emphasis on makeup because of the ability to digitally alter selfies.

"Selfie (*zipai*) is a necessary facade and first step to get their virtual identity further," said Tiffany Sum, an artist/screenwriter, who works with Ogilvy Hong Kong and splits her time between China and Los Angeles. "Whether to ultimately sell things or become a professional livestreamer on an app called Yinke, it is a very serious everyday activity."

There are more than two hundred live-streaming platforms in China. People who opt to become professional livestreamers can also earn a significant income, all from the comfort of their own homes. The industry in China differs from the US's Facebook Live or Periscope. As the *LA Times*' Yingzhi Yang reports in the story "In China, live-streaming apps soothe lonely souls and create fortunes":

Whereas Americans tend to use live-streaming platforms such as Facebook Live and Periscope to broadcast and watch events, similar platforms in China have emerged as a social-networking tool for millions of lonely hearts who are eager to seek comfort and digital companionship. Live streamers answer questions, offer advice, sing, dance, even eat their meals for all to watch.[36]

Selfie (*zipai*) is the integral element of Chinese digital culture. Dr. Gabriele de Seta, who holds a PhD in sociology from the Hong Kong Polytechnic University and is currently a postdoctoral fellow at the Institute of Ethnology, Academia Sinica, takes an anthropological approach to studying it.[37] Independent curator, researcher, and artist Michelle Proksell, who travels back and forth between China and Europe, working in both places, has also researched and written about the selfie in China.[38]

"Chinese people have experienced a very fast development of Internet infrastructure in the last ten years, and smartphones have been the most visible and evident part of this," de Seta told me when we corresponded via email.[39]

Most people in China today go online through mobile devices, and these devices have high-quality front-facing cameras. In that way, much like on the early social networking sites MySpace and Friendster, the selfie started out in China as merely utilitarian, something that people put there because they needed a profile pic. In China today, however, as Proksell explained in his interview "Decoding Culture on the Chinternet" in *Casimir* magazine, mobile technology is less "separate" from the "real world" in the way it's generally spoken of in American digital culture.[40]

"Online life here [in China] is not separate from 'real life,' it is merely an extension of every person who has a mobile device," she explained. "The physical and emotional relationships that people have to the Internet and mobile technology here only show me how much closer we are to socially accepting the Internet eventually being implanted inside of our bodies someday in our lifetime."

Proksell also notes how much faster things move both on and offline in China, which differs from slower-moving memes and Internet life in America. "The lifespan of online content here is much shorter than we see in the West," she said. "Memes come and go as fast as the sun sets sometimes." With that difference in mind, it could be easy for the American reader to consider Chinese Internet culture to be vastly different, but as de Seta writes in his essay "Selfies | 自拍," they are actually running parallel.[41]

"Just as Instagram and Snapchat support the whirling dissemination of millions of selfies in Euro-American networks, apps like WeChat, Meitu Xiuxiu, Weipai, Faceu, and a slew of other social contact platforms and image editing software provide the channels, the formats, and the filters shaping the circulation of *zipai* across Chinese media ecologies."

In the 2014 article "Is Asia Setting the Trends on Selfies?" by Angela Donald for *Ad Age,* she discusses some popular advertising campaigns in China and interviewed Carter Chow, managing director of McCann Shanghai, about why the *zipai* may be so popular in China.[42] Chow told *Ad Age* that the selfie's popularity had to do with "wanting everybody to see who you are in this society where you risk being lost among so many people, and where it's such a fast-moving environment." This echoes what de Seta and Proksell discovered in some of their research about the rapid pace of Chinese digital culture. Some of the apps that are used to personalize selfies could be "an extension of that self-expression," writes Donald.

One tongue-in-cheek selfie campaign in Chinese social media brought together fashion and the current environmental circumstances. In the Max Factor selfie makeup ad campaign "Smog, give me back my beautiful face!" which was launched on Weibo, the brand encouraged people to apply Max Factor eye makeup while wearing antipollution masks, and then post selfies. "The idea for the campaign came after the brand noticed a correlation between pollution levels and sales of eye makeup," writes LabBrand.com.[43] "Indeed when half your face is covered by an antipollution mask, your eyes are all that remain for you to make an impression."

The campaign was launched as a contest on Weibo, with the intention of showing your "most creative or most beautiful 'face mask makeup' looks," as reported by *Jing Daily*, a publication that focuses on luxury consumer trends in China.[44] The contest winner would be rewarded with eye makeup products, and a chance to be featured in *Marie Claire China*. The brand's Weibo account also showed a video with a famous eye-makeup expert offering practical advice for "smog weather beauty." In this campaign, not only does the participant post selfies to their Weibo account, but they also provide free advertising for the brand through hashtags and participation in the contest.

A selfie posted to Weibo by the highly influential celebrity Fan Bingbing operated on multiple levels: it was both a wedding engagement announcement and advertisement for a few of the brands that endorse her. There is huge power in this sort of planned selfie from this type of celebrity. An actress and TV producer who has been leading the Forbes China Celebrity List for three years, Bingbing has more than thirty-three million followers on Weibo. So in June 2015, when she announced her engagement to *The Empress of China* costar Li Chen through a single Weibo selfie with the caption "us," she made sure to also engage the clothing brands in that image.

Fan Bingbing is also notoriously secret about her love life, so this Weibo post made her announcement even more viral-worthy, capitalizing on her personal life. Fan Bingbing's influence is strong within *zipai* culture and live-streaming apps; she sets the standard of beauty in China.

"Girls and some guys, mostly wanna look like Fan Bingbing, those big doll watery eyes and sharp triangle face with pointy chin," said Sum. "They do heavy makeup to further that look. I have seen not once but multiple times that girls have apparent (poor and unnatural) plastic surgeries done to their faces. They always scared me on the bright and crowded streets of Beijing. They really look like corpses. Like corpse makeup that is very thick and laminates any facial expressions or movements."

As *Ad Age* reported in the story "Chinese Social Media Marketing Explained, Through One Super-Viral Selfie," there were three other brand nods in this single powerful selfie, which got shared 1.6 million times and received 6.6 million likes.[45] *Ad Age*'s Angela Donald breaks down the process of the ultra-endorsement through Fan Bingbing's selfie:

> Mr. Li posted the selfie first; to retweet it, Ms. Fan used Lenovo's Moto X phone. Lenovo had announced her endorsement deal just a day earlier. (The photo itself, unfortunately for Lenovo, was apparently shot with Mr. Li's iPhone 6.) Ms. Fan also wore a $530 Cleopatra-style wig from a local brand she endorses named Rebecca, which reposted the selfie and added a link to buy the hairpiece online. As for L'Oreal, which Ms. Fan also touts, it asked followers to guess which of two L'Oreal lipstick shades she used.

In addition to this selfie with four branded moments—Apple, Lenovo, Rebecca, and L'Oreal—Ms. Fan has many other endorsements. More than fifty, to be exact, from Louis Vuitton to Ganji. com, an online classified ads site. The unfolding of her engagement was another arm of an ad campaign for Ms. Fan. This selfie advertisement as both announcement and brand engagement solidified the marriage of selfie and advertisement. In other words, real-time campaigns like this are an advertiser's selfie dream come true. The ad campaign that merely uses the selfie in it is no match for real-time viral social media examples like Fan Bingbing's, which create more than just a brand—celebrities like Fan Bingbing set the precedent for *zipai* and youth who become professional livestreamers or are always using the Meitu app. She also becomes a standard of beauty in and of herself, and others imitate her.

But ultimately it is not about creating a brand—it is about being seen as beautiful. "I think instead of 'branding' themselves for the Chinese netizens, they are putting themselves into one big category of 'beauty,'" said Sum. "Branding somewhat implies standing out. These girls/boys are not doing that but exact opposite in a lot of ways. Yet, they can't really tell the difference."

Stumbling into someone else's selfie branding experience in LA

So what do selfie advertisements from other parts of the world have to teach Americans about the selfie? The selfie as used in advertising reflects back certain cultural, social, and consumerist values. It answers some questions, such as: How do people gain and claim social capital? When do people like to take a photo together? Why do people selfie? What would make people selfie more? What makes someone buy a product, and then choose to endorse it by taking a selfie with it?

As we know from individualistic approaches to social media at large, there is no one right way to selfie. The selfie is both permanent as data on the Internet yet ephemeral in nature—something shared in a moment, no matter how long it took to prepare for posting, whether that be a few seconds, minutes, or even hours. The selfie can be used as a vehicle for endorsing a product, promoting oneself, and advertising to a social network.

This reminds me of an experience I had not long ago, while leaving an event at the Hammer Museum in Los Angeles. I'd gone to see a performance series called *In Real Life* (IRL), curated by Gina Young and featuring a variety of talented artists who live and work in LA. The sketches, performance art, poetry, and monologues performed all had to do with the fluid lives we lead on and offline. Many of the performances dealt with the struggle of getting stuck online or in apps, of a distrust or fear of the Internet, social media, and apps, while others just integrated online actions like swiping on Tinder or selfie-ing into a scene. It reminded me that people are constantly negotiating what they post online and how they are seen in that space, figuring it out as they go.

As I was leaving and contemplating these questions, I ran into someone I met at the performance. She was trying to take a good selfie before getting into her car, selfie-ing in front of giant letters that said HAMMER. But she was obviously struggling with her angles and her look. Should she look cool and confident or weird and goofy? Maybe sexy? Happy? She didn't know. And she also couldn't pick a background. I suggested she just stand before the first two letters so that the image would be her face and the word "HA." How funny in a meta-selfie way, I thought to myself! I laughed out loud about this joke I'd written in my head. And I figured others had done such a thing before — it's a selfie photo op waiting to happen, after all! I encouraged her to do it.

She asked me if I wanted to join her in the selfie, and I said no. I didn't know her. She wasn't someone famous to be seen with, nor was I trying to flirt. Maybe she was just being friendly, but I didn't feel like being in the selfie. When I asked her why she was taking the selfie, she told me that it was for branding purposes, that she was trying to get better at Instagram. I nodded. What was her brand or message, anyway? She wasn't sure. It was unclear — vague, even. I watched as she self-consciously selfie-d several times in front of "HA" before settling on one of the images. A happy smile. Classic! She'd successfully captured herself, and that selfie would become both an advertisement of her brand at that moment, and also free advertising for the Hammer Museum. I nodded and gave her a thumbs-up, as if I were liking that very selfie on Facebook, rewarding her for taking the picture. Then she invited me to another party that was happening in West Hollywood. I said sure, I'll come by—maybe, we'll even talk IRL.

Chapter 6

Video Killed the Radio Star, Selfie Killed TV

STREAMING TELEVISION SHOWS ARE KEEN on reflecting back the ways that social media and technology have changed peoples' social interactions. There are two key ways that showrunners approach social media and technology. The "exterior approach" explores broader concepts of "technology," seeing it as separate from the individual, and as a vehicle for creating either an alter-ego or a new sense of "self" online. In the "interior approach," technology is not separate but integrated into everyday life. It becomes reflective of a character, a way to *express* oneself, and an opportunity to explore technology-related issues.

In this chapter I'll look at some commonalities and through-lines of the shows It's *Always Sunny in Philadelphia*, *Chasing Cameron*, *Community*, *Black Mirror*, *Lady Dynamite*, *Modern*

Family, *Master of None*, and *Broad City*. This is a book about selfies, so naturally we'll start with the ABC TV show *Selfie*. It premiered in 2014 and was canceled after one season.

"Good selfie/bad selfie" in the short-lived TV show *Selfie*

Selfie presents social media as a dumb, vapid place where sad girls go for validation. In keeping with the show's obvious title, *Selfie* takes the selfie cultural phenomena as the central focus of this television show, following the life of sad white girl Eliza Dooley (Karen Gillan), who embodies the exterior approach to technology, which considers social media/selfie culture online as a separate space where people who suck at life in the "real world" can create alter-egos and new selves online.

The exterior model in *Selfie* presents a moralistic duality: The real world is "good" and existing there is normal; the Internet is a "bad" place where people go to be dishonest and seek validation that they are unable to feel or achieve in the physical world. Setting up this dualistic world—rather than seeing technology and social media as part of a fluid IRL-URL space—makes character development easy and predictable. That is, Eliza is a lonely, pretty girl online with zero social skills in person.[1] But as she is drowning in the sadness of her Internet life, she also starts getting close to her work friend/romantic interest Henry Higgs (John Cho), who made television history as the first-ever Asian romantic lead.[2] As her interest in Henry grows, her desire for time spent on social media lessens drastically. Suddenly her huge following on Instagram is no longer important at all! She begins abandoning her Internet life for IRL, and as she does things just keep on getting better. Eliza's character development on *Selfie* is tied directly to her path of detaching from social media altogether. Only then, the show explains, does she experience "real life."

How does *Selfie* exemplify the "exterior" approach? In many ways! The show portrays social media as a space where Eliza constantly goes for validation, so much that she is socially inept in the real world and around people. Her suffering offline is pretty extreme, but it's made not-believable by the fact that she has a job as a sales rep for a big pharma company, which means her job is contingent on building strong relationships with clients. But we rarely see her doing anything at work other than flirting with men.

The show also makes many assumptions about women like Eliza who are very good at social media. Eliza takes a lot of selfies, obviously, so she knows her angles and how to hashtag pics in order to get them seen. Why wasn't her company capitalizing on this skill of hers, given how many social media influencers exist today?! They could have given her a job doing social media marketing for big pharma—at least, that's one way she could've capitalized on her social media skills rather than be an ambiguous sales rep. We also don't see her closing any deals at her job. We just see her fumbling around and being ditzy.

Instead of creating her as a social media marketing maven, Eliza's social media is portrayed negatively, as a place where she goes to experience validation through a type of separate Internet life. She posts cute selfies that get her plenty of hearts. In person, though, she is socially inept. She only knows how to self-objectify. This leads one to wonder how she got such an important sales rep job if she had no social skills. This is never explained.

Selfie could've been a show about an awkward girl who learned to navigate her life on and offline, and reflect on why she was so into social media and what it did for her. But instead, it sets up the simplistic model of "the real world is good, and the

Internet world is bad." And the only way to find life offline is, apparently, to find a romantic interest who can help her learn to socialize and be "normal" in the real world.

I think what this show really misses is the fact that most young women in America have a social media presence, selfie-ing is part of this, and it's all real life. "The normalization of the selfie, with its fake and real candor — is a real gain in the war of individuals against a future where everyone is a celebrity and kind of sucks at it," writes Zak Smith for *Artillery* magazine.[3] As a character, Eliza achieved that social media fame, one that is desired today. She was actually just embodying everything that Kim Kardashian and teen social media culture have led us to. The future is already here, and for many people this existence necessitates living life in both physical and virtual spaces. The trick is finding the balance between the two.

Reconciling technological assumptions in *Lady Dynamite* and *Modern Family*

Lady Dynamite and *Modern Family* each offer an episode in which a character's relationship to technology is what we might call "complicated." In *Lady Dynamite*, a show based on the mental breakdown of real-life comedian Maria Bamford, her character experiences some text confusion with a love interest.[4] In *Modern Family*, mother Claire (Julie Bowen) goes on a wild goose chase trying to locate her daughter Haley's (Sarah Hyland) whereabouts using "clues" left by Haley's social media presence. Both of these episodes exemplify somewhere in between exterior and interior models of characters' relationships to technology, suggesting the murkiness of the characters' actual realities.

In *Lady Dynamite*, texting is initially explored in an exterior way, but as a miscommunication deepens we see that the ways people respond via text are reflective of their character, and used as a mode of self-expression. In season 1, episode 9, "No Friend Left Behind," Maria is hanging out at Café de Leche with her friends Dagmar and Larissa. Maria goes to the bathroom and leaves her phone on the table. Larissa grabs it and sends a message with the text "How ya doin'?" to a random person in Maria's phone; in the world of the show, this type of prank has been popularized by *Anderson Cooper 360*. Unfortunately, the text was sent to Jill Kwatney-Adelman (Annie Mumolo), a friend who Maria had a falling out with years ago. When Maria returns from the bathroom and finds out who Larissa texted, she is mortified.

We get the backstory about how this friendship fell apart: Jill went to visit Maria in Duluth when she was in the mental hospital, and Maria made a remark about how she wanted to die. Jill encouraged her to end her life, and also left her with some mysterious pills and her dog, Rusty, who was supposed to help Maria with her suicide. Writes Julie Kliegman for *New York Magazine*: "This scene, designed to roast misguided right-to-die narratives that promote the offensive notion that sick people are better off dying, lands particularly well in light of disability advocates speaking out against the film *Me Before You*."

Jill leaves and Maria obviously lives; then cut to two months later, when Jill is taking credit for saving Maria from herself. That same night, more drama goes down when Jill brags about her nine-year marriage but also is affectionate toward her husband's friend, Todd (Peter Christian Hansen). Not long after that, Maria agrees to go out with Todd. Jill freaks out over that, along with the fact that Maria never got her a wedding present.

There is more to this drama in the present, when Maria meets up with Jill after Jill takes that text at face value. Maria orders pretzel bread, and Jill gets upset because she doesn't want to be around carbs because she has celiac disease. Rather than tell Jill she is being ridiculous, Maria sticks to the "no friend left behind" resolution, in which Maria does whatever she can to maintain a friendship—even if it is a toxic one.

All the while, she has neglected contacting Scott (Ólafur Darri Ólafsson), the guy she slept with not long ago. When he writes her a text that says "How ya doin'?" Maria thinks it's the same *Anderson Cooper 360* prank reference. Instead of writing back something normal, she texts him: "LOL Ha ha!!!!! Anderson Cooper 360!!!!!!" He has no idea what she's talking about so just writes back "Ok!" She doesn't get that he isn't in on the joke, and so then she responds with lots of JKs, more LOLs, a pug emoji, and a shruggy emoji. Scott sits and reads these texts, smiling to himself while he continues painting. He likes Maria, and this abundance of texts seem humorous to him. Though that text message was strange, nothing really came of it—in this show, the majority of the action takes place in person. Or, if it happens on the phone, it will eventually move offline, as in the case of other episodes that feature Maria's online dating life prior to meeting Scott.

The TV show *Modern Family* is a mockumentary sitcom that follows the lives of suburban, LA-based Jay Pritchett and his family, made up of Jay's second wife, her son, and two adult children and their families. Rather than straight sitcom, the mockumentary aspect of this means characters are speaking directly to the camera, merging documentary with sitcom. The show premiered in September 2009, and continues on through ten seasons.

The particular episode of *Modern Family* "Lost Connection" (season 6, episode 16), takes place entirely on Skype and Face-Time. It sounded so meta, that even I, queen of meta things, initially avoided checking it out. Also, how could an episode take place entirely through virtual communications, and if TV is a break from my freakin' computer, which I am on all day, why would I want to watch people interacting on their computers? Plus, how would that even work, I wondered, since the experience of switching between screens is in and of itself a dizzying, matrixlike one?

The technological conflict and resolve in this episode is much like what is seen in *Lady Dynamite*. Initially, technology is a distraction and something that seems "not real," but by the end of the episode it becomes a reflection of familial relationships. Here's the gist of the use of technology in the episode; technology guides viewers through the episode, since it takes place in real-time and through screens. Claire (Julie Bowen) is stuck at Chicago's O'Hare Airport and at the same time freaking out about an unresolved argument she had with her daughter Haley before Claire left town. When Haley doesn't return a few of Claire's panicked texts, Claire takes a turn down a techno-anxiety black hole, moving from obsessively checking her Facebook, to Face-Timing with her family members, and then searching the family's iCloud account for evidence of what her daughter is up to or what she's sending to the cloud. Claire discovers through the iCloud Find My Phone account that Haley is in Vegas, and when she notices that Haley has ordered a book about pregnancy, Claire assumes the worst: That Haley has fled to Vegas to marry some guy because she got knocked up. She assumes that all of this is also true because Haley hasn't responded to her texts.

But it turns out that none of Claire's techno-sleuthing proved to be anything more than paranoia. SPOILER ALERT: In short, Haley left her phone in someone's car and that person drove to Vegas for a trip—a quick and easy drive from Los Angeles. And the pregnancy book isn't for Haley. In fact, she was in her room sleeping the whole time. And when she emerges at the end of the episode, after her mom has gone through a total techno-spiral, she wonders why everyone seems so on edge. After all, social media and technology aren't always true reflections of somebody's whereabouts and interests. What Claire assumed about her daughter based on her social media shows that she read Haley's online presence as a literal reflection of what her daughter was up to, rather than considering that perhaps it is exterior, or separate from her daughter's actual life. Social media profiles here are misunderstood as a literal reflection of interior, interpersonal relationships. This sort of thing can easily happen on social media, where tone and the whole picture aren't usually visible. It's easy to take a modicum of information and blow it out of proportion based on one's own sensitivities at the moment.

The internal becomes external:
Community and *Black Mirror* set the dystopic tone

The shows *Community* and *Black Mirror* each took one episode to relate basically the same idea: humans all are evaluating each others' every move using Uber/Lyft-style rating systems. In that way, life is not about living, but about existing to receive validation and get good ratings from peers, thus maintaining one's hierarchical place in the user-generated social order that is disguised as "democratic"—because supposedly everyone can vote!—but is actually very much about surveillance under a techno-authoritarian state. Accumulating "likes" and quick hit validation activates the rewards circuit in the brain, and that's what keeps us all coming back—something explored in both of these shows. The scientific studies behind this prove it.

"There have been reports showing that the ventral striatum, a brain structure involved in a putative reward circuit, is recruited when participants receive monetary rewards as well as social rewards (e.g., feedback from another person such as a "you are nice"; Izuma et al., 2008)," writes Mauricio Delgado, associate professor in the Department of Psychology at Rutgers University.[5] "Extrapolating it to social media, a recent study has observed that teenagers activate similar brain circuits when they receive 'likes' or social acceptance of their posts/photos or similar by peers (Sherman et al., 2016). It makes sense and is consistent with the literature that social approval/social interactions are perceived as rewards and give us pleasure and recruit the brain's reward circuitry."

The shows reflect extreme versions of rewards/validation. At times, it's so extreme as to come off like social commentary or parody. But for those invested in sci-fi/dystopian narratives, and who realize the ways that seeming "utopian" technologies regularly go awry, it reads as extremely realistic. With this in mind, it does come back to the human level. That is, validaton, which is something internal, becomes externalized. And then it must be used for social capital within the new confines of this techno-society.

The sitcom *Community* aired on NBC from 2009 to 2015, and followed an ensemble cast of characters at a community college in the fictional town of Greendale, Colorado. Showrunner Dan Harmon created it based on his experiences at a community college. In season 5, episode 8, "App Developments and Condiments," a cutesy-seeming ratings app called MeowMeowBeenz is piloted at the college. But what seems like a "fun" way to rate your fellow students actually delves into deeper questions about the use of technology for social validation, the biological rewards systems that social media likes/gamification take advantage of, and surveillance by both peers and larger corporate entities.

Tech nerds David (Steve Agee) and Bixel (Brian Posehn) from startup company jammyPOW come to South Greendale Community College to introduce the beta-version of their seemingly innocuous new app, MeowMeow Beenz. What seems democratic at first—rating social interactions with others on a 1–5 star-as-cat-face rating system— turns out to be a way to create flawed hierarchies and manipulative social dynamics. The interior desire for social validation becomes a guiding force for how people behave toward one another. And before long, it's up to Jeff (Joel McHale) and Britta (Gillian Jacobs) to bring order back to this horrifying dystopian version of Greendale that happened entirely because all of the characters got addicted to the app's focus on getting likes, which all goes back to how the brain reads those as rewards.

Similarly, in the British sci-fi TV show *Black Mirror*, which looks at the "unanticipated consequences of new technologies," as the *New York Times*' Jenna Wortham describes it, social media rewards rule characters' lives.[6] The episode "Nosedive" (season 3, episode 1), goes deep into that theme, creating a narrative in which social media platforms and validation become the only way to survive. Though creator Charlie Brooker intends this episode as "satire," it feels eerily close to reality. Augmented reality and a single social media platform that everyone uses lets people rate all of their online and in-person social interactions using that same five-star scale ratings system. People begin envying those with higher scores. Everyone is controlled by the validation of the apps and the competition that they inspire. Rewards are pleasure. But even this scenario comes with some challenges, and real-world parallels that already exist. Writes Tasha Robinson for the *Verge*:

> The barrier for entry in "Nosedive" is fairly high. Viewers have to accept that there's no competition for the social-media app that rules everyone's lives, and no way to rate businesses or other institutions. In the real world, people who have bad experiences with airlines or car-rental companies often go straight to Twitter

or Facebook with their complaints, and often rack up instant, insincere public apologies from online customer-service reps.

Furthermore, the episode suggests that the only way to truly succeed is to project an image of perfection—and we all know that this is but an illusion, something that requires a lot of effort, particularly if everyone is always watching. In this way, the version of life on the TV show also becomes a version of what we know as reality TV—everyone is constantly spying on each other, waiting for them to break (especially the producers, who use those moments as ways to spur conflict between characters). But whereas the characters on *Community* ultimately resolve and find a way out of the ratings-ruled world, in this episode of *Black Mirror* the social control factor blows up even bigger, making it impossible to escape. In this internal model, validation via technology is a way to express oneself, but because of the dystopian effect, it becomes a broader way to explore the possible effects of technology.

Navigating emotional relationships through technology: *Master of None* and *Broad City*

In the interior model, technology takes on the role of being part and parcel of navigating emotional relationships. Checking smartphones for texts first thing in the morning, browsing social media sites, getting a swipe right from someone on a dating app, checking email and texting all day, and using apps to navigate the world are accepted parts of everyday life. Such is #modern-life. These are scenes that you'd likely see in *Master of None* and *Broad City*. In both of these shows, technology reflects ways that characters navigate emotional relationships.

Comedian and actor Aziz Ansari's Netflix show *Master of None* captures the techno-anxiety of texting, social media, and dating paranoia of twenty- and thirtysomethings who live in urban environments—well, specifically New York City, an age and place where dating is a confusing yet self-exploratory process made even more intense by the seemingly endless options of dating apps and "instant" connection.

Master of None shows an intrinsic understanding of technology that perhaps can only be realized by millennials who use it the most. It does this by focusing on the people themselves and the feelings that come up through interactions with other people through technology. Rather than portraying technology as some sort of "other," or seeing the Internet as a space where people take on alter-egos or personas, these shows use technology as part of a way to navigate emotional relationships.

In *Master of None*, characters reveal a lot about their feelings toward someone else through texts. One such example occurs in season 1, episode 2, "The Parents." Dev (Aziz Ansari) complains to his friend Brian (Kelvin Yu) that he and his dad aren't close. He uses the curt, cold tone of his dad's texts as evidence. But when we finally meet Dev's dad, the fact of the matter is that he's the same on text as he is in person; he doesn't offer up more information or overshare about anything via text, or send passive aggressive texts and then act closed-off in person. His texting conveys his emotional state, and how he feels toward his son. When their relationship changes, so do their texts. After Dev and his father start getting closer at a family dinner, his father's text messages become warmer. Where there was once a cold directness, there's now a playfulness that suggests intimacy. For the purposes of millennialism, this shift is shown via text first, and then in person. The online relationship is just a mirror of the offline relationship, and their texting was just another indication of how they felt about one another.

Throughout the show, texting and social media also play a huge role in Dev's dating life, as seen in "The Hot Ticket" (episode 3). Ghosting comes up as an extension of someone who would be emotionally unavailable in person as well. Ghosting is when you completely vanish, and it's a sad contemporary thing to experience. But sometimes people miss texts, or they're just busy and not available for a conversation in that moment. Other times, connections drift off, only to return at a later date. In this episode, Dev makes a date with Alice (Nina Arianda), a hot bartender who agrees to go with him to a concert. The show emphasizes his techno-anxiety by showing the moments when it's seventy-two, forty-eight, and twenty-four hours until the concert, and she still hasn't texted to confirm whether or not she is coming. It seems like she is ghosting.

In a last-ditch effort to get more information about Alice, Dev stalks her Instagram. He still wants a date to the concert, however, so he copy-and-pastes a generic message to a bunch of women, asking if any of them are free for the concert. We learn about Nina through her texting behavior, which reflects where she's at emotionally. In that way, technology is a mirror of how she is offline.

Similar scenarios play out in season 2, particularly between love interest Francesca (Alessandra Mastronardi), an Italian woman who Dev met earlier in the season when he was in the small town of Modena, Italy, learning how to make pasta by day and hanging out with her and other friends by night. Francesca's grandmother owns the pasta shop. And while Francesca is engaged to Pino, her boyfriend of ten years, her heart is elsewhere.

SPOILER ALERT! Dev and Francesca stay in touch after Dev returns to New York. When she comes to New York for trips with Pino, things get more intense between Dev and Francesca. Much of their flirting happens in person, but other times it plays out through texts. In one episode, at her fiancé's birthday party, she flirts with Dev via text while Pino is sitting next to her, engaged in another conversation. Francesca sends Dev a kissy emoji, which Dev and his BFF Arnold (Eric Wareheim) thoroughly analyze. Throughout the show, Francesca is consistently flirty with Dev on text, often saying more than she does in person when they are together because she's still engaged to Pino and that would feel like actual emotional cheating. Francesca's texts to Dev reveal her feelings, mirroring the type of emotional relationship they're having in person throughout the second season.

The TV show *Broad City* also explores the depths of emotional relationships through technology. The show follows twentysomething best friends Abbi Abrams (Abbi Jacobson) and Ilana (Ilana Glazer) on their adventures together living in New York City. It's a show written by millennials who are not only commenting on the surveillance elements of social media and tech, but who also accept that it is very much a part of their world. One of the most rewarding aspects of this show is that Ilana and Abbi are always in it together. Unlike most girl bestie tropes, where one eventually betrays the other, Abbi and Ilana never abandon each other, turn on each other, or ditch each other for some guy (or woman—Ilana is portrayed as queer). Instead, they're two smart, independent (Jewish) ladies who stick together, kick ass, and take names. They are a wonderful portrayal of female friendship on TV—as loving, kind, and admirable, not to mention hilarious and sex positive rather than catty, competitive, and ultimately focused on seeking attention from men or getting into a relationship with a guy and ditching each other.

When Abbi and Ilana are at home, they always call each other using Skype. The first episode of the first season opens with Abbi and Ilana on a voyeuristic bestie Skype call that's initiated by Ilana, with Ilana explaining that the two of them are "gonna be the boss bitches that they are in their minds" when they hit a concert at Bowery Ballroom together that evening. After a few moments, Abbi notices that Ilana is bouncing a little bit because, as it turns out, she's actually sitting on top of Lincoln (Hannibal Buress), fucking him while talking with Ilana. Abbi feels uncomfortable and attempts to set a boundary, then they hang up—but it's not a catty fight, and it's certainly not something that won't be resolved. It was just kinda awkward. "That was hot, that was cool—that was like a threesome in some ways," Ilana says to Lincoln, who is mostly just trying to figure out if they're dating or just fucking, an ongoing theme in the show, where sex is also sport.

It's clear that Ilana enjoyed this situation, which doesn't feel as overshare-y as, say, an episode of *Girls*. Instead, it felt like she was trying to achieve a type of sexualized bestie intimacy with Abbi, but not by being directly sexual with her (that would make their friendship more complicated). Through Skype, she's able to playfully involve her BFF in her sexual relationship, which also makes sense because they talk a lot about sex throughout the show. Most likely, this sort of thing wouldn't have happened without their Skype calls. Could it have happened IRL, or did technology create the space for this type of thing to happen? By starting the show with a Skype call, we see the ways that Skype is a vehicle for showing how Abbi and Ilana's relationship incorporates technology. There is an additional closeness between these two that otherwise wouldn't exist without the distance that technology offers.

In "Stolen Phone," the sixth episode of season 1, Abbi and Ilana decide that the real way to find guys to date is just to go through their Facebook friends, asking out dudes from high school who they already know. Cruising on Facebook is fun, and you truly never know who you'll reconnect with on there! It seems like, at the end of the day social networks are not all that different on or offline—it's just the speed at which they're accessible online. But after some deep cruising, during which they get rejected by thirty-six guys and one lady, the two say fuck it and hit the bar to meet new people. At said bar, Ilana goes home with a hot bisexual dude and Abbi gets a guy's number but then loses her phone. The episode follows Abbi and Ilana on their adventure of following the phone, which they're tracking through the Find My Phone app. They end up in parts of New York they'd not normally go to, such as the tourist-and-commercial-trap that is Times Square, and the hoity-toity Upper East Side where they encounter funny rich people stereotypes (a weekend of horseback riding upstate, anyone?). Finding the phone leads them on more adventures together. Technology shapes their escapades.

The ways that technology shapes characters' emotional lives goes one step further in season 2, episode 6, "The Matrix." After a very intense tech binge session that involves an all-nighter with the Internet, Tinder, Grindr, Instagram, FaceTime, all social media, Abbi and Ilana wake up to a Skype call from each other while sitting on the couch together! They realize they've completely disassociated and checked out into "the matrix" for the entire night.[7] To remedy this, they voluntarily decide to ditch their phones—the modern-day equivalent of going "off the grid," and hit the park with their rollerblades.

While rollerblading, they come upon a group of gorgeous, beefy, shirtless guys playing soccer, as we do over the summer in New York. As per their characters, they're both interested in meeting the dudes. Abbi exclaims that she would've "Tindered the fuck out of them" if she had her phone; Ilana suggests they just holler at the guys that they *wanna fuck*. In this weirdly revolutionary episode, Abbi and Ilana totally disregard IRL social norms, acting as cruisy in person as they would if they were Tind-ing. When the soccer ball lands at their feet, Abbi attempts to kick it back but falls down and makes an ass of herself. It's way different trying to actually flirt without the frictionless feel of technology, phones, apps, and the social media/ Internet matrix. In this episode, Abbi and Ilana admit their reliance on technology. Taking a break from social media and the Internet is important. Their dialogue at the end of the episode sums it all up:

> *Abbi: My first impression is always better on Tinder. I suck without the Internet, dude. It's like, I'm too real for it.*
>
> *Ilana: Being off the matrix is gonna help us plug in more consciously. Like that day we went off of sugar! How much sweeter were sour straws after that? So much sweeter.*
>
> *Abbi: God, you're right. One day off the matrix is gonna make us so much stronger.*

The original catfish: *It's Always Sunny in Philadelphia* mirrors the same Internet problem of *Selfie*

The sitcom *It's Always Sunny in Philadelphia* is a black comedy that's been running strong since August 2005. Created by Rob McElhenney, it follows the lives of a group of self-involved friends that run an Irish bar, Paddy's Pub in South Philadelphia. The setting at a bar reminds of the long-running show *Cheers*, and the self-absorbed nature of the gang of friends is very reminiscent of *Seinfeld*. In season 7, episode 8 "The Anti-Social Network," the gang takes on questions about how to start using Facebook for the bar. What ensues is an episode suggestive of the exterior model through which technology is separate and used to create different versions of the self. In this setup, technology does not mirror human emotions—it creates another, entirely different world that must be realized and understood as very separate from the in-person world.

The plotline suggests that characters are dismissive of Facebook because it's so "new" and "confusing." Set in 2011, a time before everyone was on the 'Book, the show reflects a turning point for the social network. Back then, businesses still registered in the same way as individual user profiles. Facebook hadn't yet rolled out pages for businesses, and the news feed was far less clogged than it is today. One could say that these were the social media behemoth's "simpler times," and therefore portrayals of it on television were, too. Except five years later, the TV show *Selfie* portrayed Instagram in the same way as *It's Always Sunny* portrays Facebook—as places where people create alter egos or new versions of the self that are separate from in person.

In "The Anti-Social Network" the gang ends up at what seems to be the city's hip gin bar. As they sit and sip gin, they begin to wonder why this place is so packed and popular, and how they even heard about it in the first place. Dee, the lone female member of this all-boys gang who always has to put up with an excessive level of come-ons from the dudes—she is like Elaine in the *Seinfeld* gang—mentions that someone sent her a link to this bar's Facebook page.

Upon hearing that they all ended up at the bar because of a "dumb Facebook link," the gang realizes that they must be missing out on some serious marketing opportunities. What if they spruced up the Facebook page for Paddy's Bar? Could this be the easy road to a ton of new fans and customers alike? "Facebook is connecting everyone these days—even people in the Middle East!" says Charlie (Charlie Day), making a weird, not-funny connection to the social media activism in the Arab Spring. "And look—people are showing up to a bar that doesn't even have a sign and serves only one, old-timey drink that nobody likes." It seems like Facebook is the real way to drive traffic to their bar. "No distractions," notes Dee (Kaitlin Olson). "Paddy's needs to get connected."

In 2011, Facebook was not yet completely mainstream. I recall that same year, I was working as a copywriter at a small marketing communications firm in Chicago, creating engaging Facebook business pages and also wasting hella time on the 'Book. My boss and I were trying to figure out what made the most sense: Create the firm as a business page and gather fans, or create it as a profile and go "friend" everyone? We were convinced that if more people became "friends" with the business rather than becoming "fans," they would be more likely to interact with it and want to get to know it. We were also skeptical. Was social media just another way to throw money at marketing? Still, a Facebook ad cost far less than a direct marketing campaign, which usually included lots of paper printouts and phone calls, and perhaps an ad in a local newspaper. What was the return on investment for a Facebook ad and maintaining a Facebook business page? There were a lot of metrics, but we didn't know for sure. Still, it felt important to make sure the business was visible on Facebook, so we did that.

This episode of *It's Always Sunny* played off that same early doubtful-yet-zealous approach to businesses joining Facebook and really thinking it would change business, because Internet! But since it's TV, the writers took some serious liberties with what happened after the gang really started "investing" in Paddy's Facebook presence. For one, a man who shushed them at the gin bar soon becomes the target of their Facebook stalking obsession, which leads to a completely tangential catfishing story. Using Facebook, they discover the rude man's name and so they friend him from the Paddy's Facebook account, and then notice on his page that he had checked into a store. They decide to go and find him in person and confront him. There's nothing like an IRL confrontation based off online interactions.

Dee and Mac perpetuate a relationship with a man who merely told them to be quiet at the bar. Thanks to the existence of Facebook, the drama can continue online, and then go back offline again if someone reveals their location, which was also pretty taboo in the early Facebook days. The location check-in feature shown in the show was a reference to the then-controversial Facebook Places feature, which rolled out in August 2010.[8]

When it turns out that Dylan's profile is a fake one created by Sally (Rosalie Ward), an angry woman with whom he had an online-only relationship, Dee and Mac (Rob McElhenney) decide to figure out who Dylan is once and for all. Sally provides Dylan's physical address; Dee then confesses to also having had an online relationship with Dylan. Turns out Dylan is not even a real person, though; he is an elderly black woman played by actress Luenell, who also creates other fake profiles of straight white men for the purpose of having Internet relationships with women. She decided to start catfishing because she was lonely, bored, and closeted, and someone had purchased a computer for her. With a sick husband in the apartment, whom the camera cuts to, and a lot of time on her hands, it seemed that the *only thing she could possibly do with her time* was to create a fake Facebook profile and hit on unsuspecting women! WTF?!

The show doesn't get into the woman's queer identity, instead portraying her as dishonest and predatory, and also bringing in a weirdly handled racial moment. In pretending to be a white man online, she experiences the types of responses he would get from women. Because she never meets them in person, she embodies a white guy dating online. Why did she decide to go catfishing, posing online as a straight white man? Who was she? How did she end up on the Internet? Did she and her husband, who is dying nearby, have some type of agreement? Were any of her victims pleasantly surprised by her seductress ways? Is she queer? Sadly, we will never know, because the show ends with this woman just being seen as someone who lies about who she is online, rather than getting into deeper questions about race, gender, sexuality, and class on- and offline.

These are the types of questions that *Master of None* addresses in season 2, episode 4, "First Date," when Dev gets sucked into the apps and goes on a million first dates (#killme). While on a date with Diana (Condola Rashad), an actor colleague whom Dev already knew, she explains some of the experiences she has as a black woman on the apps. Because when it comes to race, the same type of racism plays out in person as online. This dialogue from the episode says it all:

DIANA: Oh, being a black woman on these apps? Completely different situation. Compared to my white friends, I get way less activity. I also find that I rarely match with guys outside of my race.

DEV: Same for me. A lot of my matches are Indian women. I did read somewhere that people who do the worst on the apps are Asian men and black women.

DIANA: Well, at least white people finally have an advantage somewhere!

DEV AND DIANA CHEER, THEN SCENE CUTS TO DEV OUT WITH AN INDIAN WOMAN.

The social media influencer version of boy bands: Netflix's *Chasing Cameron*

Back in the 1990s when I was a teenager—I'm a millennial cusp, y'all, just like a person whose birthday falls between two zodiac signs!—I was obsessed with *Seventeen* magazine, *Tiger Beat*, and all the other glossy teen rags. JTT, Jonathan Brandis, and Zack (Mark-Paul Gosselaar) and Slater (Mario Lopez) from *Saved by the Bell* were my teen boy crushes. I mean, as images, and when I wasn't crushing on my friends who were girls. Obviously, I would've died if I had met Zack, aka "Preppy," in person.[9] The swoon-worthy teen magazines and TV shows were the places where I got my information about them. It was all I had! Not so for today's teen girls (and boys, and gender nonconforming folks, because gender is a spectrum so just crush on whomever you want, OK?!)

In the ten-episode Netflix series *Chasing Cameron*, viewers follow the story of Cameron Dallas, a regular kid born in Los Angeles and raised in Chino, California, who would become a social media influencer by the end of high school. His single mom, Gina Dallas, raised him and his sister, Sierra, who is four years older than he is. He didn't come from a famous family, but his social media presence brought him huge viral fame.

In the Netflix series, his sister recounts how Cameron was something of an outcast, a loner, until he discovered social media, namely Instagram, Twitter, and Vine. He began by branding himself as a model, and then also started posting funny videos to Vine. In 2014, at age eighteen, he had 8.1 million followers on Vine, 8.53 million followers on Twitter, and fifteen million followers on Instagram. Eventually, Cameron was discovered and invited to participate in MagCon, a short-lived "meet and greet convention" for social media influencers that began in 2014, ended, and was then partially revived in 2016. For his fans, this was everything. Plus, it was safer than just tweeting to fans that he was somewhere and then anticipating a swarm of them swooping in with no security present.

Through MagCon, Cameron met other teenage boys who had similarly become super successful social media influencers. "I liked getting the likes and being able to talk to all the people," said Aaron Carpenter, a social media influencer featured in *Chasing Cameron*. Aaron, Cameron, and the other boys of MagCon refer to each other and the fans as "family," and also talk about the trials and tribulations of their family, making them seem very boy band, like a social media version of the Backstreet Boys or NSYNC, minus the singing skills yet retaining the hot boy looks. Aaron tears up on-camera when discussing the loss of his father. Cameron's eyes get wet when he recalls his early days as a social media influencer, lending his image to raise money for foster kids. The majority of the show's ten episodes follow the boys through their European MagCon tour, during which we get a combination of *Real World*–style peeks into their lives, the adoring fans, and how much they love to be in the spotlight.

These guys are the teen heartthrobs for today's teens who are on social media. But unlike the teen hearththrobs of adolescence past, the boys of MagCon did it all themselves, from their homes, using their phones, computers, social media, and the Internet.

At the beginning of the series, Cameron explains that he doesn't have a business degree, he doesn't know what he's doing, he's just been learning as he goes along through the "wild wild West of social media." The boys count their likes and virality together, commenting on what types of content does the best. There were plenty of swooning tweets about how the MagCon reunion in 2016 wasn't the same as the original MagCon. Welcome to the teen future of today. Here, it's not about good guys and bad guys. It's a liking game.

Reality TV mirrors back on BRAVO's *Work of Art: The Next Great Artist*

Reality TV is intended to be emotionally manipulative in a way that feels more "real" than scripted television because its contestants are not trained actors. They are people reacting to the constraints of being placed on a reality TV show. I don't personally know Cameron or any of the MAGCON boys featured on *Chasing Cameron*, but by the end of the Netflix series (which I binge-watched in bed) I felt like I "knew" some of them more than, say, I felt I knew Dev (Aziz Ansari) on *Master of None*. Whereas Dev is a character set in a fictional world, Cameron and the boys are using their real lives as the story. I followed them both on Twitter. Cameron writes random thoughts and feelings that read as emotionally vulnerable yet crafted, and it's unclear who inspired them or whether they're subtweets, like this one: "im being real, not throwin any shade."[10] Ansari doesn't tweet much, and when he does it's usually about his show: "Master of None season 2 starts filming soon. Excited."[11] It's easier to become emotionally invested in people who seem within reach, as opposed to those that are clearly portraying themselves through a Hollywood-styled universe.

Still, reality TV felt like a faraway concept for me personally until a dear friend of mine, Peregrine Honig, was cast in season one of BRAVO's *Work of Art: The Next Great Artist*. Modeled after *Project Runway*, in which contestants compete to make it to the last round and win a grand prize—in this case, a solo show at the Brooklyn Museum—*Work of Art* featured a slew of artist contestants and judges, including art gallerists, celebrities, and *New York Magazine* senior art critic Jerry Saltz. The show ran for two seasons from 2010 to 2011. Peregrine took second place in season 1.[12] After the show ended, Peregrine became a more well-known personality through the show and on social media. And because of the reality TV component, there was an emotional connection that people felt with her that wouldn't have happened otherwise.

"Social media is really emotional, and same with reality TV," said Honig. "The people who watch and choose you become your advocates. They're following you, and that alone is kind of cult-ish—to follow someone in a TV show."

Unlike an acting gig job that you do leave when the shoot is over—though the cult of personality continues on social media—the reality TV experience is different.

"It was like living a job, or going on a road trip," said Honig. "I felt like you didn't really know where you were going, but you were always going there."

Reality TV stars are expected to have social media accounts as well, since that is a way to provide more personality, more emotional connection, more clicks and views. In short, the personal brand continues in a way that feels even more tangible than the persona on a television screen. Because even when the show ends, the reality TV star's experience is still out there and very much alive.

For a year and a half after the show ended, Peregrine told me she received Facebook friend requests from people in faraway places like Russia, Korea, and all the countries where the show had been syndicated. They wanted to #connect with her based on the version of her that they'd experienced on TV. It was a surreal social experiment that, often, played out offline, IRL.

"I remember this one moment, I had just gotten into New York, and I was putting on red lipstick, and these teenage girls started screaming," she said. "I'll never forget it. They just started screaming in the bathroom behind me. And it was so loud, it was tiled, it was this airport bathroom. And they recognized me and they couldn't believe it and they wanted to be photographed with me, and it was just such an abstract experience to be looking in the mirror and then to have these young women behind me and have them—they're seeing me in the mirror as something they've seen on television."

This experience brought up questions that relate back to the selfie—which is a mirror image of oneself. To see someone from a reality TV show, a TV show, or anything on-screen and feel such excitement, to see oneself mirrored in someone else, to feel seen and represented in a larger-than-life way. And whether that happens through a television show, a social media personality, or something else on screens, it creates an undeniable connection— though it is a one-way connection because, ultimately, it is about the viewer seeing themselves reflected back in someone else. That person is their mirror.

Chapter 7

Selfie Gazing

THE SELFIE SHOOTER'S GAZE NARRATES how you look at them. It is a self-directed image that creates a curated self/brand online.

The first person I remember actively following on Instagram is a guy I'm going to refer to as just J. When I say actively, I mean that I become emotionally invested in his narrative, I liked a lot of his content, and I read his captions. I felt #connected.

I knew J before I began following him on Instagram, however. We'd met in person at a conference and hit it off, and then went out to eat at a Japanese place with a neon sign declaring "SUSHI"—yes, they had sushi, or some semblance of it, and I remember that it was something less than fresh. It was one of those places with low-hanging tiny lights, where it's so dim that actually you're barely able to see what you are eating, let alone get a glimpse of the other person's face. Before I left for home, we became friends on Facebook. We wanted to stay in touch. We'd Gchat here and there. Eventually one or both of us dropped off.

A few years later, we rediscovered each other and #reconnected on Instagram. It was a new following experience that left me wondering about what it meant to get to "know" someone again through their curated social media presence. I was following J on Instagram when he came out as trans and requested that people use male pronouns to refer to him. J spoke openly about this transition and posted a lot of selfies about his experience. He also shared freely about navigating his relationship, his experience prepping for top surgery, all the new hormones he had been taking, and how his body had started to change. He self-disclosed frequently on social media, speaking to his experiences living with chronic illness (fibro) and PTSD, and the harassment he experienced on a daily basis. He added hashtags like #crip #translife, and talked about being hot AF. I felt connected to his narrative.

Post-top surgery, he began posting topless selfies, showing those deep scars where breast tissue had been removed and his body sewn back up. His face looked longer. He grew a moustache. He seemed defiant now. I watched on. It felt honest and emotionally raw in a way that drew me in, but also like a mixture of social media and reality TV. And like every social media storytelling experience, it was curated and carefully crafted and at times I wasn't sure if it was for me to see, really, but there it was and he allowed me to follow. Sometimes the pacing was random, and at times the emotionality of the posts felt too intense for me, the content too personal. If it was, I just didn't comment or say anything, really. But I listened as much as I could.

I was aware of my implied voyeurism as someone who followed him on Instagram. I didn't know what his transition was like. As someone who is cisgender, female, and queer, with she/ they pronouns, I have no idea what it's like to be transgender, but I do know what it is like to exist outside the gender binary. And I did learn what his particular experience was like from watching his shares. To clarify, "cisgender" means that as an individual whose gender, I feel, sometimes corresponds with my birth sex—in this case, female—and I also identify as gender nonconforming. So I am a ciswoman, with preferred traditional pronouns. I get pissed off when someone greets me with "hey, lady!" but I am fine with a sardonic, campy "hey girl" greeting that reminds me of how not-girlish I feel most of the time (#tomboy). Transgender peoples' gender identity doesn't correspond with the sex they were assigned at birth. So, "sex" is what's between your legs, and gender is what's between your ears.

When I was looking at J's selfies on Instagram, I was also aware that I was reading them through a cisgender gaze; that is, I am not trans, so I wasn't reading them through the lens of identifying with J. I was reading them as a cisperson looking at an experience very much outside of my own. But because most of J's posts were selfies, I watched his description of his gender and experience, and learned about what that was like from him. I listened rather than asking questions.

One day, J explained that he noticed some people unfollowed him after he posted his new post-top surgery scar selfies. He felt sensitive about that but he decided to keep posting them, because it felt important to share this experience and take up space. By liking them, I felt that I was offering a passive form of support, a way of saying: "I hear you, I see you." He was someone I knew on social media. I'd only met him once IRL. But somehow, that didn't matter. I was glad that I was able to bear witness to his transition; perhaps simply watching was the necessary action at that time, rather than any direct communication. I tried reaching out to talk but it didn't go anywhere. I think that sometimes, that's the main purpose of social media: To just be there and participate by bearing witness, but not directly interact, like a less removed version of reality TV.

"I think sometimes people need to feel like they are being heard more than they are being supported," said Madsen Minax, an artist who transitioned more than ten years ago. "It's complicated though, right, because that might be a kind of support. You know, human needs be weird."

This type of selfie-ing is also a form of self-disclosure—whether the selfies are visual images, photos of one's face, or self-referential status updates, typically written in a first-person narrative format. The neuroscience of sharing on social media also points to the fact that self-disclosure of this variety is intrinsically rewarding.

"There is some data that self-disclosure is intrinsically rewarding because you get some of that same activation [of the rewards section of the brain, the nucleus accumbens]," said Carrie Bearden, a professor of clinical psychology at UCLA, who primarily studies child- and adolescent-onset neuropsychiatric disorders. "Self-disclosure is not something you would think of as intrinsically rewarding, but the data would suggest that it is. You get more of that activation when it is about sharing your own personal information."

So on a scientific level, there is not only a reward happening in the brain for sharing, but there's also the social element of being validated by peers. What does this type of self-disclosure mean for someone who is disclosing their transition on social media? Rebecca Kling, Community Storytelling Advocate at the National Institute for Transgender Equality, offered her perspective about self-disclosing such vulnerabilities on social media.

"One of the things that I think we all experience but is heightened for trans folks is discomfort around photos and discomfort around the way people see us as beautiful, handsome, attractive, whatever," she said. "It can be scary to share pictures of ourselves that don't meet that ideal in our head. With trans folks, the experiences can be heightened because there is the question of am I going to be 'real' enough — but air quotes around that — am I going to be perceived the way I identify and the way I present myself?"

In this way, the selfie is an aesthetic with radical potential for bringing visibility to people and bodies that are othered.[1] It is a way to share one's own narrative, offering others a chance to learn and listen. It is less about creating a "community," a codeword for "target consumers" that is often thrown around by Facebook and corporate social media companies that are, at the end of the day, collecting users' data so that they can sell ad space, and more about being heard by others who are listening and present.

"Selfies can be powerful as a tool of validation and self care, in a sort of 'look at how great I feel today, look at how I am able to move through the world in this way,'" said Kling. "I think for a lot of trans people, during and after transition, there is an aspect of 'I want to make sure people are seeing me as me.' Sharing things on Instagram, FB, and Twitter, and getting those hearts or whatever people are calling them these days, is really important especially when you aren't getting that support from your family and coworkers, or politicians who are controlling laws in your state or country aren't giving you that support."

J's selfies create space for his own narrative — he is able to control and curate his own image the way he wants to, and to make space for his subjectivity on social media. Yet in doing so, he, and anyone else who posts personal information, is also complicit with the fact that the social network basically owns his content. Nevertheless, that opportunity for self-generated content does offer space for validation, both from peers and others who are allowed to view.

"Queer and TGNC [trans/gender nonconforming] young folks use selfies as a form of creating, mirroring, and validation outside of heteronormative spaces," said Munib Raad, LCSW, a psychotherapist and mental health graduate student training coordinator at Callen-Lorde Community Health Center in New York City.[2] "Selfies have the power to cocreate narratives with other people on the Internet that foster a self-actualization of identity, that is witnessed by community. Too many queer folks of color have very few spaces for validation and mirroring, and selfies offer a space to sustain these images and have them replicated for others to bear witness to their personhood."

Sometimes, these social media posts are just about exploring a feeling or a moment; they don't aim to answer any questions or give you a feel-good or feel-bad narrative. They just *are*—floating fragments of data that will be subsumed by the corporate social network and perhaps used to advertise products back to all of its users. Each post is a declaration, a crafted image for someone's narrative.

"I think it's powerful for anyone, but I think particularly powerful as a trans woman who certainly is through my transition, but now and probably forever, feels worried about the way people see me and worried about how I move through the world," said Kling. "That validation [that I get from social media] is really important and is really powerful."

Other types of social media–told stories are about creating a collective movement around identity, place, or politics, and have little interest in the personal. Hashtagged social media movements are less about self-disclosing or curating performative identities, and more about spreading a collective message. The sorts of posts that spread virally, fanning out in social mediated waves that resonate on a different scale than individual narratives, also make up aspects of selfie culture for queer people and others with marginalized identities.

Okay, already: #wejustneedtopee

Social media has fueled protests from the Arab Spring to Occupy, leading to in-person protests, digital organizing, and other forms of calls for social justice. How does the selfie operate within this space of social media protest, however?

A 2015 panel at SXSW, *Speaking Duckface to Power: Selfies and Activism*, offered some possible explanations. Presenters Lea Muldtofte, a PhD student at Aarhus University in Denmark, and Mona Kasra, Assistant Professor of Digital Media Design at the University of Virginia, discussed the ways that the selfie has been used as a tool for activism in the social-networked age.

"Selfies are often referred to as a perfect metaphor for our increasingly narcissistic, oversharing, and personal-branding culture, but these self-portrait images are in fact enhancing the methods by which citizens communicate, connect, and respond to the local and global event," said Kasra. Within a networked culture, people can communicate through images as well as text. Activism, she explained, can leverage this capacity to also bring personalities and faces into their message, which become a part of civic engagement. "In the 21st century, we are post-national," Kasra said. "We don't need to be in the same place at the same time." That is, for people who want to be faces of the movement; other activists do the opposite, working within security culture, which, as we know from chapter 2, is inherently antiselfie.

#wejustneedtopee is one such selfie-fueled, postnational social media movement. It began in March 2015 with a couple of trans folks on social media posting about a basic human need that law-makers were challenging. Like everyone else, they just wanted to go pee in the bathroom of their gender, but proposed laws would make this simple basic need impossible. The laws dictated that people would have to use the bathroom of the gender they were assigned at birth, unless they are trans people who have had a surgical sex change. That does not apply to people who are taking hormones but haven't had surgery, or who do not wish to have any type of surgery.

This selfie-fueled protest began in Canada and then spread to the United States, traversing national borders and moving across networked culture. The goal of the #wejustneedtopee hashtag was to speak out against repressive bills that were on the table in Canada and the United States.

It kicked off when a twenty-three-year-old trans woman from Canada named Brae Carnes started posting pics of herself on Facebook tagged with #wejustneedtopee and a sign that said "Plett Put Me Here," referencing Bill C-279 which, in 2013, sought to add gender identity to the Canadian Human Rights Act.[3] This sounded like progress, but just as the bill was about to pass, conservative Senator Donald Plett added an amendment exempting "same-sex" facilities[4] that included public washrooms, essentially killing the bill. He stated that the only trans people who could be exempt from this were those who'd had a surgical sex change; it applied to those who took hormone therapy without surgery. This left out trans people who were not planning to have surgery, either for personal or economic reasons—plus sex reassignment surgery isn't a necessary thing for someone who identifies as trans. Surgery is costly, optional, and not always something someone desires for their identity, trans or otherwise.

Courtesy of Brae Carnes.

After the #wejustneedtopee selfie action by Brae in Canada, the hashtag picked up steam and more people started selfie-ing in the bathroom that they'd be forced into if similar bills passed. A trans man in Minnesota named Michael C. Hughes shot a bathroom mirror selfie of himself in a woman's bathroom. A lady strolls out of the stall pictured behind him, causing the viewer to wonder *whatever could he be doing in there?!* The text read: "Do I look like I belong in women's facilities? Republicans are trying to get legislation passed that will put me here, based on my gender at birth. Trans people aren't going to the bathroom to spy on you, or otherwise cause you harm. #wejustneedtopee."[5]

At that time, with similar legislature on the table in Kentucky, Texas, and Florida that would fine and jail anyone "caught" in a restroom that didnt't match their biological gender, the hashtag spread. Though each person who selfie-d in the bathroom showed their face and made their statement, the message was about collective resistance to the bill, and about showing the truth of just how uncomfortable things would get not only for all of the trans people who weren't allowed to use the bathroom that matched their gender. (Where are the "all gender" bathrooms, I ask!) The hashtag went viral.

"In virality, it becomes its own language," said Muldtofte from Denmark when we spoke via Skype. It was a cold day over there; behind Lea's head on the screen there was just darkness and snow falling in this place across the globe that I'd never been to. I wondered about the self-focus of each selfie—how easy it was to identify that person's face and how, with facial recognition technology, that was becoming even easier. Showing your face and claiming your identity poses an inherent risk to any selfie-taker who decides to participate in such a decentralized social movement. Those who show face through viral campaigns are separate from people who are working within an antiselfie security culture.

It made me think of signage at protests, like the one I attended right after Election Day 2016 in downtown LA. A sign with a powerful or catchy statement and without a name or face attached to it can be easily co-opted and shared, whereas a selfie always brings it back to the individual, making them identifiable as someone practicing dissent. In the #wejustneedtopee movement, the person who is selfie-ing is already politicized by the very fact of their existence. The face and body fuel the hashtag, yet also identify the individual and make them more vulnerable to law enforcement.

I pondered this while thinking about #wejustneedtopee. Muldtofte pointed out that aside from those questions, there was a real danger in the #wejustneedtopee hashtag that transcended questions about activism, narcissism, and anonymity. No one who posted the selfie was anonymous. Everyone was publicly identifying themselves as an advocate for social justice, an activist. Part of being public about your opinions on social media, on or offline, is accepting the danger inherent in speaking out and fighting back. Social media posts are easily trackable.

Better than a #bathroomselfie: #hospitalglam & chronic babes

Browse through any selfie hashtag on Instagram and you're bound to see sexualized selfies. The most standard #mirrorselfie or #bathroomselfie typically has an element of sexy self-disclosure, of a 'look at me' quality that is eye-catching, asking for your attention. These types of selfies can also occur from inside a hospital, in a doctor's waiting room, or before being seen by an endocrinologist.

Queer disabled artist Karolyn Gehrig has been charting her experiences living with chronic illness, which include frequent trips to the hospital. She was diagnosed with Ehlers-Danlos syndrome in 2003, and also has PTSD. Her project #hospitalglam began as a way for her to document and contextualize her life within medical environments, at doctors' offices, and in other spaces as a way to advocate for her rights as a patient and for better treatment. This shifted into a movement on social media by the very nature of being hashtagged so that others could see and tag along.[6]

Images that qualify as #hospitalglam usually show the individual in a medical or clinical setting looking glamorous. #hospitalglam is *not* documentation of procedures taking place, or the environment where they are happening. "#hospitalglam is a dark wink at the ways poses of illness are often used to sell us health, beauty, and fashion in the media," Gehrig writes on the Tumblr hospitalglam.tumblr.com.[7] "We are often taxed for the efficacy of these efforts during our appointments. Representing myself as a disabled person, using the same conventions placed in a clinical environment, and labeling it #hospitalglam is, in part, an effort to examine the bias that makes it harder to access care."

Gehrig told me that she is very particular about the way she takes the #hospitalglam selfies that she shares, making sure that the images are normalizing of disabled people.

Another curious element to Gehrig's project is that, often, she doesn't "look sick" in the way that the general public thinks about people who are disabled, living with chronic illnesses, or undergoing some sort of treatment. But as it goes with photography, however, the image is whatever you want it to be—and within the context of a highly curated selfie culture, the image is always manipulated.

Courtesy of Karolyn Gehrig.

"When you are looking at these photographs of me in the hospital, a lot of the early reception from other people is that 'I couldn't possibly be that sick, I look too good to be sick,' all the stuff you hear on a regular basis," said Gehrig. "Nobody I interacted with on any basis would say that I was healthy. My avatar on Instagram was taken while there was an unsecured IV in me while I was doing a tilt table test before I threw up and passed out. You don't know that from the photo. Photos eliminate the context."

Other writers like Jenni Grover created ChronicBabe.com, a community for disabled people and people living with chronic illnesses, long before selfies were a thing. Still, she knows about the power of connecting with others who are going through similar experiences around chronic illness.

"I started Chronic Babe twelve years ago, in 2005, and putting your photo out there was a pretty unique thing," said Grover. "I didn't have a camera phone that I could use to take a selfie—I had to hire a photographer. It was just a very different time. So I have watched the community evolve so much over time and now those visuals are so powerful and important and they can also be quite shocking."

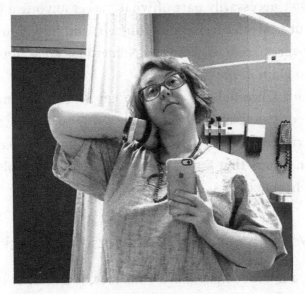

Courtesy of Jenni Grover.

In addition to the ChronicBabe community, Grover has also recently started doing Facebook Live videos every Tuesday where she talks about what's going on with her. She lives with multiple chronic illnesses, including fibromyalgia. Because of the identity she's established online, people tune in and keep up with her.

"Every single time I do Facebook Live broadcasts, I get a bunch of comments and emails from people who are so thankful to just see me in my house, in a regular way, just speaking honestly and truthfully and frankly about the experience," said Grover. "They see themselves mirrored, and in the past they might have felt completely isolated, but instead they see people who look like them and sound like them—and by looking like them I don't mean white, middle-aged, Midwestern lady—I mean just a regular person on their couch."

Sometimes, Grover glams it up. Other times, it's just her there, chilling, and she hasn't washed her hair in three days and she feels awful. But she shows up anyway. And while glamming it up is great, it isn't necessarily part of what makes anyone a babe. It is more about how you feel about yourself, and how you are practicing self-care. There is, however, something great about taking the time to glam it up.

On both ChronicBabe and through #hospitalglam, visitors and viewers can participate, engage, and see themselves and their experiences mirrored. It's a way to #connect, a way to be in touch with others that know what it's like to be disabled and/or live with chronic illness.

Vote, then share??? #ballotselfie is back

The selfie, a mirror reflection of your face, is a marker of virtual/Internet identity, a self-conscious engagement with your personal beliefs and a willingness for others to know whatever this fact is about you, too. It could be a fun consumer/shopping purchase—#newglassesselfie #nailartselfie—or it could be something as political as one's own personal politics and voting record. Because of the flatness of hashtags on Instagram, the #ballotselfie is as easily searchable as #nailartselfies.

Voting rights in America were granted by the Fifteenth, Nineteenth, Twenty-fourth, and Twenty-sixth Amendments of the US Constitution. But actually deciding to share who you vote for for is a personal and political choice. (#thepersonalispolitical)

In the 2016 election, many Democratic voters were very outspoken, donning their "I'm With Her" and "Nasty Woman" T-shirts, while supporters of Donald J. Trump covered their heads with "Make America Great Again" hats.[8] (#berniewouldvewon) Anyone who takes a selfie while wearing these clothes is pretty openly expressing their voting preferences. That's different from selfie-ing with your actual voting ballot, however.

Ballot selfies, or selfies taken with a ballot after voting, are technically an exercise in First Amendment rights—depending on what state you live in and if it is legal. According to an article on *Vox*, ballot selfies are legal in twenty-one states (and Washington, DC), and illegal in at least sixteen other states.[9]

Arguments for the #ballotselfie suggest that these images are democratic and are protected under the First Amendment. They cite studies showing that Facebook users are "more inclined to vote after seeing their friends post about voting on social media."[10] This lends itself to an idea of collectively influencing groups of people to vote through posting about voting on social media. Arguments against the #ballotselfie posit that these images could "compromise elections," which would encourage vote buying. "That is, a person who is being paid to vote a certain way can easily, and privately, prove [they] did so by taking a photo of [their] ballot."[11]

In Hawaii, a law passed that allows voters to share an image of their own marked ballot. In Arizona, though photography is banned within seventy-five feet of polling places, early ballots can be posted to social media. In California, the home of Silicon Valley and birthplace of Instagram, there was a law banning people from displaying marked ballots during the November 2016 election. A law introduced in 2016 in the state of California made ballot selfies legal; it kicked in on January 1, 2017.[12] As reported by the Associated Press, proponents of the ballot selfie, such as Nikola Jordan, a thirty-three-year-old Nebraska voter, feel that taking a #ballotselfie is a way to get other people excited about voting.[13]

Mark C. Marino, a writer and scholar of digital literature, and the Director of Communication of the Electronic Literature Organization at University of Southern California in Los Angeles, taught a writing course on selfies[14] that focused on how selfies produced and/or obscured a sense of undergraduate students' identities. Ballot selfies were a part of this conversation.

In each selfie taken for class selfie exercises, he asked students about the identity characteristics of their race-ethnicity, gender, sexuality, and socioeconomic status that they saw in those images.[15] In a *New York Times* op-ed piece, "A Case for Voting Booth Selfies," he argued that voting booth selfies are integral to identity formation for youth today.[16]

"In my class, the number of students who took selfies regularly roughly matched recent polls—more than 55 percent—and those numbers went up when we included Snapchat and other platforms."[17]

"We studied the growing body of research of selfies that shows that these images are not vehicles of vanity but contemporary modes of self-conscious communication," writes Marino. "Selfies are often written-off or devalued, however, because they're seen as something that young women do—people who have long been devalued and underestimated."

As you may have guessed, his op-ed ends with the suggestion that ballot selfies should be legal in all fifty states because who you vote for shapes your identity as well. This is a pro-#ballotselfie argument that assumes protection of voting preferences under free speech.

"Selfies reflect who you are, and shape it, too. So if we want our identity to be 'voter,' we should want Instagram in the voting booth. It marks your identity as someone engaged with the election. And it also lets you encourage your peers to vote, too."

What else could the ballot selfie mean? I got in touch with Marino.

"One of the ideas that I had—one of the ideas that they cut out from the final version of that *New York Times* article I was suggesting is that it could be used as documentation for how you voted in case there were problems down the road," Marino told me when we spoke by phone. "It couldn't be accepted in court so it's not that kind of legal documentation, but in theory you would at least have some evidence of yourself for how you voted."

Leading up to the 2016 US election, the number of voting-eligible millennials had caught up with baby boomers, with each accounting for approximately 31 percent of the voting-eligible US population.[18] America seemed as divided about the ballot selfie as they were about the actual presidential candidates.

In their book *Connected: How Your Friends' Friends' Friends Affect Everything You Feel, Think, and Do,* Nicholas A. Christakis and James H. Fowler write about the inherent socialness of voting.

A large body of evidence suggests that a single decision to vote in fact increases the likelihood that others will vote. It is well known that when you decide to vote it also increases the chance that your friends, family, and coworkers will vote. This happens in part because they imitate you and in part because you might make direct appeals to them.[19]

Certainly, this doesn't have to happen via social media—influence can come from offline networks and groups of people. But people should be able to take a #ballotselfie if they want—it's up to the individual whether or not this is information that they want to share.

In April 2016, Snapchat filed a brief amicus curiae in New Hampshire, appealing to make ballot selfies legal in the state.[20] The Snapchat case for ballot selfies suggests these are just an updated version of the social network, which has always been a part of the American political process. Part of the argument is as follows:

> The State dismisses selfies as an aberration—a new phenomenon fueled by digital photography and social media. But elections have always been a social affair. Digital media and ballot selfies are simply the latest way that voters, especially young voters, engage with the political process and show their civic pride.

In their argument for why the ballot selfie should be legal, Snapchat cites the "practice of advertising one's political pride" through selfie-ing and sending snaps. For some people who like to share their political leanings, it's natural to wear campaign buttons, or paste an "I Voted" sticker on their chest, or product promoting a certain candidate.

The decision to advertise one's political leanings also says something about their personality: That they like to share parts of their identity publicly and with their network, and they consider their political preferences as part of that identity. In other words, they like to show others how they are voting. Yet while Snapchat's argument does make sense in regard to people enjoying showing their civic pride, it naturally does not take into account the fact that wearing a pin or pasting an "I Voted" sticker is dissimilar to a ballot selfie.

For one, a ballot selfie posted to a public social network can be repurposed and reshared in any other context. Once it's out there, anyone can use it. Depending on networked levels of privacy, the ballot selfie could be for a Snapchat social network of a few friends or a group, an entire Facebook network, or the entire network on Instagram. The ballot selfie also becomes part of an individual's personal brand, which in turn shapes their networked identity.

It's also something that, depending on who you are, could get screengrabbed and stuck on the Internet forever, like Eric Trump's ballot selfie where he voted for Daddy Trump, posted it, and then deleted because he lives in New York, where ballot selfies are illegal. Though technically this was not a selfie because his face wasn't in it, the tweet did clearly show whom he voted for. Even though he deleted it after he realized it was illegal, some amazing people on the Internet were sure to screenshot it.[21]

Justin Timberlake almost took a hit for his ballot selfie in Tennessee, a state where the ballot selfie's legality is unclear.[22] His was an actual selfie—a photo of himself at a voting booth in Memphis. Timberlake had flown from California to Tennessee to cast his vote there.[23] He took this ballot selfie to encourage his fans to vote. After realizing that he may have broken the law Timberlake took it down.[24]

To document and share yourself doing something such as voting means way more than just putting an "I'm with Her" pin on your jacket. It's an image that will stay on the Internet for a very long time. It's more than a declaration of one's political leanings at a certain period in time. It is both documentation and archive of a political moment, both personal and public. To find some ballot selfies, simply go to Twitter or Instagram and search for #ballotselfie.

But aside from the vast difference of a networked identity and a political identity before the Internet, Snapchat does have a point. There is an important social draw to sharing your ballot selfie with friends through a network. People are using these tools to communicate visually with one another. Surely, sharing a ballot selfie with friends will encourage them to vote, and it will also make you seem patriotic. If nothing else, at least it shows that you care about the future of America and are practicing your right to vote.

But other than the social factor, did ballot selfies sway the 2016 election results, or were they merely a part of it? As of this book's writing, there is no conclusive evidence that ballot selfies are responsible for the election results. (That's all you, Russia![25]) But the pollsters' predictions about who might win the election were completely wrong. Certainly, the ballot selfie represents freedom of speech and promoting a candidate through posting about them, but selfies don't win elections. Politicians do.

For all the debate about ballot selfies, I believe that a self-consciously posted one can act as both documentation and evidence of an entire thought process, and something to mark a specific historical moment.

I wanted to talk with someone who had posted a ballot selfie for some reason, particularly looking at why they shot it and what it meant to them. Never mind all the legalities — you can always take a selfie before or after. I actually also took a

#votingdayselfie after the fact, to let people know that I had voted.

Matthew Simon, a New York-based software developer for the software development company We Also Walk Dogs, answered my question about why he took this selfie after voting.[26] His story goes far beyond the surface of the selfie's supposed surfaceness.

I'm a longtime Green Party voter, and a couple of years ago switched my party registration to Green as well. I've never voted for the designated presidential candidate of a major party and didn't particularly plan on doing so in the future. However by the start of November, the tone of the campaign season and the possibility of a Trump administration had me second-guessing myself.

For the last year I'd been entirely sure I was going to vote Green again, but then in the last week or two before the election, as the polls started to look sketchy, I lost my confidence. On election day I was still undecided, and put off going to vote until the afternoon, hoping I'd make up my mind. As the clock ticked down, my wife urged me out of the house, and I headed out still unsure of my vote.

What probably tipped the scales was an interaction I had on the steps of the polling station, just as I was headed in. I ran into our neighborhood pharmacist, who I hadn't seen recently, and who asked me how my mom and dad were doing. I told him my mother had died a couple of years ago, suddenly, of cancer—an awkward moment, soon over, but it got me thinking about my mom and what she would have said about my indecision.

She had been a fiery radical in her youth, but had mellowed into a bit more of a pragmatist in her later years, and while she would have agreed with my many criticisms of Clinton, the utter horror show of the Trump campaign would have left her with little patience for any waffling.

I stood there for a long time, with my ballot almost completed, every race decided except the top of the ticket, before I decided to vote for Hillary. I took the picture [the ballot selfie] at that moment to help me remember the experience, and how uncomfortable it was. In all honesty, I thought Hillary was going to win, and the picture would be a reminder that I had come around to supporting her because the alternative was so much worse.

In the context of the Trump administration, I'm not sure what to think of it. Maybe it's a record that, when the chips were down, I was ready to hold my nose and settle for a flawed candidate over one that was truly horrific. Or maybe it shows the moment when I got suckered into supporting a flawed politician who never should have been the nominee and was destined to lose.

I spoke with another person about taking a selfie on Election Day—Sam Cohen, a writer and PhD student at USC, had a particular experience with selfie-ing. She told me all about it via Facebook Messenger:

> i hadn't felt super caught up in Hillary enthusiasm during the election--just anti-Trump fear--but on election day, I was overwhelmed by the feeling of *this is historic* and *today we elect a woman for president* -- my polling place was full of women, poc, queer people, and i spent a long time talking to this girl who used to live in my building while we waited, and i felt overwhelmed by this feeling that i hadn't let myself feel, like it wasn't until the day at the polls that i realized how much electing a woman meant to me

i posted a selfie with my i voted sticker in the car. i had dressed up for the polls and was wearing a blazer and button up with purple lipstick, like, i just woke up with this feeling of women seize power today! and i wore that.

i remember my friend's teen daughter in iowa liking it immediately and thinking how much this would mean to some-one like her. idk. and then I came home and Nikki Darling picked me up to go to school and was like spewing out tid-bits of women's history from the driver's seat and crying and maybe i started crying but i can't remember, and when we got to the campus of USC we took another selfie there. I remember she put on red lipstick for the selfie.

and i felt really happy to be able to take that selfie together because i love nikki, and usc kind of saved both of our lives, and we had red and purple lipstick on (respectively), and we were in this moment of extreme optimism and like giddy empowered joy

These are both touching stories. Reading them now, they feel nos-talgic and hopeful, a memory from a time when there was less fear in the air. Like the many #ballotselfies and #ivoted selfies, they are a reminder of the power of the vote. The selfie, like the vote, are personal declarations.

38 likes

mrmosquedasjhs As promised, a #ballotselfie #channelone #channelonenews #election2016

View 1 comment

NOVEMBER 8, 2016

Brian Mosqueda, EdM, Santan Junior High School
"I teach 7th and 8th grade Social Studies at Santan Junior
High School in Chandler, Arizona. I took the ballot selfie in
response to a story that my students saw on Channel One
News (a daily news program for middle and high school
students). They ran a story about how ballot selfies are illegal
in some states. We were discussing this issue, and my students
suggested I take one on election day, and so I did."

YOLO, fer real

I've heard the selfie generation and millennials referred to as
the "trash generation," taking up space and posting images and
yelling into the void. Getting the backstory behind all of those

#ballotselfies made them feel more narrative, however, and less like floating fragmentary images. When selfies are used to speak up, celebrate, or participate in social movements, they're empowering as a way to connect, show solidarity, or just share something vulnerable. Consider the GLSEN "Day of Silence Selfie Sign," in which individuals printed out signs, fill in their names, and share what they are doing to end anti-LGBT bullying and harassment.[27] It's a way of showing solidarity via social media.

The selfie-taker as relatable
The selfie-taker as consumable
The selfie-taker as narcissist
The selfie-taker as activist
The selfie-taker as behaving badly
The selfie-taker as self-representing
The selfie-taker as political
The selfie-taker as turning away from the event
The selfie-taker as inside the event
The selfie-taker as making demands
The selfie-taker as representative
The selfie-taker as empowered
The selfie-taker as resister
The selfie-taker as perpetrator
The selfie-taker as surveilled
The selfie-taker as sousveilled
The selfie-taker as celebrity
The selfie-taker as grievable
The selfie-taker as victim
The selfie-taker as brand
The selfie-taker as not working
The selfie-taker as deserving
The selfie-taker as over-sharing
The selfie-taker as filtered
The selfie-taker as vulnerable
The selfie-taker as authentic
The selfie-taker as hoax
The selfie-taker

"Selfie Station" by JB Brager

Now consider this powerful selfie from a woman named Brenna Mae, who lives with agoraphobia, a disorder that causes anxiety in places or spaces that appear difficult to exit. On a particularly triumphant day, she was able to leave home on her own for the first time in three years. She was so excited about this that she took a selfie in front of her intended destination, Trader Joe's. Then some bus driver drove by and almost ruined her moment, yelling at her to quit taking selfies, assuming that she was just some dumb millennial selfie-ing for no reason. Little did he know that this was a huge day for her, and so she took her freakin' selfie and also posted her reason for doing so. At the end of her letter-style post, she wrote: "I'm sorry that you see my generation, documenting our lives, as something to be scorned. I'm sorry you don't hear the stories we have to tell."[28]

This instance is so entirely typical of how the selfie generation is perpetually misunderstood. The woman's act of taking a selfie means something entirely diferent from how it is perceived. Her selfie is telling a narrative that the assumptive onlooker cannot glean from the very act of selfie-ing. Indeed, he would never know what a powerful moment this was for her.

Chapter 8

Fake News and Selfie Journalism! Read All About It!

NOT LONG AGO, A FRIEND tweeted a link to me about "selfie journalism."[1] What could that mean? I wondered. The article explained that "selfie journalism" included a lot of things, including the devastating "last goodbye" videos from Aleppo, and people Snapchatting their anger about Trump winning. But those selfie vids weren't journalism at all—they were reactions to emotional events, to life-threatening experiences, to impending death, as in the videos from Syrians that came pouring out of eastern Aleppo, where more than fifty thousand civilians were trapped in a last enclave of rebel-held Syria as government forces closed in.[2]

Elsewhere on social media, individuals shouting their anger about Trump winning had a similar, yet less immediate fear attached, the underlying concern being that Trump would start a war with Russia, China, Iran, or all of the above, and nuke us all to death. Those videos from Aleppo and the postelection snapchats aren't selfie journalism—they were last goodbyes, cries for help, and just devastating to watch.

So what is selfie journalism? I argue that selfie journalism breaks with the tradition of the selfie as images of oneself shot with a smartphone camera. Instead, selfie journalism is a type of social media commentary through recontextualized images, posted through an individual's social media account.

Selfie journalism

Obama's former photographer, Pete Souza, has an Instagram account. Every time Trump does something Souza finds inane, Souza finds a contrasting image of what Obama did on that day instead, and then posts it to his Insta.[3] It throws major shade on Trump, pointing out the disparity in how they both handled situations. For example, on April 10, on the day when Trump was absent from the White House's Passover Seder, Souza posted a photo of last year's White House Seder, full of people, with Obama in the middle, celebrating the Jewish holiday.[4] Examples like this of selfie journalism offer contrasting images or tweets, posted to a social media account, to offer criticism or observations. It recontextualizes the images against current events, and it is responsive in the moment.

"Alt" Twitter accounts became a site of selfie journalism shortly after the Trump Administration attempted to put a gag on the social media accounts of government agencies including the EPA, the National Park Service, and Badlands National Park because they were tweeting real, scientific facts about climate change. The agencies immediately recognized this as an authoritarian move. A former Badlands National Park Service employee took it upon himself to set the record straight and get the facts out there through a new "unofficial" or "rogue" Twitter account.[5]

What began as @AltUSNatlParkSer transformed into @NotAltWorld, a vehicle for continuing to share facts about climate change. It spawned an entire Twitter movement in support of continuing climate change science, with other accounts following suit.[6, 7] Nearly every government agency created their own "alt" account, from Centers for Disease Control and Prevention to the Food and Drug Administration. The list goes on.[8] The best tweet about the proliferation of alt park accounts fighting back against the Trump Administration came from a random social media producer at Kenyon College named David Hoyt, who tweeted: "The thing the dystopian novels could never predict was the sudden rebellion of the national park social media managers."[9]

This kind of selfie journalism was a direct response to the propaganda-promoting machine that is Trump's Twitter account, where he rants about his greatness and his ratings, gets angry at people who disagree with him, and blames others for the state of affairs. In April 2017, Twitter sued the federal government after it demanded that Twitter unmask accounts that were tweeting against the Trump Administration. The account that they went after was @ALT_uscis, which writes tweets about Trump's immigration policies. Twitter had received a summons to reveal the identity of that account.[10] This brings up more questions about digital privacy and protections under the First Amendment.

Twitter wrote in its filing: "The rights of free speech afforded Twitter's users and Twitter itself under the First Amendment of the US Constitution include a right to disseminate such anonymous and pseudonymous public speech."[11] Twitter dropped the lawsuit the following day, after the request to reveal the identity of @ALT_uscis was withdrawn.[12]

The alt accounts @AltUSNatlParkSer and @NotAltWorld continue to fight back against the climate change-denying Trump Administration. Their tweets are responsive, pushing back in a similar way as Souza does with his contrasting Obama Administration images on Instagram.

How news spreads

In a social media-driven media landscape, news spreads through shares, and people with similar friends and interests will likely be reading the same thing. This creates filter bubbles, a result of personalized searches that give search engines more information for their algorithms, thus the ability to better serve you more of what you want.

Eli Pariser both coined the term "filter bubble" and writes about it extensively in his book *The Filter Bubble,* which explains how algorithms and social media shape the information we consume and, ultimately, shape our knowledge. Rather than read news and information that counters our viewpoints, or read things that we wouldn't necessarily encounter in our online communities, social media and search engine filter bubbles ensure that we will continue reading the content that we want, which reinforces our points of view. The algorithms feed us what it knows we want to read.

This happens on Google Search and on Facebook. It's one of the reasons we love getting news from our Facebook friends whose status updates, links, and pictures we click on: The algorithm reads it, and then serves us more of the same friend. It's far easier to go to a reliable friend's profile, which also gives a sense of #connection, and receive news and updates and jokes from them rather than tapping a news site for information. Oh why yes *of course* I'd love to stop by my savvy FB friend's wall and read their commentary about what's going on, along with bits and pieces of their personality and humorous commentary on the news! Each friend who posts regularly like this, who feeds the network, also becomes an online personality within the context of their social media filter bubbles.

Although it's easy to spend hours scrolling Facebook reading what you like, there is a downside. Pariser's book talks about the dangers of such filter bubbles, and calls on the powerful tech companies of Facebook, Google, and Microsoft to provide users with more than just what they want, and instead give them information that will actually inform them. He makes the comparison of consuming only the news you want all the time to eating junk food nonstop. That is, you need a balance. But can you really ever fuck with the algorithm, which is just delivering more of what you want based off what you tell it you like? No, not unless the algorithm is reformulated. In a *New York Times* review[13] of Pariser's book, Evgeny Morozov writes:

> Google looks to your previous queries (and the clicks that follow) and refines its search results accordingly. If you click on gossip blogs like Gawker rather than Netflix after searching for the names of movie stars, links to Gawker may feature more prominently. Likewise, if you have hundreds of Facebook friends, you see relevant updates only from the closest of them; Facebook relies on your earlier interactions to predict what, and who, is most likely to interest you. Thus, if you're a conservative who clicks on links only from other conservatives, you may never see updates from your liberal acquaintances, even if you do "friend" them.

In the divisive aftermath of the 2016 election, a few more glaring issues came up that further complicated the filter bubble. First, people who supported Hillary or a third-party candidate felt so infuriated by Trump supporters that many requested Trump supporters defriend them immediately, or went ahead and did it themselves. The more glaring issue here is that social media is not a productive space for discussing politics. Polarizing arguments tend to end in blocking or defriending someone, or some other form of virtual silencing. By defriending a Trump supporter, however, it wouldn't be possible to see their news feed or understand where they were coming from. But after the election, it didn't seem to matter. The filter bubble effect was amplified as politics became exceedingly polarizing.

In addition to the socially-driven filter bubble, actual fake news sites had shaped how people became informed during the election. The fake news site ChristianTimesNewspaper.com, created by Cameron Harris, a college graduate who was committed to Maryland Republican politics and wanted to make fast cash, produced headlines like "BREAKING: Tens of thousands of fraudulent Clinton votes found in Ohio warehouse."[14] Trump kept ranting about a "rigged election" and that it would "cause him to lose"—don't worry, bro, Comey had your back there!—and so he took it upon himself to shake undecided people to side with Trump. "I had a theory when I sat down to write it," the twenty-three-year-old Mr. Harris, a college grad, former quarterback, and frat leader, explained to the *New York Times*.[15] "Given the severe distrust of the media among Trump supporters, anything that parroted Trump's talking points people would click. Trump was saying 'rigged election, rigged election.' People were predisposed to believe Hillary Clinton could not win except by cheating."

Harris appeared both proud of his antics, and somewhat guilty about spreading lies; after all, this "part-time gig" did score him about $1,000 per hour in web advertising revenue. Yet as the story went viral, eventually it did reach the board of elections in Franklin County, Ohio, which investigated the fraud claims and proved that they were false. Harris insisted that he wrote the fake news for the money, not because of the politics, but that story sounded very dubious. Eventually, Google announced[16] that it wouldn't be placing ads on sites that created fake stories, and soon Harris's moneymaking scheme was over.

There were plenty of other fake news headlines, like "FBI Agent Suspected In Hillary Email Leaks Found Dead in Apparent Murder-Suicide," which was published on DenverGuardian. com, another fake news site. It got shared more than half a million times on Facebook, yet was completely false.[17] A reporter tracked down the owner of the site, with assistance from John Jansen, head of engineering at Master-McNeil Inc., a tech company in Berkeley, California. Eventually, the website's creator agreed to talk with NPR reporter Laura Sydell, who reported:

> Jestin Coler is a soft-spoken 40-year-old with a wife and two kids. He says he got into fake news around 2013 to highlight the extremism of the white nationalist alt-right. "The whole idea from the start was to build a site that could kind of infiltrate the echo chambers of the alt-right, publish blatantly or fictional stories and then be able to publicly denounce those stories and point out the fact that they were fiction," Coler says.[18]

From there, it became pretty clear that Coler could get an audience for his fake news on Trump-supporting Facebook groups that were eager for content they could use to uphold their theories.

One such conspiracy theory hit me closer to home, falsely involving an artist/musician friend of mine, Arrington de Dionyso. He got sucked into the #Pizzagate conspiracy theory through the most bizarre of circumstances.

Six years prior, he helped paint a mural at Comet Ping Pong, a pizza restaurant and music venue in Washington, DC. In the wake of the #Pizzagate conspiracy theory, he became a target of alt-right harassment online after completely fake news spread via

4chan message boards populated with far right extremist trolls and white supremacists. The theory going around went something like this: "Hillary Clinton and her former campaign chair, John Podesta, were running a child-trafficking sex ring at Comet Ping Pong." I put this in quotes to ensure that it's read as just a theory. It seemed completely insane, but those on the far-right who wanted to believe it did exactly that, buying into the mayhem and chaos thereafter. The #Pizzagate conspiracy targeted any artists who had been associated with Comet Ping Pong, including de Dionyso. It became part of a queerphobic witch hunt that targeted artists, musicians, and supporters. In an interview with *Hyperallergic*, Dionyso addresses the ways that the fake news about him spread throughout Facebook communities:

> For as much as we talk about the echo chambers and bubbles we're living in, every time I've made any kind of statement [on Facebook] about the harassment I'm experiencing, the support has been thunderously loud and unanimous. And I really do believe that we who reject this type of flagrantly immoral witch hunt and spread of misinformation, those of us who oppose that are clearly in the majority. I think no matter what happens we really have to keep reminding ourselves of that. We are in the majority.[19]

The fake #Pizzagate conspiracy news went so far that on December 4, 2016, a twenty-eight-year-old man named Edgar M. Welch actually drove six hours to DC, armed with an AR-15 rifle. Upon arriving, he fired shots into the restaurant.[20] Thankfully, no one was hurt, but this fake news apparently hit the dude so hard that he would kill for it.

On either side of the American political spectrum, the same idea of *homophily* is true: We are influenced by the people around us.

Pizza selfie courtesy of Arrington de Dionyso.

People posting false information and not fact-checking leads to something resembling "post-truth," the idea that we are living in a culture that has no grasp on what is happening. Maybe so. But keep in mind that the idea of "post-truth," much like the selfie phenomena, has been around since the dawn of social networks like MySpace circa 2006. It's just that now, with more advanced and widespread social media, it can reach people more quickly than ever before. Alexis Mantzarlis, of Poynter.org and leader of the International Fact-Checking, challenges the assertion of "post-truth" in his post:

> Perhaps due to my own confirmation bias, I am quite unimpressed with the post-truth trope. It implies there was once a golden age when politics and the media were dominated by facts (ignoring almost identical terms popularized 11 years ago), falsely presumes that people will never change their minds

when fact-checked on a partisan issue and absurdly reduces political action to purely rational choices.[21]

As Mantzarlis explains in his article "Fact check: This is not really a post-fact election" in the *Washington Post*, politicians haven't changed one bit: "Politicians have always lied, post-truthers concede: The difference now is that voters don't care. Yet a surging appetite for fact-checking and a newly released study of its impact indicate that facts may still have some fight left in them." It's been for the last ten years or so, from Paul Krugman's writing about "The Post-Truth Campaign" in 2011 to a blog post by David Sirota in 2007, welcoming the "post-factual era."

Contextless comedy on social media: Is it "fake news"?

I enjoy writing social media commentary and narrative-esque posts that cast me as a character in my own life, as I see fit. It seems to work—on social media, people like emotional content that is also personal and eccentric, and I think I've done a good job of amplifying my quirks in a way that is funny, relatable, and distinguishable from the other content out there. I'm just here to make friends and make jokes, especially about the current political climate.

I wondered if this was the same logic that makes showing clips of newscasts and poking fun at political events on social media work for the Left. But satire is obviously different from news. And when I was writing political comedy/jokes on social media, at times it *did* border on being read as "fake news." I began receiving messages about whether or not something I wrote was true. Were I onstage at a comedy venue, this would not be the case because that space is intended for satire. But out in the wild west of social media, there is no context, only content.

Read all about it! Six types of fake news!

Around the same time that fake news rocked the 2016 election, I met a writer named Mark Marino, who coincidentally was teaching a course on fake news at University of Southern California (USC),[22] who we encountered last chapter on the topic of #ballotselfies. He described it as an "elective," and the entire three-week course, based off his background in netprov (or, improv for the Internet), revolved around the creation and dissemination of fake news. Mark and I talked ballot selfies by phone and then emailed for a while before eventually meeting up at Canter's Deli, a classic Jewish deli in Los Angeles. I was interested in his fake news course. I followed the course through a Google Group. Much of it involved reacting to the constant stream of lies coming out of the Trump Administration. In his post *Fake News Reader*, Marino lays out the "six types of fake news" as he sees them:

1. **Fantasy Fake:** The otherworldly stories of Bat Boy and Elvis sightings from *Weekly World News*, *Inquirer*, et cetera. This is fake news designed to entertain. (Incidentally, it's some of the most carefully wrought from a legal perspective — though that's not exactly the full story.)

2. **Funny Fake:** Good Ol' Satire, as in the *Onion*, *The Daily Show*, *National Lampoon*, the *Oxford Mutton Chops*, the *Congressional Reporter*, *Bunk* magazine, et cetera. This is fake news designed to entertain, but with a slant, a point of view.

3. **Fony Fake:** Hoaxes designed to prank or punk the foolish and entertain the bored. Like Funny Fake, these Fony Fake stories may ape the forms and styles of news, but like Fantasy Fake, they're more interested in offering diversions to their

audiences than critically sending up the fourth estate. Think: War of the Worlds. People pretending to be Spencer Pratt.

4. **Fallacious Fake:** (propaganda lite) These misleading or sensationalized news whose job it is to rile-up and whose primary color is yellow. Twenty-four-hour news channels (Fox News, CNN, MSNBC) can trip or dive into this bog, as can government press offices.

5. **Flat Fake:** (full-strength propaganda) A more direct form of propaganda, this news pretends to be satire, even posts on sites marked as fake news outlets, but it's not particularly funny. In fact, it's not trying to make people laugh but instead to make people click on the link, like, retweet, and share it for the generation of ad revenue. (ex. Pope Endorses Trump — not exactly a knee-slapper).

6. **фальшивка Fake (Falshivka Fake):** (propaganda de ruski) Fake news originating in Moscow.[23]

Selfie with Mark C. Marino at Canter's Deli in Los Angeles.

Courtesy of Mark C. Marino.

Vice President Mike Pence purportedly "never said" that he condoned conversion therapy for gay people, the "practice of trying to change someone's sexual orientation or gender identity," according to an article in the *New York Times*, in which his spokesperson Marc Lottner denied that Pence supports the practice, stating instead that a past campaign statement had been misinterpreted.[24] But judging from his horrific record of anti-LGBTQ everything, it is not safe to believe that any of this is true. In this case, technically it is speculation on the parts of LGBTQ activists like myself to say that he is most likely for conversion therapy. It doesn't feel like fake news. It seems like the one as-of-yet unspoken step away from the truth. We need facts.

Sometime after the election, there was a parody petition going around on Change.org called "Electrocute Mike Pence Until He Knows He is Gay."[25] Yeah, I signed it. Based on what Pence has said, this wasn't fake news—this was speculation-as-comedy, a way of exaggerating the truth. Or just recognizing it for what it is. I searched for it again after the inauguration had taken place, but it was gone.

Fake news: Now and then

It is painfully unironic that Trump made a joke on Twitter about how we're "living in Nazi Germany" but then horrifyingly didn't mention the death of six million Jews who perished in the Holocaust. A statement issued by former White House Press Secretary Sean Spicer—who was constantly parodied on *SNL*—did not mention the murders of Jews during the Holocaust.[26] At other times, Trump has called the rise of anti-Semitism "horrible" and "painful," but clearly has no grasp on what anti-Semitism truly is, its long history, or how he is perpetuating it.[27, 28] Much of fake news history is rooted in anti-Semitism that is ultimately upheld by histories of white supremacy.

In Jacob Soll's essay "The Long and Brutal History of Fake News" published on *Politico*, he recaps an event that occurred on Easter Sunday 1475 in Trent, Italy.[29] The story begins like the plot of a horror movie, with a two-and-a-half-year-old kid named Simonze, who had gone missing. Quickly accusations came from Franciscan preacher Bernardino de Feltre, who claimed that the Jewish community had murdered the child and then drained his blood and drank it to celebrate Passover. Rumors erupted on the basis of anti-Semitism, and Prince-Bishop of Trent Johannes IV Hinderbach ordered the Jews arrested and tortured. Fifteen would be "found guilty" and burned at the stake even though there was no evidence that they committed these crimes. In fact, the papacy had attempted to halt the convictions—but Hinderbach wouldn't hear it. Instead, Simonize became Saint Simon, one hundred miracles were attributed to him, and fifteen Jews were killed all thanks to the spreading of fake news. Writes Soll:

> Fake news is not a new phenomenon. It has been around since news became a concept 500 years ago with the invention of print—a lot longer, in fact, than verified, "objective" news, which emerged in force a little more than a century ago. From the start, fake news has tended to be sensationalist and extreme, designed to inflame passions and prejudices. And it has often provoked violence.

In his article, he discusses the various other ways that fake news has spread, rooted in anti-Semitism, from Nazi propaganda about Jews—we all know where that led—as well as the "cottage industry" of fake news in Antebellum America, which focused on bizarre untrue stories of African-American people "spontaneously turning white." Sensationalism is a driving force of fake news and yellow journalism, which eventually sent the public into a search for "objective news." That is, news that wasn't slanted one way or another, and that purported to report just the facts. Writes Soll:

> While partisan reporting and sensationalism never went away (just check out supermarket newsstands), objective journalism did become a successful business model—and also, until recently, the dominant one. In 1896, Adolph Ochs purchased the *New York Times*, looking to produce a "facts-based" newspaper that would be useful to the wealthy investor class by providing reliable business information and general news. Ochs showed that news did not have to be sensationalist to be profitable, though the paper was accused of being a mouthpiece for "bondholders."

To return to World War II and anti-Semitism, however, even "objective" journalism did not do the American public justice. As Hitler rose to power in Nazi Germany and the Red Scare struck Americans thanks to Joe McCarthy's anti-Communist propaganda machine, the role of reporters seemed murky. What was the truth? Meanwhile, a story in the *New York Times* in 1922 mentions Hitler as a "new popular idol" rising in Bavaria. This was a fact. Yet this article downplayed Hitler's anti-Semitism, something that would never be forgotten.[30]

But the fake news of yesteryear differs in dissemination from the fake news of today. Mostly, it has to do entirely with speed. Much of fake news is easily believed and not really questioned because of how fast it is being read on mobile phones, and the websites' designs look plausible. In Kyle Chayka's article "Facebook and Google Make Lies as Pretty Much Truth" for *The Verge*, he writes about the ways that AMP and Instant Articles actually camouflage fake news as something real.[31] "On a

Facebook timeline or Google search feed, every story comes pre-packaged in the same skin, whether it's a months-long investigation from the *Washington Post* or completely fabricated click-bait," writes Chayka.

One such example he uses is an article about Trump's false popular vote win on the generic URL "70news.wordpress.com," which Chayka writes "looks just like a piece from the *New York Times* or *Bloomberg*. It has the bare basics of a headline, prominent thumbnail image, publish date, and source. Clicking through to the story on a mobile browser, as the majority of US Google searchers would, brings up the post-Web 2.0 standard: boxes of well-proportioned text in an empty white field with branding at the top and bottom. It looks pretty normal, though odd capitalizations and bolding hint that something might be off."

Certainly, without a clearer investigation of this site, and with a quick reading of it on the train on the way home from work, or maybe sitting at a cafe waiting for a friend, or even at a restroom break while on a great American road trip, this fake news could be quickly absorbed and read as truth.

But unlike recognizable mainstream news sites with well-established brand identities, one thing that usually gives away fake news sites is the shoddy design, which is unimportant because traffic and social media shareability are the only advertising goals.

And so, ultimately, as Pariser argues, the onus is on Facebook and Google, the places where fake news is read and shared, often through communities that are super hungry for this content. In this new day in the age of information wars, Facebook has pledged to fight fake news. To start, Facebook hired outside fact-checkers like Snopes and Politifact to sift through and flag fake news stories and other fakenesses from the news feed.[32] Writes Rob Horning on Twitter of fake news and filter bubbles:

> fake news and filter bubbles are symptoms of a larger issue: the
> way social media incentivizes performances of loyalty, us vs.
> them[33]

It is just about monetizing. As Horning writes in this tweet—Facebook is not "focused on engagement"; it is focused on selling ads—we must remember what the real incentive for Facebook is.[34] It is not to bring together people in any sort of a benevolent, sharing "community"—it is to make money, create revenue, keep people on there, which is no different from any publication of the past. So if the revenue incentive includes weeding out fake news, then surely Facebook will keep on it.

This social media landscape is all a fake news performance anyway

In some ways, however, amid a sea of fake news and real news and facts and fiction, the selfie resurfaces as a break from the news, an aspirational image with only one purpose: creating yourself as you want to be seen by friends and onlookers in your network. The selfie is self-imaging, a performance on social media, a brief glimpse of an individual with Internet access who is telling their own story in this moment, and inviting you, dear viewer/voyeur, to observe, and to judge if you feel like, ignore if you want, comment, fuck off, reshare, whatever.

Courtesy of Amalia Ulman from the series
"Excellences & Perfections" on @amaliaulman IG
and Arcadia Missa Gallery (London)

The selfie can also be its own curated version of fake news, or performed identities for social media. I think of the artist Amalia Ulman, who used her Instagram account to create a performed version of herself that was influenced by "extreme makeover culture" as found on IG. The performance lasted five months, ultimately blending fact and fiction. The piece was technically titled *Excellences and Perfections*, and she let all who followed her at @amaliaulman know about it from the beginning. But those who started following along later didn't know it was all social media performativity. The series included a large number of selfies, naturally. It was eventually archived and presented as an online-only exhibition series at Rhizome, in both a way to showcase it as art and also preserve it.[35] As Rhizome describes on the exhibition's homepage:

On April 19, 2014, Amalia Ulman uploaded an image to her Instagram account of the words "Part I" in black serifed lettering on a white background. The caption read, cryptically, "Excellences & Perfections." It received twenty-eight likes.

Courtesy of Amalia Ulman from the series
"Excellences & Perfections" on @amaliaulman IG
and Arcadia Missa Gallery (London)

It's important to note the small amount of likes that she received on this initial post, whereas the actual images that people bought into, in which she commented on extreme makeover culture on IG, received likes into the hundreds; ultimately, she got almost ninety thousand followers on her account as a result of the performance. Those well-liked images crafted a narrative of her social media personas, proving the artifice of social media and learning what people really "liked." But thus began her performance, in which she replicated images of herself in manipulated versions of the "Hot Babe"—she faked a breast augmentation, posting images of herself laid up in a hospital with bandages around her chest. The performance was staged and distributed to the network. Then there are other shots like one of her posing, leaning toward the camera wearing only underwear and sticking her ass up so it's clear she's wearing a thong, and wearing a black hat with the words BAE across the front in white. They are all performances of curated identies on social media.

The fictional version of herself that she played in this account that was based in Los Angeles brought in elements of selfie celebrity and Instagram model culture. There is no better place to do this than LA, home of the entertainment industry, the glut of glamour and hypercommercialization, the place (other than New York) where people go to hopefully make it as actors, comedians, or some other type of celebrity.

I came to Los Angeles to write this book and to better understand the construction of celebrity, what it means to work toward fame, and to constantly create aspirational images and performances of oneself within the context of the entertainment industry, rather than just within the microcosm that is the selfie world/social media influencers. Though of course, the two go hand-in-hand, often overlapping, as in the case of Cameron Dallas, a social media influencer who makes a living off this, and got his own Netflix show about how he became a "self-made" man.[36] Ultimately though, Ulman's project comments on the lengths people go to to create themselves for social media consumption. Her goal wasn't to become a social media influencer—it was to comment on those who create personas for social media:

> Through judicious use of sets, props, and locations, *Excellences and Perfections* evoked a consumerist fantasy lifestyle. Ulman's Instagram account is a parade of carefully arranged flowers

and expensive lingerie and highly groomed interiors and perfectly plated brunches . . . . And Ulman went to great lengths
to replicate the narrative conventions of these privileged feeds,
from her use of captions and hashtags (#simple, #cutegasm), to
the pace and timing of uploads, to the discerning inclusion of
"authentic" intimate or emotional content (a photo of a lover
or a moment of despair).[37]

The most fascinating part of this project, to me, is that some people
were outraged when they found out that this was social commentary
and not "real." It was real in as much as they invested in the character
that they were following. If the emotions are real, is it not real?

In March 2016, the *Telegraph* ran an article that played up
the meanness of her "lying" with the headline "Female Instagram
artist who hoaxed thousands with her fake profiles is exhibited
in London," suggesting once again that social media presents a
"true" version of oneself, and that seeing is believing.[38] Wrong! The
article announced an offline exhibition of these formerly online-
only images in London, at Whitechapel Gallery and Tate Modern.
It seemed that the original social media fans of the project, that
became emotionally invested in Ulman's character, were the most
"hurt" by this "deception" because they wanted a character that
they could #connect with. But did they not already #connect?

> While Ulman's project was criticised by users of Facebook and
> Instagram—most of whom she had fooled—as a "hoax," she
> has also received widespread praise for drawing attention to
> the double standards that allow women to be simultaneously
> valued and shamed for how they present their bodies online.[39]

Ultimately, the project won her thousands of Instagram followers, but of course that wasn't the point. Instead, it was about the

performance, bringing out the flattened Instagram #hashtagged characters, and discussing the ways that women perform their personas online. In an interview with *New York Magazine*, Ulman describes the ways that she developed her Insta character:

> I began by researching the cosmetic gaze and the beauty myth, then I prepared a script and timeline that followed the rhythm of social media. I identified three popular trends: the Tumblr girl (an Urban Outfitters type); the sugar-baby ghetto girl; and the girl next door, someone like Miranda Kerr, who's healthy and into yoga. Part of the project was about how photography can be a signifier of class, and how cultural capital is reflected in selfies.[40]

Personally, I was interested in the idea of how, in creating a fictional narrative on social media, Ulman clarified the ways that social media allows people space to construct personas, and to play with those for an audience that's ready to consume content. More than anything, social media is about getting a reaction, about sharing and #connecting without actual in-person human interaction, about getting someone else to buy into your image and, ultimately, the version of you that you present. To ever meet offline—to actually connect—would be an added bonus; ultimately, social media becomes entertainment, especially in the context of these types of projects.

What if Ulman's project was seen as "fake news" about a girl's life? To users who devoutly followed her, that's what it was. But the joke's on them for believing everything they see. On social media, it's perfectly simple for anyone to create a "fake" narrative. In fact, I once staged a fake relationship with a high-profile political personality—let's just refer to her as "our SLOTUS." Many people bought into the narrative, believing and enjoying it, even participating and leaving comments on my "relationship" with this woman. Of course, my project was far less realistically believable; it was more like anti-fan fiction or alt-erotic fantasy. Ulman's project creates a potentially "real" girl. My story was an unbelievable situation, which made it all the more fun. Ulman's came off as more "true."

The performative nature of Ulman's project goes against findings from a new report published in *Frontiers in Psychology*."[41] This study refers to the more banal selfies, not the "Hot Babe" type selfies that Ulman created for her project. Curiously though, the questions of "authenticity" in relation to the selfie do in fact reappear. As reported by Laura June for *The Outline*:

> Termed the "selfie paradox" by the study's author, Sarah Diefenbach at Ludwig-Maximilians-University Munich, the research suggests that while people often view their own selfies as "ironic" and "authentic," they are likely to view the selfies of others as self-promotional and inauthentic. This may explain how everybody can take selfies without feeling narcissistic.[42]

If this is true, the selfie paradox makes clear that no one feels narcissistic when taking selfies because taking selfies would suggest an attempt to show one's "authentic" self though even that sense of "authenticity" is performed. The selfie is an aspirational image. Never before has it been easier, cheaper, and faster to share how we want to be seen.

Chapter 9

The Authentic Selfie

THE SELFIE IS AN ASPIRATIONAL image, but it also an integral aspect of socializing, interacting, and being seen by others online. In an attention economy of likes that demands performance and absolute connectivity, the selfie is a way to visually grab someone's attention, mimicking a face-to-face interaction. In order to exist, the selfie most be produced by the individual, and consumed by the network. Even though the selfie is a singular image object, it exists as a continual piece of content when posted to the network because of the people on the network who interact with it. Yet upon posting, it also becomes an archive of one's presence on the network. Unless it's just on an Instagram Story or a Snap—then it will be gone after twenty-four hours. The selfie that is posted to the network is always about being seen the way you want others to see you. (#putyourbestfaceforward)

Though the selfie is a millennial phenomenon, there are noticeably different selfie-ing habits between older millenials such as myself, who grew up using AIM and then joined Friendster and early MySpace; younger millenials who had Facebook in high school; and members of Generation Z who, born after 1996, are teens now or in their early twenties and regularly use Instagram, Snapchat, and Tumblr. One thing that distinguishes older and younger millennials and Gen Z is the question of online privacy. Older millennials remember a time when there *was* such a thing as online privacy, whereas younger Gen Zs do not.

"One of the reasons I (and a lot of us 'older millennials' in tech) get so nostalgic for the old days is because we believed in the power of living in public and the tools we used never got in the way of that; and the tools were for the most part, super naive about the potential privacy violations they presented," said Harlo Holmes, director of newsroom digital security at Freedom of the Press Foundation.

Infinite mirror // selfie-ing

The selfie is perpetually here and now, but where is it headed? Madison Malone Kirscher writes regularly about selfies for *New York Magazine*'s section Select All, which asks questions about how we live online. I was intrigued by her stories about sealfies (selfies with seals), handless selfies (selfies taken with a timer in front of the mirror while the phone is flying in the air) and ballot selfies, and figured she'd have some answers to these questions.[1]

"Anytime anybody whips out a phone to take a photo, people will call it a selfie," said Kirscher when we spoke by phone. "If you can put 'selfie' in a headline, people will click it and people will care." The word "selfie," as we saw in chapter 4, is buzzy, cute, and clickworthy.

"When I think about people like my parents, they know what [the selfie] is," Kirscher said. "Suddenly, this trend that maybe they don't give a damn about—people taking pictures in their bedroom mirrors throwing their phones in the air, which is this ridiculous teen thing—there's a touchstone there now because everyone knows what a selfie is this side of point-and-shoot cameras circa 2003."

The social appropriateness of the selfie is constantly in flux. It was intensely vilified during its upswing, but now it has settled in to being an accepted aspect of how we live.

The selfie is fun. When shared, it becomes a social image. Ultimately, self-imaging is enjoyable and something that most every millennial does at some point, to see how they look on-screen and to connect with friends.

Madison M. K. ✓
@4evrmalone

Following ˅

Willingly returned to my high school to see this year's musical so now I'm hiding out in the bathroom because time is a flat circle.

4:10 PM · 11 Mar 2017

"I have this series of tweets where I take a selfie every time I wear tech fleece—[the other day, I was doing it, and] I watched some person who was probably thirty to thirty-five years older look at me and then pantomime, 'Are you kidding me?'" said

Kirscher. "And that's not even an inappropriate setting. I'm just walking up 1st Avenue, I'm not bothering anyone, I'm not impeding on anything—I'm just taking a picture of my face."

That's one way of selfie-ing, and it's also specific to millennials who are in their 20s. Because selfie-ing is largely a teen phenomena, as discussed in chapter 1, what about kids who are part of Generation Z, people who were born after 1996? If we're talking about the future, this is who will determine it.

"I don't use Facebook because Facebook is boring," said George Yocom, thirteen, who's in the eighth grade and lives in Minneapolis. "That's where all the old people go and write about weird weather and stuff. I don't want to hear about what you are doing right now."

I'd been on Facebook just moments before talking to George. After talking with him, I felt incredibly lame. I'd met his mom the week before when she came by the *Star Tribune* of Minneapolis, where I work, to give a talk to journalists about covering the trans community.

George and I talked about his social media—he really only uses Instagram, Snapchat, and Tumblr because that's where his friends hang out, and that's mostly who he follows on social media. He goes on every day, often first thing in the morning, and of course social media does affect his friendships and how he sees people in the world. It's also important for him to post about the stuff he cares about and is doing.

"As a trans activist, I am more like trying to get people to support this organization, or do stuff and not just sit there and think about it—which is good, but to actually go out there and do stuff," he said.

But really, I just wanted to talk with George about his selfies. Maybe, I wrote this whole book just so I could get to this part of it. I asked him, how often do you post selfies and why? These are the questions that launched by investigation into the selfie in the first place.

"I feel like, mainly I probably do because I don't know what else to post and I don't have any other pictures and like, why not?" he said. The selfies that he notices get the most likes are ones where he's wearing really cute outfits, and doesn't have his face in them.

"[When people see those photos they] are like, 'Oh cute,' and I'm like, 'I know.'"

There's an assumption out in the world, as mentioned in Nancy Jo Sales' book *American Girls* that social media is affecting the lives of teenage girls in a negative way, and that they would leave the network if they could. Certainly, social media is changing the social behavior of teens today. When I asked George if social media has been a helpful way for him to connect with friends, he replied, "It definitely helps me connect with people because obviously I can't be with people 24/7, but I want to know what they're doing," he says. "And like, sometimes it's hard to talk to people because I have social anxiety, so it's cool to see them online and be like, 'Hey, you're having a good time, that's great!'"

Two artists of the selfie generation: RaFiA Santana & Brannon Rockwell-Charland

Selfies are a completely mainstream phenomenon. And like any pop culture phenomena, they are ripe for critique by artists of the selfie generation. Artists of the selfie generation use social media as part of building their persona or brand, and they also use themselves in their work. In this IRL-URL fluid space, artists of the selfie generation criss-cross from the digital to the physical, exploring and playing with the overlap between the two.

Artists of the selfie generation are diverse, geographically scattered about (location independent!), and connected by the Internet and social media. Artists of the selfie generation engage with intersectional feminism, a term originally coined by Black feminists to point out the unique intersection of oppression that they experience both as women and people of color. It now has come to include anyone who experiences oppression under white supremacist, capitalist, patriarchal society. As the blog *Intersectional Feminism 101* writes: "Those with disabilities, mental illness, non-Western religious identities, nonwhite ethnic or racial identities, nonthin bodies, non-Eurocentric features, low income, those who are not alloromantic, allosexual, heterosexual, or cisgender [specifically cis male by Western standards], or those who simply do not adhere to a Western model of gender or sexuality all experience oppression due to their relative 'disadvantage.'"[2]

One such artist who uses the selfie as one of her many means of self-expression is Brooklyn-based artist RaFiA Santana, age twenty-six. She is a millennial who selfies as a way to both create an archive of herself, and to make sure she is seen the way she wants to be seen. On social media she has said that she has a separate account just for people of color, and one where she creates a persona that's read more by non-POC folks. Creating such distinct personas on social media is one way to navigate fluid social media identities.

Her selfie art is also a necessity in part because of systemic racism that she experiences. Santana knows that someone who takes her photo will come to it with their own visual memory and baggage of historical images of Black people. Santana works across platforms, and often uses herself in her work. She comes from a family of artists—her mother is a photographer and archivist, and her father is a photographer and filmmaker—and she started using a camera as a teenager.

On the top of her website, she has category for "selfie," but this wasn't on purpose. It just happened because she tagged a lot of images with #selfie, and that created a larger tag cloud on the top of her website.

"I have a ton of images of myself, and it does stretch across photography, graphic design, and just like Instagram pictures," said Santana. "That was a way of categorizing it and putting it into different compartments—how to show it. Somebody picked it up as a series, and I was like, 'Oh I guess it's kinda like that, but I was like, oh wait it's not a self-portrait series,' but whenever I post a picture of me that I made, I put it under 'selfie.'"

The main draw of the selfie, especially for people who have seen results they aren't happy with when turning over the lens to a photographer, is that we can shape our own narratives based on how we want to be seen.

"You get these narratives with photography but if somebody else is taking your picture they are seeing you through their lens, and a lot of what I have been taking issue with and just noticing with a lot of Black photography in major magazines—a lot of the photographers are white and if they shoot Black people they are not conscious about the inherent biases they have—because they've been seeing Black people through the white lens forever. That's like all they've been seeing—they'll still photograph Black people the same way, making them look demonic or just the standard ghetto and not lit properly, they don't understand how Black people want to look—they don't understand the Black aesthetic."

For Santana, she's often had to go back and retouch photos that were taken of her at major magazines, because the photographer didn't know how to photograph her. With the selfie, such issues don't come up because she's taught herself how to shoot, she knows what looks good, and she knows how to make it so.

"The selfie has been super empowering in that way, just being able to show myself as I am," she said. In addition, selfie-ing is a way for her to self-reflect—she sees selfie-ing and self-reflection as overlapping.

"Self-reflection is important because you need that to grow," she says. "If you don't know where you're at you don't know where you need to be. Even if you are in a bad place, you usually want to get out of that bad place. You want to think about that and break down all the things that you do like and things that you don't like, how do I change this, enhance this, the selfie is very important to me in that respect—it's sort of like a record."

It's not impossible to get an image of yourself that you like that wasn't taken by you, but it's definitely harder. Finding a photographer who not only gets your aesthetic, but gets the essence of you and can bring that out in an image—heighten it to ensure that you look even better than you would in everyday life—is a rarity.

"I want to show myself how I wanted to be seen and that's not going to happen if I let someone else take over my image," said RaFiA. "Unless we have that relationship and are close with each other, and they know what I want to look like."

Similarly, Brannon Rockwell-Charland, twenty-four, is an artist working on her MFA in the interdisciplinary studio program at UCLA. She engages often with the selfie, and for her it is a way to connect with herself and assert a sense of power. Rather than tell you more, I asked Brannon for her thoughts on her relationship to the selfie. Here's what she shared:

Every time I make an image of myself, whether I make it in a darkroom or on an iPhone, I feel that I am reclaiming some kind of power. Selfies give me a sense of control in the face of the always-impending fetishization of black women's bodies.

The way I'm "read" by others visually is at the center of my work, and there's a lot at stake for me when I render myself. I'm attempting to clear some space to be able to express my full range of humanity while engaged with whatever aspects of my history I choose but without respectability politics.

I think about history all the time—my own personal history and the contentiousness with which we tend to view images of black woman-ness throughout time. Jezebel. Mammy. Slut. Superwoman. Tragic Mulatto. The list goes on. I'm as tired of that list as I am intrigued by that list. I want to be able to be all of those women simultaneously and at will. I want to be able to be none of them.

I resist erasure by redefining, by embodying, by existing artistically in spaces that are amazing and problematic when it comes to the image of the black woman.

The thing about selfies as a form of image-making that is so tied to social media is that, as we discussed in our queer Tumblr article, we are wrapped up in this paradox of self-reclamation and the social capitalist currency of the Internet.[3] "We are subject to market logic."

I think maybe I used to be more concerned with resisting and transcending late capitalism. But these days, having just moved to LA, having just started an MFA program, still feeling very uprooted in my art practice, wondering how I'll afford to live in this city, I find myself wanting to engage with capitalism like I want to engage with the labels of black womanhood. I find myself wondering if I should make my Instagram public. Instagram is where I post most of my selfies; it's the online space where I am my weirdest self. I find myself wondering

*how to sell my work. I am in my work. I'm sitting in this per-
petually ambivalent space.*[4]

Courtesy of Brannon Rockwell-Charland.

For Brannon, selfies are a continual part of her work, ever
evolving and complicated in their multifacetedness. As an artist, she curates her image online as well, making her selfie collection unique to her aesthetic and sense of self. By being what
she describes as her "weirdest self," Brannon creates a type of
artist persona through selfies and other content she posts to
Instagram, while also recognizing that the images she is making are connected to capitalizing on one's own body and image
likeness.

In this way, there is a projected and curated vulnerability displayed through selfies that traverses issues of privacy online. "When I talk about our 'right to privacy,' I usually frame it as a choice, or a positive action, rather than a defense," said Harlo Holmes, of the Freedom of the Press Foundation. "There is indeed a lot of power in creating a public self; everyone is going to share stuff, but make sure you use technology in a way that only you get to choose which version of yourself exists for public consumption."

Genevieve Gaignard is another artist who creates work around complicated racial identities. As a self-identified mixed-race woman, she contends with different stereotypes and personas in her work, creating alter-egos in a way that is more Nicki Minaj and less Cindy Sherman. She also takes many, many selfies.

As I wrote in a review of her exhibition "Us Only" at Shulamit Nazarin Gallery in Venice, California, for *CRAVE* magazine, I discussed how her "high yellow femme" identity complicates her relationship to Blackness and how she is read out in the world, yet isn't necessarily a conversation about what it's like to "pass."[5] In her show she explores the multiple identities that she could embody based on the ways she is perceived.

I wrote about Gaignard's art several times in Los Angeles. In a review of her exhibition *Smell the Roses* at the California African-American Museum for *Hyperallergic*, I was curious to think about her work as more than either selfie or self-portrait, and more like creating new mythologies that blend autobiography and fiction.[6]

Because of their shared interest in characters, Gaignard's work is often compared to Cindy Sherman. But whereas Sherman reveals nothing about herself, Gaignard reveals a lot. And instead of working with female archetypes in the media, Gaignard makes the personal explicitly political.

She's also damn funny. So I'll leave you with this tongue-in-cheek work of hers. It's called "Selfie Stick," and points to the selfie's origins: the mirror.

Genevieve Gaignard, *Selfie Stick*, 2017,
Found mirrors, Dimensions variable.
Courtesy of the artist and Shulamit Nazarian, Los Angeles.

No selfies allowed but plenty of rewards received at Jumbo's Clown Room

Speaking of the production and consumption of (cis)female bodies, there are no selfies or other types of photography allowed at Jumbo's Clown Room, a strip club on Hollywood Boulevard in Los Angeles. I had driven by it many times while cruising to the through Hollywood, noticing the bouncer who eyed IDs at the door. The red-brick facade reminded me of how few brick buildings there are in Los Angeles because of earthquakes. There are no windows in the facade of Jumbo's. There are no free shows for passersby.

I initially resisted going to Jumbo's. I had seen amateur burlesque shows in Chicago, at dimly-lit dive bars on makeshift stages, and at storefront theaters squeezed between warehouses on diagonally directional streets. I didn't want to pay an admission fee to see women's bodies commodified, and then throw dollar bills at them, which felt even more demoralizing. Even though I am a cis queer woman, I grapple with questions of objectifying women. Also, why go watch live when this commodification is so readily available on TV, the Internet, and in porn? With all this screened play, why would anyone go see girls, like, real human beings, simulating what we are already seeing on screens all the time already?

Jumbo's was different from other strip clubs. Unlike the plethora of other XXX nude girl joints, which I noticed the most when I first moved to LA, this one has been around since 1970, it's not nude, and it is burlesque. It is rumored that workers there are treated more ethically. As with any strip club though, there are still plenty of dollar bills that patrons throw onto the stage, ready to be swept up after the dance is over. It's the business of selling bodies, sex, desire, pleasure.

Curious and open to this new experience, I decided to go—but not on my own, of course. BFF Che Landon, who you remember from previous chapters, thought it would be hilarious to take our eight-months-pregnant-and-about-to-pop friend to Jumbo's. What funnier place to spot a pregnant woman, *am I right??* And who knows, maybe the baby would decide to make an appearance that evening!

There are no photos allowed inside the red-brick facade of Jumbo's. A packed bar and a stage with a single golden pole erected into it sandwich the available seating area. A series of chairs lined the perimeter of the stage, just beyond the rail that separated the dancer and the audience members who have decided to sit right there in front of the stage and fling bills at the dancers rather than lounge on a black leather booth or on stools at a high stooled circular table further away. The bar that wraps its way around the stage is painted red, and dotted with yellow stars. Mirrors line the back wall of the stage, the ceiling above the stage, and another side of the wall adjacent to the stage.

No matter where you are sitting in the audience, you can see the dancer from multiple angles. Or you can just look straight ahead at her. There is no screen or screened bodies. Just sit back and look into the mirror—see yourself watching her, see her reflected back in the mirror, see reflections of bodies in space.

Sitting in the front row that night at Jumbo's, I had the overwhelming sense that I'd experienced this dynamic before—this wanting to sit in the front row and look but not be seen looking. I turned to my left, watching as one of my friends gleefully dispensed dollar bills like a blissed-out bank teller to a happily receiving customer.

That's when it hit me. I remembered this experience. My desire to look but not be seen reminded me of being at a comedy show and making the bold choice to sit in the front row, experiencing that same sensation—hoping that the comedian would make eye contact with me and single me out, put me on the spot with eye contact, but not actually acknowledge my presence. I was there to listen and be an objectified voyeur, but not to be seen.

There's another important element of Jumbo's that I mentioned earlier, but I want to reinforce. There are no phones allowed. No one can photograph the girls. They cannot photograph themselves, either. In essence, they are protected against the threat of social media and the Internet. Their bodies will not exist in data form. Their essence will never leave that room. The memories of their bodies will exist only in the minds of visitors that evening, hundreds of eyes gazing in, skin-deep, on the surface. They can only be seen directly, never in a meta-way or through a third-party app. They can only ever be performers and reflections in mirrors, various angles, ass, face, right here, right now.

Anyone seen with their phone out is reprimanded. I took mine out at one point just to check an app quick, and immediately a bouncer noticed and approached me, yelling: "No phones!" I was putting the phone away when the dancer on stage who donned an obviously sexy Halloween costume that included a fake bloodied sword moved toward me. I played along with her slashing role-play motion. Then she slunk off, dropping to the floor where she gyrated awhile, then wrapped her legs around a pole, sliding up and down it until the song ended and she exited.

While she did this, I watched the mirrors. They created multiple reflected versions of her in this physical space that replicated the infinite reflection of a sexualized selfie put out on the Internet, available for anyone to see through the smartphone in their hands, a face appearing in the palm of your hand. Except instead of direct gazes and dollar bills landing on her as she moved across the stage, such a selfie would garner likes and retweets and comments, shares and often creepy @ messages. Every click is feedback, a like, a reward. Every dollar dropped on-stage is a monetary reward.

"The human reward system tends to be responsive to a variety of things that lead to a subjective pleasurable response," said Dr. Mauricio Delgado, associate professor in the Department of Psychology at Rutgers University. "This includes the most basic of rewards such as food or money. This also includes more social rewards; things such as a simple smile, receiving compliments, or feeling accepted by peers."

I was thinking about this effect of the body and face as a woman's first and last weapon in the digital age and IRL, online as a selfie-er versus in-person as a body. In both spaces, the body becomes not just a brand or a means of gaining social capital, but a literal commodity.

I tell this story not to take issue with strip clubs, burlesque/erotic dancers, or the act of voyeurism. My experience at Jumbo's made me think more deeply about some of the recurring critiques of selfie culture, particularly those aimed at young women who find the act of selfie-ing to be empowering, experimenting with their bodies and sexuality in the way that they want to, being seen in the way that they want to be seen. It is empowering as a way to capture attention and to connect quickly, but it comes with the reality of literally releasing one's selfie as data to the network.

Often, the young women who are purveyors of selfie culture replicate the same types of sexual submissiveness that wouldn't be seen as "strong" or empowering at all. Women's bodies are always sexualized. This becomes even more complicated within the realm of selfie culture, because while the image is of her and for her, it becomes something that is also consumed by others who see her as a sexualized object. It's impossible to escape the gaze or the commodification of bodies under patriarchy.

Can the selfie ever be radical?

I'm a millennial who voted and then selfie-d about voting. I felt conflicted about this. Why did I need to share something I did? If a tree falls in the forest and no one is there to hear it, did it really fall? (#picsoritdidnthappen) Similarly, if I voted and didn't take a selfie of that instance, did I ever vote? (#ballotselfieoritneverhappened)

The answer is obviously yes, but considering that it's only 2017 and women only gained the right to vote in 1920, not even one hundred years ago, I decided that I wanted to be part of the voting selfie moment on social media. This begs the question: Are selfies tools of empowerment for women in the digital age, or for other people and bodies that are usually othered? Is it meaningful to post a photo like this?

Professor Derek Conrad Murphy makes a case for selfies as a "means to resist the male-dominated media culture's obsession with and oppressive hold over their lives and bodies."[7] Murray pulls out the ways that selfie-ing and self-imaging for women on and for the Internet do *feel* revolutionary, like a sea of faces all rallying together, even if there is no political motivation behind the selfie-ing. "Even if there is no overt political intent, they are indeed contending with the manner in which capitalism is enacted upon their lives," writes Murray in his paper *Notes to self: the visual culture of selfies in the age of social media.*[8]

Murray is self-aware of this generous read on selfie culture, a seemingly ostentatious remark against the blanket accusations of narcissism. Despite the view that your dad might give about "the kids these days being such narcissists," Murray disagrees, instead taking a more positive approach to the phenomena on the whole, noting the ways that it can be used to dismantle the repression and control of female sexuality.

"Teaching a lot of young women, I see them struggling with societal expectation around how they should behave and look, which often grates against their own desires," Murray said to me, when we emailed about these questions.[9] "For many women, pornography is very liberating, while others feel demeaned by it, and that's OK. Antiporn stances, however, often exert just another form of moralistic control and shaming—and often strip women who participate in and consume it of their agency. In terms of the selfie, seeing young women in control of their own image and expressing an unapologetically bold form of sexuality, simply grates against a very repressive social role that women are meant to perform."

In an attention economy on and offline that demands performance and absolute connectivity, a young woman must continue defining herself. At the end of the day, the selfie is a way to visually grab someone's attention, mimicking a face-to-face interaction. It is a way to hold space.

The approval of others is not meaningless. I've long since wondered if taking and posting a selfie connotes anything beyond surface likes. Self-imaging ultimately comes down to a desire, perhaps even a need, to see oneself—not for someone else's enjoyment, but just for oneself, to be seen. It is a mechanism for survival, a truly stark negation against invisibility, an action against erasure.

Get selfie-aware

On social media, narratives are fragmented and stories drift off, consumed by the network. Facebook was originally conceived as a way to "tell your life story online," which seems laughable at this point in time. Who except the people closest to you give a shit about what you ate today? (As I write this, the friend who sits next to me at this café is taking a picture of the cupcake she is about to eat. But she's a foodie, so . . .) Yet the networks demand content, and everyone has their niche online.

To cast a social media narrative like a screenplay, reality TV show, memoirlike narrative, or series of jokes at a standup comedy show requires constant checking and posting. Plus, the narrative flow is much harder to accomplish on social media. Doing so would mean constantly anticipating reactions. Not everyone has time or interest to strategize that, unless there is a monetary incentive. Think back to chapter 5, the women in China who earn money livestreaming themselves on one ore more of the two hundred livestream platforms. But in the United States, this is less common. Becoming a believable character on social media is to create oneself as a character that is consumable for an audience of social media onlookers, and it is work. Plus, on social media there is an expectation of giving away content for free.

For those who do put time and energy into their social media realms, the article "Social Media Got You Down? Be More Like Beyoncé" by Jenna Wortham for *New York Times Magazine* rings true.[10] Wortham takes a more optimistic approach to creating a persona or character for yourself online, especially if the rawness of just posting your life to the Internet is bumming you out. (#truth) Taking the time to figure out how to craft your own image, how you want to be seen, is also decidedly individualistic in nature.

Things got more live on social media in 2016, upping the possibilities for content creation. In Spring 2016, Facebook introduced Facebook Live, which allows anyone anywhere to broadcast anything they want to their network.[11] Similarly, in August 2016, Instagram introduced Stories, which are like public versions of snaps, varying in length, but created throughout the day and logged as tiny videos or photos with stickers, locations, music, and visual effects galore, and perhaps direct message someone about.[12] Quick emoji reactions—a heart-eye, fire, 100 percent, all make responding to someone's Instagram Story frictionless and low-risk. Instagram described Stories as a way to "share all the moments of your day, not just the ones you want to keep." By November 2016, Instagram introduced live videos on their Stories feature. Facebook owns Instagram, but no matter—this is always more content for the network. There are also archival features, such as highlighted stories and a way to save or archive posts for later. You might forget this, but the network won't forget—much like with Facebook Memories.

In Wortham's article, she argues that this ability to share practically further toes the line of what is socially acceptable. In other words, what's something to talk about and work out with people IRL, and what's something to post about as part of one's online brand?

"There's nothing necessarily *wrong* with either example—but they each clearly underline the ways that social media has stripped away our ability to tell what is OK to share and what is not," writes Wortham. "It's not just that watching people vie for your attention can feel gross. It's also that there's a fine line between appearing savvy online and appearing desperate."

Wortham suggests that actually, if people thought more about creating a persona for themselves online—in other words, more showing and less telling—audiences could spend more time just enjoying projecting a fantasy. She cites various examples of ways that Beyoncé has quelled rumors about her sister Solange and her marriage to rapper Jay Z through either playing into the drama or creating more of it for the sake of wonderment. In short, Beyoncé has found a way to create a fantasy, holographic selfie through her creative work and Internet presence that leaves people guessing based on what she shows them rather than what she tells them.

"Most people treat social media like the stage for their own reality show, but Beyoncé treats her public persona more like a Barbie—she offers up images and little more, allowing people to project their own ideas, fantasies, and narratives about her life onto it," writes Wortham.

This is one way to go about creating the selfie, one that will get you the attention you want. It's Creative Writing 101, to show the story, not tell it. Let the joke unfurl on its own—don't give away the punchline up front. When it comes to just easily learning how to "be more like Beyoncé," as Wortham suggests, making it seem like a casual, easy, fun-filled adventure for a leisure class that has time to even think about this, the joke is actually on anyone who thinks that it could be this easy to be like Beyoncé. She's a celeb. You better believe that she's got a PR team that guides her through the treacherous swamps, nooks, and crannies of the Internet's social media landscape.

Despite the controversial nature of presenting any personal information online through social media, we keep doing it. The social media companies that house our selfies and accounts are using our personal data in ways we are not entirely aware of.

"So, while selfie-taking can be a powerful, radical means for expressing and championing forms of identity that have been historically rejected by a racist/patriarchal mainstream culture (think, queer selfies, selfies at BLM protests, hijab selfies, fourth wave soft nude selfies) all selfies shared on social networks are inadvertently participating in capitalism—the same structures that are marginalizing their identities in the first place," said Alexis Avedisian, Communications Manager at the NYC Media Lab.[13] "Digital formats of activism (like radical selfies) allow for inclusivity within that user's network, but fully honoring inclusivity is made difficult due to the often apolitical, commercial goals specific to the social media platforms which host the activist action."

The selfie is the most easily accessible and powerful image for asserting a sense of personhood and connecting with others in a fragmented, networked, and hyperconnected world. It is done without any cost other than the agreement that your image becomes quantifiable data, demonstrative of complacency within techno-capitalism. We cling to the selfie: It is a mode of self-expression and immediacy, an opportunity to create space online, and to connect for (the illusion of) free in a digital age that will transform our personalized interests, purchases, browsing history, and social relations into currency for them. The only social requirement is you.

Peregrine Honig, "Golden Mirror Selfie" (2017).
Commissioned for Alicia Eler.

The Selfie Generation: Afterword

*A selfie comes, a selfie goes,
a new selfie takes its place.*

THE SELFIE GENERATION CAME OUT two years ago, and since then many new iterations of the selfie have appeared. The burning of Notre Dame in France signaled a wave of nostalgia-induced pre-disaster selfies, posted by people who remembered the cathedral before it was charred (#notredame). After the tragedy died down, people stopped posting those types of selfies, and Notre Dame just became another backdrop for tourist selfies. Meanwhile, new research about deaths by selfies has surfaced. A total of 259 deaths involving selfies around the world have occurred between the years of 2011–2017, which is worrisome.

In selfie celeb land, Kim Kardashian posted a happy Mother's Day selfie with her mom, with a generic caption "to the best mom in the entire world" and "I love you so much!" For the selfie queen, this holiday simply wouldn't exist if she didn't also post about it, publicly performing familial sentimentality for her fans.

Instagram's handy translation tool helped me decode comments on an #aftersexselfie written in Russian. A guy lying in bed somewhere on the other side of the world selfies, shirtless. In a comment, someone asked why his partner wasn't there with him and he responded, according to a halfway translated post, that "she's shy about that too." It's an awkward #aftersexselfie if your partner isn't there to prove that you've actually done it. Selfies like this come off as #humblebrags. In the land of selfie, you frame yourself as you want to be seen.

I've noticed my own fickle social media habits. These days, I go through phases of posting many Instagram Stories, but then get busy and drop off the network all together. Stories to me are both a way to connect and a reaction to the *ennui* of a hyperconnected postmodern existence. Since the publication of this book, I've also experienced sending and receiving nudes on Snapchat. I've since deleted my Snapchat account. The selfie world keeps spinning round and round.

But I keep coming back to the most alarming trend: Death by selfie.

Despite my worry, the number of deaths by selfie, technically categorized as "accidental deaths," are a very low total of 259, as mentioned above. But it is a legitimate cause for concern because "death by selfie" is its own category—that enough people have died while selfie-ing to make it quantifiable.

This information came out in the 2018 study "Selfies: A boon or bane?" published in the *Journal of Family Medicine and Primary Care*.[1] It reported that one-fourth of those deaths happened because the selfie-taker was engaged in "non-risky" behavior, like being hit by a wave and drowning while hanging out in an otherwise peaceful sea. The other three-fourths of the deaths were "risky," in which someone took a selfie and lost their life, and the majority were by men. More than half of the females in the study were taking "non-risky" selfies when they met their end. The most selfie deaths were caused by drowning—trying to take a selfie when a boat was capsized, or getting washed away by waves. Transport and fall were the second and third top selfie death-related cause. The most selfie deaths occurred in India, Russia, US and Pakistan.

"Selfies are themselves not harmful, but the human behavior that accompanies selfies is dangerous," the study concluded.

Indeed, this is yet another reason why I refuse to give a judgment of "good" or "bad" on the selfie in general. The context of the selfie affects the meaning and the risk associated with the act of selfie-ing. A selfie taken with family and friends at dinner is completely different than a selfie shot in front of an oncoming train.

Certainly, our focus when selfie-ing is on the phone and not the world around us. To die by selfie-ing is technically accidental.

According to data from the Centers for Disease Control and Prevention there were a total number of 161,374 unintentional injury deaths in the United States in 2016, which include 34,673 deaths by unintentional falls, 40,327 motor vehicle traffic deaths, and 58,335 unintentional poisoning deaths.[2] The top ten causes of death in 2016 around the world included 1.4 million deaths caused by road injuries.[3]

So, if this total number of selfie-related deaths were broken down annually, it would equal an average of forty-three selfie-related deaths per year, still an incredibly small number in relation to the number of accidental deaths that occur overall.

I understand the impulse people have to blame social media for the world's problems—it's easy. After all, Trump, while tweeting away propaganda and nonsense, is a national embarrassment and social media bully. Facebook's privacy rules are constantly changing, and for some reason, people trusted this free service in the first place. Instagram and Snapchat are a place where many teens socialize, and so they're on their phones more often. Anyone who grew up before smartphones is angsty about this. And selfies, well, selfies must just be more evidence for the impending END. OF. THE. WORLD. Right?

Truly, it is much harder to look at the negative human behavior that causes these tragedies. That's why artists exist.

UK-based artist Stephanie Leigh Rose's project STEFDIES touches on the human behavioral aspects of the selfie. For her project, she goes to a random place, often a tourist attraction, sets up her camera nearby, and then lies facedown on the ground. Once ready, she shoots the photo of her looking "dead." The photos are all on her Instagram @STEFDIES, which she describes as "A photographic performance art series that chronicles a life."

Of course, selfie pops up in her work.

"Most don't even notice me because they are so self-absorbed in their selfie," she told me via Skype. "They don't even know that someone is on the ground next to them."

In her STEFDIES photo at the Brunate Lighthouse in Italy, we see the view of a giant wooden cross, a gorgeous viewing platform overlooking city, hills, and blue sky.[4] She's facedown on the cement while two tourists just sit there on a bench. One guy looks at her and appears concerned, and another woman gazes out over the rail, completely oblivious of her "death." They appear somewhat confused but also just absorbed in their tourism.

But this is also a single moment in time. We aren't privy to what happened next—we just see what the photograph shows us. In another @STEFDIES pic at Cenontes Dos Ojos, Mexico, a well-known diving site in the Yucatan peninsula that's also one of the world's largest underwater cave systems, she wears a bikini and floats facedown in the water while a guy nearby completely ignores her.[5]

Despite the seeming self-absorption captured in these photos, they are not meant to be commentary on the selfie or tourism. Instead, they let the viewer come to their own conclusions about both Stef and the other people in the photo.

"Well what are we really here for— this thing we want to get likes for, or are we here for this monument or natural beauty?" she said. "The pictures are no comment on what's better or worse."

So what *are* we here for? Certainly, that is the selfie-taker's decision. For me, I'd rather be there for the experience, the natural beauty, or the monument. But if the perfect selfie moment, sunrise, or just sentimental image arises, I'm not gonna miss that, either. I'll take a photo. To post or not to post is another decision. For that, I must pause and decide if I want to participate in the network, or keep this moment for myself.

Taking photos on our phones is also a part of this experience we call life. It doesn't have to be all pro-selfie or anti-selfie—it can be somewhere in-between, with some selfies and a lot of being present. The camera in all its forms gives us a chance to document life as we know it. The selfie is just another iteration of that desire—to document, to share, to remember, to be seen.

Acknowledgments

THANK YOU, EVERYONE!

The idea for this book began in 2013 when I was a staff writer for New York art blogazine *Hyperallergic*. My editor, Hrag Vartanian, asked me if I'd like to do a weekly column of some sort, and I jumped at the opportunity. Being fascinated with cultural trends, I had been following the selfie since it started becoming a regularly written about thing. I call it a thing because it is both a noun and a verb, an object and an action—a selfie, to selfie, selfie-ing. The column began with the post "I, Selfie: Saying Yes to Selfies" and from there it became loosely known as "The Selfie Column." It ran for about a year, from June 2013 to May 2014, and gave me the opportunity to follow and analyze selfie news while also soliciting selfies from readers, along with a paragraph about why they shot the particular selfie and what it meant to them.

Naturally, my first huge thank you must go to Hrag and friends at *Hyperallergic*, who took a chance on the selfie column idea.

Next big thanks go out to my agent Caitlin McDonald at Donald Maass Literary Agency. We worked through many book proposal revisions together, which ultimately led to the sale of *The Selfie Generation* to Skyhorse Publishing in 2016. Thanks, Caitlin, for your tenacity and belief in the project!

Editors are amazing and I have been lucky to have only the best. Thank you to my editor, Maxim Brown, at Skyhorse for your tireless and enthusiastic edits on *The Selfie Generation*. It's been so fun working with you. I hope one day we can meet IRL, lol.

Thank you to my brilliant friends who generously offered their time and editorial realness that helped me sort out many ideas and ditch others: Desirée Salomone, Shera L. Morgan, Lauren Elizabeth Neal, Janna Avner, Thea Sircar, and Svetlana Kitto.

Thank you to the editors who have made me the writer I am today: Hrag Vartanian, Abraham Hyatt, Jillian Steinhauer, Peter Koechley, Bill Adee, Curt (Curtis) Hopkins, Max Read, Alex Huntsberger, Rob Horning, Amana Fontanella-Khan, and Drew Tewksbury.

Thank you to my inspiring and beautiful creative collaborator friends Peregrine Honig and Eve Peyser.

Thank you to my parents, Ihsan and Marge Eler, my little sister, Jenny Eler, and my aunt Hülya Eler.

Thank you to JB Brager, artist and fellow selfie theorist, for always being down to text about selfies and send actual selfies, lol. Your snark and problematizing brings me lifeeeeee.

Thank you to Elaine Romero. I'm so grateful that we happened to meet that random day at the Coffee Studio in Chicago, and have been friends ever since!

Thank you to amazing friends for your support and kindness throughout this selfie book journey: Theo Downes-Le Guin, Ray Anthony Barrett, Tiffany Sum, Samira Yamin, Genevieve

Gaignard, Julie Perini, Lauren Ross, Dorothy Santos, An Xiao Mina, Anne Orchier, Claire Potter, Che Landon, Ani Raya-Flores, Alex Carrillo, Nikita Gale, Munib Raad, Hannah Cox, David Prince, Maria Bamford, Scott Marvel Cassidy, Todd Coleman, Dana Duff, Andrea Gyorody, Sarah Bendix, Karen Krausen, and Vicki Simon.

Thank you for sharing your selfies with me, Brannon Rockwell-Charland! #tbt to our studio visit at Oberlin College, and our epic email letter writings. #Aqueerius #lol

Thank you to Café Tropical in the Silver Lake neighborhood of Los Angeles!

Thank you to Los Angeles.

Special shout-out to my awkward and brilliant teen girl self who took SOOOO many self-portraits in an attempt to figure out how she looked and how other people saw her.

Notes

An Introduction to the Selfieverse

1. @evepeyser. "mom just tweeted at me, 'tweets are verbal selfies.' She is an accidental web theorist and she's smarter than us all." *Twitter.* 13 Oct 2015, 9:47 p.m., https://twitter.com/evepeyser/status/654126282549129216.

2. Blas, Zach. *Facial Weaponization Suite.* 2011–2014, www.zachblas.info/works/facial-weaponization-suite.

3. Tinder is another story for this series of essays, see Eler, Alicia and Eve Peyser. "How to Win Tinder." *New Inquiry.* 26 August 2015, https://thenewinquiry.com/how-to-win-tinder; and Eler, Alicia and Eve Peyser. "Tinderization of Feeling." *New Inquiry.* 14 January 2016, https://thenewinquiry.com/tinderization-of-feeling.

Chapter 1: Screen Kween!!!

1. Curry, Ruth. "Toward a Unified Theory of Kim Kardashian." *Brooklyn Magazine.* 14 September 2014, http://www.bkmag

.com/2014/09/10/toward-a-unified-theory-of-kim -kardashian-hollywood.

2. Sales, Nancy Jo. *American Girls: Social Media and the Secret Lives of Teenagers*. Alfred A. Knopf, 2016.

3. Bakhshi, Saeideh, Eric Gilbert and David Shamma. "Study: Face It: Instagram Pictures With Faces are More Popular." *George Tech News Center*. 20 March 2014. http://www .news.gatech.edu/2014/03/20/face-it-instagram-pictures -faces-are-more-popular.

4. Rutledge, Pamela B., PhD, MBA. Positively Media, a column on *Psychology Today* magazine. https://www.psychologytoday .com/blog/positively-media/201406/bundle%3Ablog?page=3.

5. Hinchliffe, Emma. "It's the end of the line for Yik Yak." *Mashable*. 29 April 2017. http://mashable.com/2017/04/29 /yik-yak-shuts-down.

6. Douglas, Marissa. "5 Tips to Keep Your Long Distance Relationship Healthy." *Odyssey Online*. 2 August 2016. https://www.theodysseyonline.com/5-tips-long-distance -relationship-healthy.

7. Eler, Alicia. "Stop Freaking Out About Funeral Selfies." *Hyperallergic*. 4 November 2013. https://hyperallergic.com /91660/stop-freaking-out-about-funeral-selfies.

8. Weitz, Julie. Artist homepage. http://www.julieweitz.com.

9. Weitz, Julie. "Re: real brief questions for the selfie book—." Received by Alicia Eler, 4 May 2017.

10. Brazil, Ben. "UCI class looks at the history behind selfies." *Los Angeles Times*. 4 June 2016. http://www.latimes.com /socal/weekend/news/tn-wknd-et-teaching-selfies-20160604 -story.html.

11. Mowlabowcus, Sharif. "Of Selfies and Queer Folk." *Photoworks UK.* 27 January 2014. http://photoworks.org.uk /selfies-queer-folk.

12. Like "latinx," the "inx" ending in this descriptor is used to be more gender inclusive.

13. geoff. "Selfies of the Marginalized Body: Acts of Resistance, Disruptions of the Expected." *Living Not Existing.* 27 November 2013. http://livingnotexisting.org/2013/11/27 /selfies-of-the-marginalized-body-acts-of-resistance -disruptions-of-the-expected.

14. Berger, John. *Ways of Seeing.* Penguin Books, 1973.

15. Another friend of mine, Janna Avner, who is quoted later in this book, overuses hashtags as a semi-ironic commentary on marketing via social media. Lol.

Chapter 2: Privacy Settings

1. I know what you're thinking, but no, this is not a reference to coming out of the closet.

2. *Merriam-Webster,* definition of "privacy." https://www .merriam-webster.com/dictionary/privacy.

3. *Black's Law Dictionary,* definition of "privacy." http:// thelawdictionary.org.

4. Harcourt, Bernard. *Exposed: Desire and Disobedience in the Digital Age.* Harvard University Press, 2015.

5. Ibid, 167.

6. United States. Cong. House of Representatives. *Uniting and Strengthening America by Providing Appropriate Tools Required to Intercept and Obstruct Terrorism (USA PATRIOT ACT) Act of 2011.* 107th Congress. H.R.3162. Washington. Accessed via https://www.congress.gov/bill /107th-congress/house-bill/3162.

7. Ratner, Michael and Margaret Ratner Kunster. *Hell No: Your Right to Dissent in Twenty-First Century America.* The New Press, 2011.

8. Ibid, pg 18.

9. Risen, James and Eric Litchtblau. "Bush Lets U.S. Spy on Callers Without Courts." *New York Times*. 16 December 2005. http://www.nytimes.com/2005/12/16/politics/bush-lets-us -spy-on-callers-without-courts.html.

10. Ratner, Michael and Margaret Ratner Kunster. *Hell No: Your Right to Dissent in Twenty-First Century America*. The New Press, 2011.

11. Macaskill, Ewen and Gabriel Dance. Produced by Feilding Cage and Greg Chen. "NSA Files: Decoded. What the revelations mean for you." *Guardian*. 1 November 2013. https:// www.theguardian.com/world/interactive/2013/nov/01 /snowden-nsa-files-surveillance-revelations-decoded #section/1.

12. Rudolph, Harrison. "DHS Is Starting to Scan Americans' Faces Before They Get on International Flights." *Slate*. 21 June 2017. http://www.slate.com/blogs/future_tense/2017 /06/21/dhs_s_biometric_exit_program_is_starting_to_scan _americans_faces_before.html.

13. Macaskill, Ewen and Gabriel Dance. Produced by Feilding Cage and Greg Chen. "NSA Files: Decoded. What the revelations mean for you." *Guardian*. 1 November 2013. https:// www.theguardian.com/world/interactive/2013/nov/01 /snowden-nsa-files-surveillance-revelations-decoded #section/1.

14. Whittaker, Zack. "'Dark mail' debut will open door for Lavabit's return, says Ladar Levison." *ZDNet*. 2 November 2015. http://www.zdnet.com/article/dark-mail-debut-to-open -door-for-lavabit-return-ladar-levison.

15. Zetter, Kim. "A Government Error Just Revealed Snowden was the Target in the Lavabit Case." *WIRED*. 17 March 2016. https://www.wired.com/2016/03/government-error-just -revealed-snowden-target-lavabit-case.

16. Ball, James. "NSA collects millions of text messages daily in 'untargeted' global sweep." *Guardian*. 16 January 2014. https://www.theguardian.com/world/2014/jan/16/nsa -collects-millions-text-messages-daily-untargeted-global -sweep.

17. United States. Cong. House of Representatives. *USA FREEDOM Act of 2015*. 114th Congress. H.R.2048. Washington. Accessed via https://www.congress.gov/bill/114th -congress/house-bill/2048/text.

18. Siddiqui, Sabrina. "Congress passes NSA surveillance reform in vindication for Snowden." *Guardian*. 3 June 2015. https:// www.theguardian.com/us-news/2015/jun/02/congress -surveillance-reform-edward-snowden.

19. Kelly, Erin. "Senate approves USA Freedom Act." *USA Today*. 2 June 2015. https://www.usatoday.com/story/news /politics/2015/06/02/patriot-act-usa-freedom-act-senate-vote /28345747.

20. Siddiqui, Sabrina. "Congress passes NSA surveillance reform in vindication for Snowden." *Guardian*. 3 June 2015. https:// www.theguardian.com/us-news/2015/jun/02/congress -surveillance-reform-edward-snowden.

21. ACLU. "Senate Passes USA Freedom Act. https://www.aclu .org/news/senate-passes-usa-freedom-act.

22. Brager, JB. "Selfie Control." *New Inquiry*. 17 March 2014. https://thenewinquiry.com/selfie-control.

23. Fung, Brian. "The House just voted to wipe away the FCC's landmark Internet privacy protections." *Washington Post*. 28 March 2017. https://www.washingtonpost.com/news/the -switch/wp/2017/03/28/the-house-just-voted-to-wipe-out-the -fccs-landmark-internet-privacy-protections/?utm_term =.031ae339e382.

24. *Electronic Frontier Foundation.* "NSA Spying." https://www.eff.org/nsa-spying.

25. Kravets, David. "NSA Leak Vindicates AT&T Whistleblower." *WIRED.* 27 June 2013. https://www.wired.com/2013/06/nsa-whistleblower-klein.

26. *Electronic Frontier Foundation.* "NSA Spying: How it Works." https://www.eff.org/nsa-spying/how-it-works

27. "U.S. agency denies data center to monitor citizens' emails." *Reuters.* 15 April 2013. https://www.reuters.com/article/us-usa-security-nsa-idUSBRE93E11O20130416.

28. Bamford, James. "The NSA is Building the Country's Biggest Spy Center (Watch What You Say)." *WIRED.* 15 March 2012. https://www.wired.com/2012/03/ff_nsadatacenter.

29. Waugh, Rob. "Half of Facebook users 'can't keep up' with site's snooping policies as privacies rules change EIGHT times in two years." *Daily Mail.* 3 November 2011. http://www.dailymail.co.uk/sciencetech/article-2057000/Half-Facebook-users-sites-snooping-policies-site-changes-privacy-rules-EIGHT-times-years.html.

30. Johnson, Bobbie. "Privacy no longer a social norm, says Facebook founder." *Guardian.* 10 January 2010. https://www.theguardian.com/technology/2010/jan/11/facebook-privacy.

31. Kirkpatrick, Marshall. "Facebook's Zuckerberg says the Age of Privacy is Over." *ReadWriteWeb.* 2010. http://www.readwriteweb.com/archives/facebooks_zuckerberg_says_the_age_of_privacy_is_ov.php.

32. *Facebook.* Privacy settings. www.facebook.com/settings/privacy.

33. Xiong, Chao and Andy Mannix. "Case file in Philando Castile shooting released, dashcam video shows shooting." *Star Tribune.* 21 June 2017. http://www.startribune.com/case-file

-in-philando-castile-shooting-to-be-made-public-today
/429659263.

34. Vankin, Deborah. "Made in L.A. 2014': Jennifer Moon continues phoenix rise at Hammer." *Los Angeles Times*. 30 July 2014.

35. Eler, Alicia. "An Artist Turns Surveillance into Affection." *Hyperallergic*. 12 February 2015.

36. Davlin, Ann. "History of Cameras: Illustrated Timeline [Updated in 2015]." *Photodoto*. 2015.

37. Harcourt, Bernard. *Exposed: Desire and Disobedience in the Digital Age*. Harvard University Press, 2015.

38. Ibid.

39. @aliciaeler. "Without privacy we cannot have social change or even democracy." —Nate Cardozo @EFF @Snowden. Twitter. 9 November 2015. 11:08 p.m. https://twitter.com /aliciaeler/status/663946302355456005.

40. Timberg, Craig and Elizabeth Dwoskin. "Facebook, Twitter and Instagram sent feeds that helped police track minorities in Ferguson and Baltimore, report says." *Washington Post*. 11 October 2016.

41. "After promises to restrain Twitter use, Donald Trump tweets rant on New York Times." CBS News. 13 November 2016. http://www.cbsnews.com/news/twitter-use-restraint-60 -minutes-donald-trump-tweets-new-york-times.

42. Lee, Micah. "Surveillance Self-Defense Against the Trump Administration." *Intercept*. 12 November 2016.

43. Hulette, Elisabeth. "Police can require cellphone fingerprint, not pass code." *Virginian-Pilot*. 30 October 2014. https:// pilotonline.com/news/local/crime/police-can-require -cellphone-fingerprint-not-pass-code/article_25373eb2 -d719-5a6e-b677-656699a50168.html.

44. Giroux, Henry A. "Selfie Culture in the Age of Corporate and State Surveillance." *Third Text*. Volume 29, Issue 3, 2015, pp. 155–164. http://www.tandfonline.com/doi/abs/10.1080/09528822.2015.1082339.

45. Ackerman, Spencer and Ewen MacAskill. "Privacy experts fear Donald Trump running global surveillance network. *Guardian*. 11 November 2016. https://www.theguardian.com/world/2016/nov/11/trump-surveillance-network-nsa-privacy.

46. "The Oxford Dictionaries Word of the Year 2013 is 'selfie.'" *Oxford Dictionaries Blog*. November 2013. https://blog.oxforddictionaries.com/2013/01/fore-for-four.

47. @aliciaeler. "MONO APP CULTURE." Twitter. 13 April 2017, 11:46 a.m. https://twitter.com/aliciaeler/status/852563575294001152.

48. Naylor, Brian. "Firms Are Buying, Sharing Your Online Info. What Can You Do About It?" NPR, *All Tech Considered*. 11 July 2016. http://www.npr.org/sections/alltechconsidered/2016/07/11/485571291/firms-are-buying-sharing-your-online-info-what-can-you-do-about-it.

49. "Big data, financial services and privacy." *Economist*. 9 February 2017. https://www.economist.com/news/finance-and-economics/21716621-should-our-bankers-and-insurers-be-our-facebook-friends-big-data-financial.

50. "Getting to know you." *Economist*. 11 September 2014. https://www.economist.com/news/special-report/21615871-everything-people-do-online-avidly-followed-advertisers-and-third-party.

51. Victor, Daniel. "Selfies in the Voting Booth? Snapchat Fights for the Right." *New York Times*. 26 April 2016. https://www.nytimes.com/2016/04/27/us/politics/voting-booth-snapchat-selfies.html.

52. NSA Archive. http://nsarchive.gwu.edu/NSAEBB /NSAEBB441/docs/minaret%20after.pdf.

53. Bedoya, Alvaro M. "The Color of Surveillance." *Slate*. 18 January 2016.

54. Joseph, George. "Undercover Police Have Regularly Spied on Black Lives Matter Activists in New York. *Intercept*. 18 August 2015. https://theintercept.com/2015/08/18/undercover-police -spied-on-ny-black-lives-matter.

55. @Snowden. "Organize. Compartmentalize to limit compro-mise. Encrypt everything, from calls to texts (use Signal as a first step)." Twitter. 12 October 2015, 7:05 p.m. https:// twitter.com/Snowden/status/653723172953583617.

56. Joseph, George. "NYPD officers accessed Black Lives Matter activists' texts, documents show." *Guardian*. 4 April 2017. https://www.theguardian.com/us-news/2017/apr/04/nypd -police-black-lives-matter-surveillance-undercover.

57. Eler, Alicia. "An L.A. Art Show Was the Backdrop for a Major Discussion About the Future of Standing Rock." *LA Weekly*. 19 December 2016. http://www.laweekly.com /content/printView/7727333.

58. Goodman, Amy. "Standing Rock Special: Unlicensed #DAPL Guards Attacked Water Protectors with Dogs & Pepper Spray." *DemocracyNow!* 24 November 2016. https://www .democracynow.org/2016/11/24/standing_rock_special _unlicensed_dapl_guards.

59. *Black Lives Matter: Solidarity with Standing Rock*. http:// www.blacklivesmatter.com/solidarity-with-standing-rock.

60. Howard, Dorothy. "The Performance of Activism: Facebook Check-Ins to Standing Rock." *Medium*. 1 November 2016. https://medium.com/@anacreon_club/the-performance-of -activism-facebook-check-ins-to-standing-rock-6c54579a2e2c.

61. Kent, Jo Long. "Police Scan Social Media to Fight Crime." NBC Connecticut. 19 November 2012. http://www .nbcconnecticut.com/troubleshooters/Facebook-Twitter -Instagram-Social-Media-Police-179734571.html.

62. "What is Security Culture?" *CrimethInc*. https://crimethinc .com/2004/11/01/what-is-security-culture.

63. Ibid.

64. *Decolonize this Place*. http://www.decolonizethisplace.org.

65. #birdsofafeatherflocktogether.

Chapter 3: Consenting to the Image

1. Soat, Molly. "Social Media Triggers a Dopamine High." *American Marketing Association*. https://www.ama.org /publications/MarketingNews/Pages/feeding-the-addiction .aspx

2. Instagram. "Terms of Use." https://help.instagram.com /478745558852511.

3. Lizerbram, David. "Rules for Using Images Online." David Lizerbram & Associates. 7 February 2017. http://lizerbramlaw .com/2017/02/07/rules-using-images-online/.

4. Eler, Alicia. "A Leimert Park Performance Artist Weaves Together Social Media and South L.A. History." *LA Weekly*. 27 January 2017. http://www.laweekly.com/arts/a-leimert -park-performance-artist-weaves-together-social-media-and -south-la-history-7867002.

5. Vukovic, Adam. "Fair Use Lawyers." *Legal Match*. https:// www.legalmatch.com/law-library/article/fair-use-lawyers .html.

6. Boboitz, Sara. "A Brief History Of 'F**kboy,' The Internet's Favorite New Man-Bashing Slur." *Huffington Post*. 3 June 2015. http://www.huffingtonpost.com/2015/06/03/f--kboy -definition-take-that-haters_n_7471142.html.

7. Bahadur, Nina. "'Bye Felipe' Beautifully Calls Out Online Dating's Worst Guys." Huffington Post. 29 October 2014. http://www.huffingtonpost.com/2014/10/29/bye-felipe -instagram-account_n_6068182.html Tinder. "Terms of Use." https://www.gotinder.com/terms.

8. Lewis, Maddi. "15 of the Most Shocking Exchanges From the 'Bye Felipe' Instagram." *Buzzfeed*. 4 June 2015. https:// www.buzzfeed.com/mlew15/15-of-the-most-shocking -exchanges-from-the-bye-fe-h0se.

9. *Tinder in Brooklyn*. http://tinderinbrooklyn.tumblr.com.

10. *Male Feminists of Tinder*. http://malefeministsoftinder .tumblr.com.

11. *YOLOCAUST*. Yolocaust.de. No images are available for publishing because every image was found online and taken without permission. The only text left about the project exists on the website and reads as such: "The crazy thing is that the project actually reached all 12 people who's selfies were pre-sented. Almost all of them understood the message, apolo-gized and decided to remove their selfies from their personal Facebook and Instagram profiles."

12. Courbet, Gustave. *The Origin of the World*. Musée d'Orsay, Paris. http://www.musee-orsay.fr/en/collections/works-in -focus/search/commentaire/commentaire_id/the-origin-of -the-world-3122.html.

13. Newell-Hanson, Alice. "ann hirsch is a horny lil feminist." *VICE i-D*. 12 June 2015. https://i-d.vice.com/en_gb/article /ann-hirsch-is-a-horny-lil-feminist.

14. "Revenge." *Wikipedia*. https://en.wikipedia.org/wiki /Revenge_porn.

15. "What Is Rape Culture?" WAVAW Rape Crisis Centre. http://www.wavaw.ca/what-is-rape-culture.

16. Bisignani, Dana. "Normalizing Violence Against Women: Rape Culture." *Gender Press*. 11 February 2015. https://genderpressing.wordpress.com/2015/02/11/normalizing-violence-against-women-rape-culture.

17. Talbot, Margaret. "The Attorney Fighting Revenge Porn." *New Yorker*. 5 December 2016. http://www.newyorker.com/magazine/2016/12/05/the-attorney-fighting-revenge-porn.

18. "Senate Passes Kean/O'Toole 'Upskirting' Bill." *Senate New Jersey*. 14 March 2016. http://www.senatenj.com/index.php/tomkean/senate-passes-keanotoole-upskirting-bill/26205.

19. Ibid.

20. O'Hara, Mary Emily. "A federal revenge-porn bill is expected next month." *The Daily Dot*. 11 December 2015. https://www.dailydot.com/layer8/federal-revenge-porn-bill/.

21. Blake, Andrew. "House bill would criminalize 'revenge porn,' carry penalties for nonconsensual sharing." *Washington Times*. 15 July 2016. http://www.washingtontimes.com/news/2016/jul/15/house-bill-seeks-criminalize-revenge-porn-carries.

22. Ibid.

23. Shaban, Hamza. "Congress Wants to Criminalize Revenge Porn." *Buzzfeed*. 14 July 2016. https://www.buzzfeed.com/hamzashaban/congress-wants-to-criminalize-revenge-porn?utm_term=.kpLEvgpGKM#.kdLvlwdAzx.

24. Dejean, Ashley. "This guy thinks revenge porn laws are unconstitutional and is suing Oregon for violating his 'free speech.'" *Fusion*. 3 December 2016. http://splinternews.com/this-guy-thinks-revenge-porn-laws-are-unconstitutional-1793864116.

25. Lizerbram, David. "Rules for Using Images Online." David Lizerbram & Associates. 7 February 2017. http://lizerbramlaw.com/2017/02/07/rules-using-images-online.

26. "VIDEO : New Epic Pro-Trump Ad Hitting Swing States" *Truthfeed*. 28 July 2016. http://truthfeed.com/video-new -epic-pro-trump-ad-hitting-swing-states/13814.

27. Bauer, Kelly. "Trump's Ad Featuring Chicago-Area Business Leaves Owner Miffed." *DNA Info*. 8 August 2016. https:// www.dnainfo.com/chicago/20160805/downtown/trump -used-chicago-business-ad-but-owner-supports-clinton.

28. Frank, Priscilla. "Artist Photoshops 400 Nude Selfies To Explore the Future of the Online Image (NSFW)." *Huffington Post*. 4 November 2014. http://www.huffingtonpost.com /2014/11/04/jillian-mayer_n_6064116.html.

29. Johnson, Ted. "Hacker Sentenced Over Celebrity Nude Photo Leak." *Variety*. 27 October 2016. http://variety.com /2016/biz/news/jennifer-lawrence-nude-photos-hacker -sentenced-1201902819.

Chapter 4: The 24/7 Selfie News Cycle

1. @victomato. "2016, ya'll." Twitter. 25 September 2016, 11:59 a.m. https://twitter.com/victomato/status /780119655423676416.

2. Matyszczyk, Chris. "Astonishing pic of Hillary Clinton shows what we've become." *CNET*. 26 September 2016. https://www.cnet.com/news/hillary-clinton-astonishing -picture-shows-our-selfie-centered-life.

3. Gallucci, Nicole. "This Hillary Clinton campaign photo brilliantly sums up 2016." *Mashable*. 26 September 2016. http:// mashable.com/2016/09/26/hillary-clinton-campaign-selfies /#T7eNa3owRmqE.

4. @KimKardashian. "I got my selfie!!! I really loved hearing her speak & hearing her goals for our country! #Hillary ForPresident." Twitter. 6 August 2015, 9 p.m. https://twitter .com/KimKardashian/status/629502260607725569.

5. Jones, Jonathan. "Those taking selfies with Hillary aren't narcissists—but our best hope." *Guardian*. 26 September 2016. https://www.theguardian.com/commentisfree/2016/sep /26/taking-selfies-hillary-clinton-not-narcissists#img-1.

6. Eler, Alicia. "I, Selfie: Saying Yes to Selfies." *Hyperallergic*. 24 June 2013. https://hyperallergic.com/73362/saying-yes -to-selfies.

7. I recognize that I am also a member of the media. This isn't meant as an attack on the media—I am just clarifying the state of things.

8. Fausset, Richard and Yamiche Alcindor. "Video by Wife of Keith Scott Shows Her Pleas to Police." *New York Times*. 23 September 2016. https://www.nytimes.com/2016/09/24/us/charlotte -keith-scott-shooting-video.html?_r=0.

9. Jeffries, Adrianne. "How to die while taking a selfie." *Outline*. 17 November 2016. https://theoutline.com/post/233 /death-by-selfie.

10. Lamba, Hemank et. al. "Me, Myself and My Killfie: Characterizing and Preventing Selfie Deaths." Carnegie Mellon University, USA. https://arxiv.org/pdf/1611.01911v2.pdf.

11. Hastings, Deborah. "Woman in North Carolina killed while driving and texting about being 'happy.'" *New York Daily News*. 26 April 2014. http://www.nydailynews.com/news /national/north-carolina-woman-dies-behind-wheel-texting -happy-article-1.1769965.

12. In North Carolina, state laws do not allow people to operate a vehicle while using a mobile phone for texting or emailing, but they can use it for GPS or voice communication.

13. Unlawful use of mobile telephone for text messaging or electronic mail. GS 20-137.4A. North Carolina General Assembly. 2009. http://www.ncleg.net/EnactedLegislation/Statutes /HTML/BySection/Chapter_20/GS_20-137.4.html.

14. "Crazy Selfie From Hong Kong Skyscraper." YouTube, uploaded by Frank Wu. 21 August 2014, https://www .youtube.com/watch?v=82SDk1kInvI.

15. "25 Most Dangerous Selfies Ever!" YouTube, uploaded by Keepin it Karl. 12 February 2015, https://www.youtube.com /watch?v=A_aPgPq6hMM.

16. Uttam, Payal. "Death by selfie? Russian police release bro-chure after spate of fatal accidents." CNN. 8 July 2015.

17. "Man Takes Selfie Moments Before Deadly Shark Attack." *World News Daily Report*. Date unknown (spoof website). http://worldnewsdailyreport.com/man-takes-selfie-moments -before-deadly-shark-attack.

18. @petewentz. "Rest In Pete: http://worldnewsdailyreport .com/man-takes-selfie-moments-before-deadly-shark -attack/" *Twitter*. 8 August 2014, 2:34 p.m.

19. "I know the human being and fish can coexist peacefully." YouTube, uploaded by Goth Pop TV. 9 July 2008. https:// www.youtube.com/watch?v=20Jcrk6jGfo.

20. *Selfies at Serious Places*. http://selfiesatseriousplaces.tumblr. com; *Selfies at Funerals*. http://selfiesatfunerals.tumblr.com; *Selfies With Homeless People* http://selfieswithhomelesspeople .tumblr.com.

21. Chayka, Kyle. "Why Social Media Turns to Images to Help Us Cope with Tragedy." *New York Magazine*. 4 December 2015. http://nymag.com/selectall/2015/12/why-we-turn-to-viral -images-to-cope-with-tragedy.html.

22. Eler, Alicia. "I, Selfie: Saying Yes to Selfies." *Hyperallergic*. 24 June 2013. https://hyperallergic.com/73362/saying-yes-to -selfies.

23. Hakala, Kate. "Why Are Couples Posting #Aftersex Shots on Instagram?" *Nerve*. http://www.nerve.com/love-sex/aftersex.

24. Aldridge, Gemma and Kerry Harden. "Selfie addict took TWO HUNDRED a day – and tried to kill himself when he

couldn't take perfect photo." *Daily Mirror*. 23 March 2014. http://www.mirror.co.uk/news/real-life-stories/selfie-addict -took-two-hundred-3273819.

25. Kreisinger, Elisa. "No Shame in a Selfie." Audio blog post. *Refinery29*. N.p., n.d. Web. https://soundcloud.com /user-88808584/no-shame-in-a-selfie.

26. "Baseball announcers poke fun at group of sorority girls taking selfies." ABC 7 News. 2 October 2015. http://abc7news .com/society/baseball-announcers-poke-fun-at-group-of -%20sorority-girls-taking-selfies/1013853.

Chapter 5: Meta-Selfie Advertising, lol

1. Guardian staff. "Selfie is Oxford Dictionaries' word of the year." *Guardian*. 19 November 2013. https://www .theguardian.com/books/2013/nov/19/selfie-word-of-the -year-oed-olinguito-twerk.

2. Australian Associated Press. "Selfie: Australian slang term named international word of the year." *Guardian*. 18 November 2013. https://www.theguardian.com/world/2013 /nov/19/selfie-australian-slang-term-named-international -word-of-the-year.

3. Eler, Alicia. "I, Selfie: Saying Yes to Selfies." *Hyperallergic*. 24 June 2013. https://hyperallergic.com/73362/saying-yes -to-selfies.

4. Tait, Amelia. "The march of the micro-influencers: why your friends are promoting toothpaste." *New Statesman*. 5 April 2017. http://www.newstatesman.com/science-tech/social -media/2017/04/march-micro-influencers-why-your-friends -are-promoting-toothpaste.

5. Stryker, Sam. "I Tried The Tea The Kardashians Post On Instagram, And This Is What Happened." *Buzzfeed*. 31

May 2016. https://www.buzzfeed.com/samstryker/i-tried
-kardashians-fit-tea?utm_term=.bhmzROrgny#
.phYRyrxNV8.

6. @BerniceKing. "If only Daddy would have known the power of #Pepsi." Twitter. 5 April 2017, 9:15 a.m. https://twitter .com/BerniceKing/status/849656699464056832.

7. Zhang, Michael. "Samsung Camera Ads Imagine Famous Self-Portrait Paintings as the Result of Selfies." *PetaPixel*. 17 December 2014. https://petapixel.com/2014/12/17/samsung -camera-ads-imagine-famous-self-portrait-paintings-result -selfies.

8. "Dove Selfie | Redefining Beauty One Photo At A Time." YouTube, uploaded by Dove US. 20 January 2014. https:// www.youtube.com/watch?v=_3agBWqGfRo.

9. trauma_kmart. "'IDK' 'TOTES' 'SELFIE' This Chick-Fil-A ad totally appeals to the radical youth of today." *Reddit*. https://www.reddit.com/r/FellowKids/comments/4sjc0x/idk _totes_selfie_this_chickfila_ad_totally.

10. @joshgondelman. "Thank goodness. Too many people have gone ketchupless for too long." Twitter. 30 January 2017, 4:30 p.m. https://twitter.com/joshgondelman/status /826226224968130560.

11. *Heinz Ketchup: Stop Hunger Now*. #SelfieForGood cam-paign. http://www.heinzketchup.com/StopHungerNow.

12. *Public Art in LA*. "Social Media is selling your shit." Stencil graffiti on sidewalk, 2016. Pico Boulevard west of Hauser Boulevard, Los Angeles. http://publicartinla.com/LA_murals /Hollywood/social_media_stencil.html; *Up In The Valley*. "Tag Archives: Social Media is Selling Your Shit." http:// upinthevalley.org/?tag=social-media-is-selling-your-shit.

13. ABPHY.com. "#socialmediaissellingyourshit." http://abphy .com/hashtag/socialmediaissellingyourshit.

14. Redondo, Brian. "Hanksy: The Next Viral Street Art Sensation." *UTMOST.US*. 10 June 2016. https://www.brianredondo.com/written.

15. @jmudrums. "4 hours sleep, Day 2 starts now @dangerbirdrecords @hollymiranda." Instagram. 1 August 2016. https://www.instagram.com/p/BIkv5QUDA5W.

16. Najafi, Leila. "Here's the Lowdown on All Those LA Places that Keep Popping Up on Your Instagram." *Thrillist*. 30 August 2016. https://www.thrillist.com/lifestyle/los-angeles/best-places-los-angeles-la-instagram-pictures.

17. Colette Miller. "Spirit Paintings." http://colettemiller.com/about#.

18. Eler, Alicia. "Interview | Kate Berlant: Comedy from the Other Side." *CRAVE* magazine. 27 November 2015. http://www.craveonline.com/culture/928521-kate-berlant-comedy-side.

19. @kateberlant. "Contempt-orary art." Twitter. 21 June 2017, 11:28 a.m. https://twitter.com/kateberlant/status/877594103407460352.

20. @kateberlant. "Just bombed so hard I tried to recover by reciting a tweet." Twitter. 6 August 2016, 12:37 p.m.

21. @kateberlant. "Actually I'M Terry Gross, and THIS is Fresh Air." Twitter. 28 April 2016, 8:29 p.m. https://twitter.com/kateberlant/status/725889811882479616.

22. @kateberlant. "I wonder how many whites are meditating in their Sundance hotel rooms right now." Twitter. 22 January 2016, 2:49 p.m. https://twitter.com/kateberlant/status/690667748133867520.

23. Mansfield, Aaron. "'Jeopardy!' Has Officially Killed 'Woke.'" *Complex*. 30 June 2017. http://www.complex.com/pop-culture/2017/07/jeopardy-officially-killed-woke.

24. Wilson, Chris. "The Selfiest Cities in the World: TIME's Definitive Ranking." *TIME*. 10 March 2014. http://time .com/selfies-cities-world-rankings; To discover the "selfiest" cities across the world, *TIME* magazine assembled a database of more than 400,000 Instagram photos that had been hashtagged "selfie" and included geographic coordinates, ranking 459 cities to determine what they call the "selfiest places on Earth." While this database builds strong evidence of the selfiest places on earth, it does leave out selfies that have not been hashtagged because they do not want to be part of being labeled as a selfie.

25. Santos, Dorothy R. "Re: Thoughts on Filipino culture & selfie-ing for my book." Received by Alicia Eler, 17 December 2016.

26. "Enjoy McDo's Everyday McSavers." YouTube, uploaded by McDo Philippines, 28 July 2014, https://www.youtube .com/watch?v=lmWrdxFRe-Y.

27. Francisco, George. "Interview—selfie-ing in the Philippines for forthcoming book, THE SELFIE GENERATION." Received by Alicia Eler, 2 December 2016.

28. Kine, Phelim. "Rodrigo Duterte: The Rise of Philippines Death Squad Mayor." *Human Rights Watch*. 17 July 2015. https://www.hrw.org/news/2015/07/17/rodrigo-duterte-rise -philippines-death-squad-mayor.

29. Mallonee, Laura C. "An Art Museum Designed for Taking Selfies." *Hyperallergic*. 16 March 2015. https://hyperallergic .com/191194/an-art-museum-designed-for-taking-selfies.

30. Rusli, Evelyn M. "Facebook Buys Instagram for $1 Billion." *New York Times*. Dealbook blog. 9 April 2012. http:// dealbook.nytimes.com/2012/04/09/facebook-buys-instagram -for-1-billion.

31. Issac, Mike. "Facebook Said to Create Censorship Tool to Get Back Into China." *New York Times*. 22 November 2016.

https://www.nytimes.com/2016/11/22/technology/facebook
-censorship-tool-china.html?_r=0; As of this book's writing,
Facebook is working on a censorship software to get back
into the Chinese market. According to reports from the *New
York Times*, the tool would "suppress posts from appearing
in people's news feeds in specific geographic areas," which
would "comply with government requests to block certain
content after it is posted."

32. Newman, Lily Hay. "Meitu, a Viral Anime Makeover App,
    Has Major Privacy Red Flags." *WIRED*. 19 January 2017.
    https://www.wired.com/2017/01/meitu-viral-anime-makeover
    -app-major-privacy-red-flags.

33. Kane, Clare. "What Selfies in America vs. China Can Tell Us
    About Beauty Standards." *MIC*. 26 January 2016. https://
    mic.com/articles/133484/what-selfies-in-america-vs-china
    -can-tell-us-about-beauty-standards#.mBj7NM4Bp.

34. Ibid.

35. Rauhala, Emily. "These viral selfie apps with 1 billion down-
    loads are shaping China's start-up culture." *Washington Post*.
    3 August 2016. https://www.washingtonpost.com/world
    /asia_pacific/a-viral-selfie-app-with-1-billion-downloads-is
    -shaping-chinas-start-up-culture/2016/08/03/c89e985a
    -4348-11e6-b34c-ced7e11f0ca6_story.html.

36. Yang, Yingzhi. "In China, live-streaming apps soothe lonely
    souls and create fortunes." *Washington Post*. 5 January
    2017. http://www.latimes.com/world/asia/la-fg-china-live
    -streaming-20161128-story.html.

37. Gabriele de Seta. About. http://paranom.asia/about.

38. Michelle Proksell. http://michelle.yexl.de.

39. de Seta, Gabriele. "Introducing Alicia Eler, and Selfie
    Research." Received by Alicia Eler, 5 September 2016.

40. Cowie, Alix-Rose. "Decoding Culture on the Chinternet." *Casimir.* 18 December 2015. http://casimirtv.com/decoding -culture-on-the-chinternet.

41. de Seta, Gabriele. "Selfies | 自拍." Paranom.asia. 17 February 2016. http://paranom.asia/2016/02/selfies.

42. Donald, Angela. "Is Asia Setting the Trend on Selfies?" *Advertising Age.* 15 December 2014. http://adage.com /article/global-news/asia-world-s-trend-setter-selfies/296191.

43. *Labbrand.* "Digital in China: WeChat, Baileys, MaxFactor." 21 March 2014. http://www.labbrand.com/brandsource /digital-china-wechat-baileys-maxfactor.

44. Lu, Jasmine. "China: This Week In Digital Luxury Marketing." *Jing Daily.* 5 March 2014. https://jingdaily.com/china -this-week-in-digital-luxury-marketing-41.

45. Donald, Angela, "Chinese Social Media Explained, Through One Super-Viral Selfie." *Ad Age.* 11 June 2015. http://adage .com/article/digital/chinese-social-media-marketing -explained-super-viral-selfie/298969.

Chapter 6: Video Killed the Radio Star, Selfie Killed TV

1. It's important to keep in mind this show would be very different if the lead were *NOT* white. That is, she would experience racism on her Instagram all the time.

2. Sullivan, Gail. "John Cho of 'Selfie': 'I experienced racism.'" *Washington Post.* 9 October 2014. https://www .washingtonpost.com/news/morning-mix/wp/2014/10/09/john -cho-of-selfie-wants-roles-outside-any-asian-stereotype-2.

3. Smith, Zak. "Selfie Conscious." *Artillery* magazine. 3 May 2016. https://artillerymag.com/decoder-9.

4. Kliegman, Julie. "*Lady Dynamite* Recap: Adventures of a Sheep-Herding Pug." *Vulture.* 4 June 2016. http://www

.vulture.com/2016/06/lady-dynamite-recap-season-1
-episode-9.html.

5. Delgado, Mauricio. "Social media rewards quote for my book 'The Selfie Generation.'" Received by Alicia Eler, 21 April 2017.

6. Wortham, Jenna. "Black Mirror and the Horrors and Delights of Technology." *New York Times Magazine*. 30 January 2015. https://www.nytimes.com/2015/02/01/magazine/black-mirror-and-the-horrors-and-delights-of-technology.html.

7. It makes one wonder if perhaps one day there will be a twelve-step program for social media. I guess more will be revealed. Lol.

8. This was around the same time that a then-twenty-five-year-old Mark Zuckerberg, at the Crunchies in San Francisco, announced that privacy was no longer a social norm: "People have really gotten comfortable not only sharing more information and different kinds, but more openly and with more people," he said. "That social norm is just something that has evolved over time." This was a great plug for Zuckerberg to say that "the people" were requesting less privacy, when really this shift occurred as a result of Facebook gaining enough influence as a company to shape peoples' attitudes about online privacy. That is, that it somehow wasn't important. Facebook location services and the ability to "check in" further amplified this new attitude toward being OK with a lack of digital privacy. Now you could know where your friends were and what they were doing, as if it were appealing and *somehow not stalkerish* to show up there unannounced. Furthermore, this would act as an attempt to stamp out serendipity, those wonderful occurrences when people just happen to cross paths at the right time and place. At the end of December 2011, Facebook purchased location-based social app Gowalla to further

boost their Timeline options. Facebook figured that they would then build upon the nature of publicizing your location to your friends and whomever you'd like, making location-based check-ins even more socially acceptable.

9. I remember learning that Mario Lopez was a radio disc jockey when I heard him on the radio, as I was driving up the 1 in Los Angeles, shortly after I had moved there. That was definitely less exciting to hear about, as an adult.

10. @camerondallas. "im being real, not throwin any shade." Twitter. 16 July 2017, 3:43 p.m. https://twitter.com /camerondallas/status/886718020260777984.

11. @azizansari. "Master of None season 2 starts filming soon. Excited." Twitter. 3 August 2016, 5:55 p.m. https://twitter .com/azizansari/status/761002490443681792.

12. #Peregrineshouldvewon

Chapter 7: Selfie Gazing

1. Eler, Alicia. "The Feminist Politics of #Selfies." *Hyperallergic*. 25 November 2013. https://hyperallergic.com/95150/the -radical-politics-of-selfies.

2. Raad, Munib. "Quote about queer/trans kids and selfies for my book?" Received by Alicia Eler, 21 December 2016.

3. King, Robin Levinson. "Activists angered by change to transgender rights bill." *Star*. 26 February 2015. https://www.thestar .com/news/canada/2015/02/26/activists-angered-by-change-to -transgender-rights-bill.html

4. Wee, Darren. "Trans woman shows how 'ridiculous' bathroom bans are with urinal selfie campaign." *Gay Star News*. 9 March 2015. https://www.gaystarnews.com/article/trans -woman-shows-how-ridiculous-bathroom-bans-are-urinal -selfie-campaign090315/#gs.j756quk.

5. Kohner, Claire-Renee. "Trans Man Behind #WeJustNeed-toPee Isn't Selfie-Centered." *Advocate*. 17 March 2015. https://www.advocate.com/politics/transgender/2015/03/17/trans-man-behind-wejustneedtopee-isnt-selfie-centered.

6. Sicardi, Arabelle. "#HospitalGlam: The Chronic Illness Social Movement." *Buzzfeed*. 11 January 2015. https://www.buzzfeed.com/arabellesicardi/hospitalglam-the-chronic-illness-social-movement.

7. *HospitalGlam* FAQ. https://hospitalglam.tumblr.com/post/123920547604/faq.

8. Margolin, Emma. "'Make America Great Again' — Who Said It First?" NBC News. 9 September 2016. http://www.nbcnews.com/politics/2016-election/make-america-great-again-who-said-it-first-n645716; This slogan was originally coined by Ronald Reagan for his 1980 campaign, as reported here.

9. Crockett, Zachary. "Your ballot selfie could get you arrested in these states. Here's where it's legal and illegal." *Vox*. 8 November 2016. https://www.vox.com/policy-and-politics/2016/10/25/13389980/ballot-selfie-legal-illegal.

10. Corbyn, Zoe. "Facebook experiment boosts US voter turnout." *Nature*. 12 September 2012. https://www.nature.com/news/facebook-experiment-boosts-us-voter-turnout-1.11401.

11. Ibid.

12. Myers, John. "Sorry, Californians, you still can't take ballot selfies on Nov. 8." *Los Angeles Times*. 13 October 2016. http://www.latimes.com/politics/essential/la-pol-sac-essential-politics-updates-state-elections-officials-are-still-1476379986-htmlstory.html.

13. Shipkowski, Bruce. "Posting a ballot selfie? Better check your state laws first." AP. 23 October 2016. https://apnews.com/709338e5557a49e7ad5c68109ffecfca/posting-ballo

-selfies-personal-choice-or-illegal-act; Ballot selfies are actually illegal in Nebraska, however, resulting in a $100 fine if caught.

14. Marino, Mark C. "Know Thy Selfie — An exercise in Selfie Reflection. An essay assignment—for #SelfieClass at USC." *BuzzAdemia Now!* on Medium.com. 26 January 2015. https://medium.com/buzzademia-now/know-thy-selfie -8c0c023372b.

15. Ibid.

16. Marino, Mark C. "The Case for Voting Booth Selfies." *New York Times*. 8 November 2016. https://www.nytimes.com /interactive/projects/cp/opinion/election-night-2016.

17. Pew Research Center. "Generations and 'Selfies.'" 5 March 2014. http://www.pewsocialtrends.org/2014/03/07/millennials -in-adulthood/sdt-next-america-03-07-2014-0-04/.

18. Fry, Richard. "Millennials match Baby Boomers as largest generation in U.S. electorate, but will they vote?" Pew Research Center, Fact Tank: News in the Numbers. 16 May 2016. http://www.pewresearch.org/fact-tank/2016/05/16 /millennials-match-baby-boomers-as-largest-generation-in -u-s-electorate-but-will-they-vote.

19. Christakis, Nicholas A. and James H. Fowler. *Connected: How Your Friends' Friends' Friends Affect Everything You Feel, Think, and Do*. Little, Brown and Company. 2009.

20. Brief Amicus Curiae of Snapchat, Inc. in Support of Appellees and Affirmance. 22 April 2016. http://electionlawblog .org/wp-content/uploads/Snapchat-Ballot-Selfie-Amicus-With -ECF-Stamp.pdf.

21. Judge, Monique. "Eric Trump Tweets, Then Deletes, Illegal Ballot Selfie Showing He Voted for Dad." *Root*. 8 November 2016. http://www.theroot.com/eric-trump-tweets-then -deletes-illegal-ballot-selfie-1790857632.

22. In Tennessee, voters are not allowed to take photos in polling places, but photos of mail-in ballots are less legally clear.

23. "Justin Timberlake's Ballot Selfie Raises Some Important Questions." AP. 25 October 2016. http://fortune.com/2016/10/26/justin-timberlake-ballot-selfie-laws/?iid=sr-link1.

24. Farber, Madeline. "Justin Timberlake Avoids Jail Time after Taking a Ballot Selfie in Memphis." *Fortune*. 27 October 2016. http://fortune.com/2016/10/27/just-timberlake-ballot-selfie/.

25. Sanger, David E. "Obama Strikes Back at Russia for Election Hacking." *New York Times*. 29 October 2016. https://www.nytimes.com/2016/12/29/us/politics/russia-election-hacking-sanctions.html?_r=0.

26. @matthewsimon. "This is the glum face I made when I finally decided to vote for the presidential candidate of a different party. #Sad." Twitter. 8 November 2016, 3:07 p.m. https://twitter.com/matthewsimon/status/796096722632081408.

27. GLSEN. "Selfies for Silence." http://action.glsen.org/page/s/selfies.

28. Lorenz, Andrew. "Women With Agoraphobia Pens Powerful Post After Being Harassed for Taking a Selfie." *The Mighty*. 13 June 2016. https://themighty.com/2016/06/woman-uses-selfie-to-fight-agoraphobia-and-harassment/.

Chapter 8: Fake News and Selfie Journalism! Read All About It!

1. *Videostrategist*. "Q&A: Yusuf Omar on the Power of 'Selfie' Journalism in the Newsroom." 11 January 2017. https://videostrategist.com/q-a-yusuf-omar-on-the-power-of-selfie-journalism-in-the-newsroom-daaf46a515bd.

2. Mackintosh, Eliza. "Syrians post 'goodbye' messages from eastern Aleppo." CNN. 12 January 2017. http://www.cnn .com/2016/12/13/middleeast/syria-aleppo-goodbye-messages/.

3. @petesouza. Instagram. https://www.instagram.com /petesouza/.

4. Kircher, Madison Malone. "Former Obama White House Photographer's Instagram Shade Reaches New Heights in Honor of Trump's First 100 Days." *New York Magazine*. 25 April 2017. http://nymag.com/selectall/2017/04/100-days -ex-obama-photographer-is-still-insta-shading-trump.html.

5. Epstein, Kayla and Darryl Fears. "Rogue Twitter accounts spring up to fight Donald Trump on climate change." *Washington Post*. 25 January 2017. https://www.washingtonpost .com/news/energy-environment/wp/2017/01/25/rogue-pro -science-protest-sites-are-sticking-up-for-federal-research /?utm_term=.32e9a8bf40e3.

6. @AltNatParkServ. Twitter. https://twitter.com/AltNatParkSer.

7. @NotAltWorld. "Can't wait for President Trump to call us FAKE NEWS. You can take our official twitter, but you'll never take our free time!" Twitter. 24 January 2017, 9:07 p.m. https:// twitter.com/NotAltWorld/status/824091198457573376.

8. Noe, Rain. "Here's a List of All the U.S. Govt's Rogue Twitter Accounts Fighting Trump's Crackdown on Science." *Core77*. 25 January 2017. http://www.core77.com/posts /60230/Heres-a-List-of-All-the-US-Govts-Rogue-%20Twitter -Accounts-Fighting-Trumps-Crackdown-on-Science.

9. @DavidJHoyt. "The thing the dystopian novels could never predict was the sudden rebellion of the national park social media managers." Twitter. 24 January 2017, 7:28 p.m. https:// twitter.com/DavidJHoyt/status/824066409995137025.

10. @ALT_uscis. Twitter. https://twitter.com/ALT_uscis.

11. Complaint filed by Twitter against U.S. Department of Homeland Security; U.S. Customs and Border Protection; John F. Kelly, in his official capacity as Secretary of Homeland Security. Filed 6 April 2017. https://www.documentcloud.org/documents/3538057-Show-Multidocs-Pl.html.

12. Titcomb, James. "Twitter drops lawsuit against US government as order to unmask anti-Trump account withdrawn." *Telegraph*. 7 April 2017. http://www.telegraph.co.uk/technology/2017/04/07/twitter-sues-us-government-order-unmask-anti-trump-account.

13. Morozov, Evgeny. "Your Own Facts." *New York Times*. Sunday Book Review. 10 June 2011. http://www.nytimes.com/2011/06/12/books/review/book-review-the-filter-bubble-by-eli-pariser.html.

14. Shane, Scott. "From Headline to Photograph, a Fake News Masterpiece." *New York Times*. 18 January 2017. https://www.nytimes.com/2017/01/18/us/fake-news-hillary-clinton-cameron-harris.html.

15. Ibid.

16. Wingfield, Nick, Mike Issac and Katie Benner. "Google and Facebook Take Aim at Fake News Sites." *New York Times*. 14 November 2016. https://www.nytimes.com/2016/11/15/technology/google-will-ban-websites-that-host-fake-news-from-using-its-ad-service.html.

17. Mikkelson, David. "FBI Agent Suspected in Hillary Email Leaks Found Dead." *Snopes*. 5 November 2016. http://www.snopes.com/fbi-agent-murder-suicide.

18. Sydell, Laura. "We Tracked Down a Fake-News Creator In The Suburbs. Here's What We Learned." NPR, *All Things Considered*. 23 November 2016. http://www.npr.org/sections/alltechconsidered/2016/11/23/503146770/npr-finds-the-head-of-a-covert-fake-news-operation-in-the-suburbs.

19. Murphy, Blair. "Artist Targeted by #Pizzagate Conspiracy Theory Speaks." *Hyperallergic.* 23 December 2016. https://hyperallergic.com/347458/artist-targeted-by-pizzagate-conspiracy-theory-speaks.

20. Kang, Cecilia and Adam Goldman. "In Washington Pizzeria Attack, Fake News Brought Real Guns." *New York Times.* 5 December 2016. https://www.nytimes.com/2016/12/05/business/media/comet-ping-pong-pizza-shooting-fake-news-consequences.html.

21. Mantzarlis, Alexios. "The dangers of crying wolf with 'post-truth.'" *Poynter.* 19 November 2016. http://www.poynter.org/2016/the-dangers-of-crying-wolf-with-post-truth/439353.

22. #coincidences #LA #thingsthathappentome #thingsthathappeninLA.

23. Marino, Mark C. "Fake News, a look back and I made you look." Fake News Reader on *Medium.* 20 January 2017. https://medium.com/the-fake-news-reader/fake-news-a-look-back-and-i-made-you-look-294e0560a234.

24. Stack, Liam. "Mike Pence and 'Conversion Therapy': A History." *New York Times.* 30 November 2016. https://www.nytimes.com/2016/11/30/us/politics/mike-pence-and-conversion-therapy-a-history.html.

25. RussianVodkaSux. "Petition: Electrocute Mike Pence Until He Knows He Is Gay." *Lip Stick Alley.* https://www.lipstickalley.com/threads/petition-electrocute-mike-pence-until-he-knows-he-is-gay.1106629/.

26. "Statement by the President on International Holocaust Remembrance Day." 27 January 2017. https://www.whitehouse.gov/the-press-office/2017/01/27/statement-president-international-holocaust-remembrance-day.

27. Davis, Julie Hirschfeld. "In First, Trump Condemns Rise in Anti-Semitism, Calling It 'Horrible.'" *New York Times.* 21

February 2017. https://www.nytimes.com/2017/02/21/us /politics/trump-speaks-out-against-anti-semitism.html?_r=0.

28. Carroll, James. "What Donald Trump Doesn't Understand About Anti-Semitism." *New Yorker*. 23 February 2017. http://www.newyorker.com/news/news-desk/what-donald -trump-doesnt-understand-about-anti-semitism.

29. Soll, Jacob. "The Long and Brutal History of Fake News." *Politico*. 18 December 2016. http://www.politico.com /magazine/story/2016/12/fake-news-history-long-violent -214535.

30. Beauchamp, Zack. "The New York Times' first article about Hitler's rising is absolutely stunning." *Vox*. 3 March 2016. https://www.vox.com/2015/2/11/8016017/ny-times-hitler.

31. Chayka, Kyle. "Facebook and Google Make Lies As Pretty Much Truth." *Verge*. 6 December 2016. https://www.theverge .com/2016/12/6/13850230/fake-news-sites-google-search -facebook-instant-articles.

32. Heath, Alex. "Mark Zuckerberg: Facebook will 'proceed carefully' with fighting fake news and won't block 'opin- ions.'" *Business Insider*. 16 December 2016. http://www .businessinsider.com/mark-zuckerberg-on-how-facebook -will-fight-fake-news-2016-12.

33. @robhorning. "fake news and filter bubbles are symptoms of a larger issue: the way social media incentivizes per- formances of loyalty, us vs. them." Twitter. 21 February 2017, 1:56 p.m. https://twitter.com/robhorning/status /834129679409958914.

34. @robhorning. "Facebook is not 'focused on engagement'; it is focused on selling ads." Twitter. 21 February 2017, 1:36 p.m. https://twitter.com/robhorning/status/834124718928166916.

35. *Amalia Ulman: Excellences & Perfections*. New Museum. Online-only exhibition. Accessible at http://www.newmuseum .org/exhibitions/view/amalia-ulman-excellences-perfections.

36. For more discussion of this, revisit chapter 5.

37. Ibid, New Museum exhibition.

38. "Female Instagram artist who hoaxed thousands with her fake profiles is exhibited in London." *Telegraph*. 11 March 2016. http://www.telegraph.co.uk/women/life/female-instagram -artist-who-hoaxed-thousands-with-her-fake-profi.

39. Ibid.

40. Corbett, Rachel. "How Amalia Ulman Became an Instagram Celebrity." *Vulture*. 18 December 2014. http://www.vulture .com/2014/12/how-amalia-ulman-became-an-instagram -celebrity.html.

41. June, Laura. "People Only Like Selfies of Themselves." *Outline*. 13 February 2017. https://theoutline.com/post/1072 /people-only-like-selfies-of-themselves.

42. Ibid.

Chapter 9: The Authentic Selfie

1. Kircher, Madison Malone. "Court Rules in Favor of Ballot Selfies." *New York Magazine*. 28 September 2016. http:// nymag.com/selectall/2016/09/ballot-selfies-ruled-legal-in -new-hampshire.html.

2. *Intersectional Feminism for Beginners*. "FAQ." http:// intersectionalfeminism101.tumblr.com/faq.

3. Eler, Alicia and Brannon Rockwell-Charland. "Naming a Radical Queer Girl Tumblr Aesthetic." *.dpi Feminist Journal of Art and Digital Culture*, Issue 32. https://dpi.studioxx.org /en/no/32-queer-networks/naming-radical-queer-girl-tumblr -aesthetic; *Naming a Radical Queer Girl Tumblr Aesthetic* focuses on Tumblr as a space of safety, creativity,

self-expression, and escape for young queer women and women of color while considering the paradox of the Internet as subject to market logic. It is a fluid, deeply personal space wherein girls/gurls/grrrls of any age can be raw, vulnerable, emotional, and sexual. Tumblr resists subjugation and creates a potentially utopic space for oppressed people. "Naming a Radical Queer Girl Tumblr Aesthetic" (available at https://dpi.studioxx.org/en/no/32-queer-networks/naming -radical-queer-girl-tumblr-aesthetic) expanded on a previous version of the essay, "The Teen-Girl Tumblr Aesthetic," that was coauthored by Alicia Eler and Kate Durbin and published on *Hyperallergic* as part of the world's first-ever Tumblr as Art Symposium in 2013, shortly after writer Ben Valentine published the essay "Tumblr as Art." This updated version explores the IRL-URL connections of racial and queer identity politics.

4. Rockwell-Charland, Brannon. "Re: quote for The Selfie Generation book!!" Received on 11 November 2016 by Alicia Eler.

5. Eler, Alicia. "Review | Genevieve Gaignard: For Us Only." *CRAVE* magazine. 26 November 2015. http://www .craveonline.com/art/928457-review-genevieve-gaignard -coded-for-us-only#r8TwKP05ZKTYlciJ.99.

6. Eler, Alicia. "An Artist Reinvents Herself to Mine the Fictions of America." *Hyperallergic.* 9 January 2017. https:// hyperallergic.com/338452/an-artist-reinvents-herself-to -mine-the-fictions-of-america.

7. Murray, Derek Conrad. "Notes to self: the visual culture of selfies in the age of social media." *Consumption Markets and Culture*, Vol. 18, No. 6, 2015, pp. 490–516.

8. Ibid.

9. Murray, Derek Conrad. "Re: Interview with you for my book, 'The Selfie Generation.'" Received by Alicia Eler on 7 November 2016.

10. Wortham, Jenna. "Social Media Got You Down? Be More like Beyoncé." *New York Times Magazine.* 27 September 2016. http://www.nytimes.com/2016/10/02/magazine/social -media-got-you-down-be-more-like-beyonce. html?_r=0.

11. Zuckerberg, Mark. "Today we're launching Facebook Live for everyone – to make it easier to create, share and dis-cover live videos . . ." Facebook. 6 April 2016. https://www .facebook.com/zuck/posts/10102764095821611.

12. "Introducing Instagram Stories." Instagram Blog. 2 August 2016. http://blog.instagram.com/post/148348940287 /160802-stories.

13. Avedisian, Alexis. "Interview with you for my book, The Sel-fie Generation." Received by Alicia Eler on 20 November 2016.

Afterword

1. Bansal, Agam, Chandan Garg, Abhijith Pakhare, and Samik-sha Gupta. "Selfies: A boon or bane?" *Journal of Family Medicine and Primary Care,* 2018 Jul-Aug; 7(4): 828-831. https://www.ncbi.nlm.nih.gov/pmc/articles/PMC6131996/

2. Center for Disease Control and Prevention, National Cen-ter for Health Statistics: https://www.cdc.gov/nchs/fastats /accidental-injury.htm.

3. World Health Organization, "The top 10 causes of death," 24 May 2018. https://www.who.int/news-room/fact-sheets /detail/the-top-10-causes-of-death.

4. STEFDIES at Brunate Lighthouse. #stefdies #stefdiesinitaly #antiselfie #lakecomo #brunate #italian #lifeanddeath #contemporaryphotography #mortality

#femalephotographer #performanceart #performanceartist #femaleartist #faceplant #makeartnotwar #travelphotography #seetheworld #artexhibition #corpsepose #londonartist #galleryart #exhibitionist #photogallery #photoexhibition #coffeetablebook #streetart #streetartist." Instagram, tagged with location Capo Circeo Lighthouse, Italy. https://www.instagram.com/p/BZYWEpJgIKE.

5. STEFDIES at Cenotes Dos Ojos. #stefdies #stefdiesinmexico #mexico #telum #cenotes #cenotesmexico #cenotestulum #streetphotography #photography #travelphotography #femalephotographer #performanceart #performanceartist #contemporaryart #contemporaryphotography #antiselfie #faceplant #leaveamark #femaleartist #travelphotography #artexhibition #celebratelife #humour #photogallery #photoexhibition #coffeetablebook. https://www.instagram.com/p/BwxCdhIFo_6/.